HERACLES TO ALEXANDER THE GREAT

HERACLES TO ALEXANDER THE GREAT

Treasures from the Royal Capital of Macedon,
a Hellenic Kingdom in the Age of Democracy

A collaboration between

the Ashmolean Museum, University of Oxford

and the Hellenic Ministry of Culture and Tourism,
17th Ephorate of Prehistoric and Classical Antiquities

ASHMOLEAN
MUSEUM OF ART AND ARCHAEOLOGY UNIVERSITY OF OXFORD

2011

HERACLES TO ALEXANDER THE GREAT:
Treasures from the Royal Capital of Macedon,
A Hellenic Kingdom in the Age of Democracy

Ashmolean Museum, Oxford
7 April–29 August 2011

Copyright © Ashmolean Museum, University of
Oxford and the Hellenic Ministry of Culture and
Tourism, 2011

The authors and contributors have asserted their moral
right to be identified as the authors of this work.

British Library Cataloguing in Publications Data

A catalogue record for this book is available from the
British Library

EAN 13: 978 1 85444 254 3

Catalogue designed by Stephen Hebron
Typeset in Minion Pro and Foundry Sans
Printed and bound in Belgium by DeckersSnoeck Ltd.

Front cover illustration: Gold Medusa – originally
attached to the linen cuirass of King Philip II
Back cover illustration: A celestial or solar symbol
became the emblem of Macedonian royal power
Frontispiece: Detail from the back of the marble throne
and eternal seat of the Queen Mother Eurydice
(Illustrations courtesy of the Hellenic Ministry of
Culture and Tourism – Archaeological Receipts Fund)

For further details of Ashmolean titles please visit:
www.ashmolean.org/shop

HELLENIC REPUBLIC
Ministry of Culture and Tourism

HELLENIC EXHIBITION ORGANISATION

17th Ephorate of Prehistoric and Classical Antiquities:

Archaeologists
Dr Angeliki Kottaridi
Ioannes Graekos
Eva Kontogoulidou
Niki Kakoulidou
Elena Kavoukopoulou
Dimitris Papoudas

Conservators
Panagiotis Kamatakis
Manolis Achladianakis
Vangelis Chrysostomou
Anna Tsamakda

Directorate of Museums, Exhibitions and
Educational Programs:

Archaeologists
Harikleia Lanara
Alexandra Alexopoulou

ASHMOLEAN EXHIBITION ORGANISATION

Ashmolean Exhibition Curator and Editor
Dr Yannis Galanakis

Catalogue
Declan McCarthy
Elizabeth Stone
Emily Withers

Exhibition
Aisha Burtenshaw
Sadie Pickup
Agnes Valenčak

Exhibition Design
London Atelier (Pouya Zamanpour and Ralf Eikelberg)
Graeme Campbell
Greg Jones

Ashmolean Press Office
Susie Gault
Claire Parris

Catalogue edited by Dr Angeliki Kottaridi and Dr Susan
Walker on behalf of the Hellenic Ministry of Culture and
Tourism and the Ashmolean Museum

Contents

Acknowledgements

This exhibition is under the aegis of the Prime Minister of the Hellenic Republic, Mr George A. Papandreou

The exhibition was realised with the help and assistance of the staff at:

The Hellenic Ministry of Culture and Tourism
The 17th Ephorate of Prehistoric and Classical Antiquities
The Museum of the Royal Tombs at Aegae
The Greek Embassy in London
The Ashmolean Museum and the Faculty of Classics,
    University of Oxford

We are grateful to the following individuals, institutions, companies and their staff for their immense efforts and help:

LEAD SUPPORTER

The George Economou Collection

EXHIBITION SUPPORTERS

Aegean Airlines
The A G Leventis Foundation
Coutts & Co
Mr and Mrs Nicholas Egon
The Friends of the Ashmolean
The Hellenic Centre, London
Greek National Tourism Organisation
Associated events supported by Jaymount Investments Ltd,
    an affiliate of The Onassis Foundation
Malcolm Hewitt Wiener Foundation
Meyvaert Glass Engineering

HONORARY COMMITTEE

Mr Pavlos Yeroulanos (Chair), Minister of Culture and Tourism of the
Hellenic Republic

His Excellency Mr Aristidis Sandis, Ambassador of Greece to the
United Kingdom

Dr Lina Mendoni, General Secretary, Hellenic Ministry of Culture
and Tourism

Dr Maria Andreadaki-Vlazaki, General Director of Antiquities and Cultural
Heritage, Hellenic Ministry of Culture and Tourism

Professor Sir John Boardman, Emeritus Lincoln Professor of Classical Art
and Archaeology, University of Oxford

Dr Christopher Brown CBE, Director, Ashmolean Museum,
University of Oxford

Mr Dimitris Dondos, Chairman, Saint Catherine Foundation

Mr Nicholas Egon and Mrs Matti Xylas-Egon

Mr Stamos Fafalios, Chairman, Hellenic Centre

Mr Robin Lane Fox, Fellow and Tutor in Ancient History, New College,
University of Oxford

Mr George Lemos, Secretary, Hellenic Foundation

Mrs Edmée Leventis, The A G Leventis Foundation

Mr Haralambos K Leventis, The A G Leventis Foundation

Professor Chrysoula Saatsoglou-Paliadeli, MEP, Director of excavations
at Vergina, the Aristotle University of Thessaloniki, Greece

The Rt Hon The Lord Sainsbury of Preston Candover KG,
The Butrint Foundation

SCIENTIFIC COMMITTEE

Dr Angeliki Kottaridi, Director of the 17th Ephorate of Prehistoric and
Classical Antiquities

Dr Elena Kountouri, Head of the Secretariat of the Central Archaeological
Council of Greece

Dr Maria Lilimpaki-Akamati, Emeritus Director of the 17th Ephorate of
Prehistoric and Classical Antiquities

ORGANISING COMMITTEE

Dr Angeliki Kottaridi, Director of the 17th Ephorate of Prehistoric and
Classical Antiquities

Dr Susan Walker, Keeper of Antiquities, Ashmolean Museum,
University of Oxford

Dr Victoria Solomonidis FKC, Minister Counsellor (Cultural Affairs),
Embassy of Greece to the United Kingdom

Mrs Agatha Kalisperas, Director, the Hellenic Centre

Mrs Louisa Leventis-Williamson, the A G Leventis Foundation

Dr Maria Stamatopoulou, University Lecturer in Classical Art and
Archaeology, Fellow and Tutor of Classical Archaeology at Lincoln
College, University of Oxford

Our thanks go to the catalogue contributors:

Dr Harikleia Brekoulaki, Assistant Researcher in the Research Centre for
    Greek and Roman Antiquity, National Hellenic Research Foundation.
Professor Stella Drougou, Professor of Classical Archaeology, Aristotle
    University of Thessaloniki.
Dr Yannis Galanakis, Ashmolean Exhibition Curator and Editor for the
    'Heracles to Alexander the Great', Department of Antiquities, Ashmolean
    Museum, University of Oxford.
Mr Ioannes Graekos, Archaeologist of the 17th Ephorate of Prehistoric and
    Classical Antiquities.
Professor Miltiades Hatzopoulos, Director of the Research Centre for Greek
    and Roman Antiquity, National Hellenic Research Foundation.
Dr Angeliki Kottaridi, Director of the 17th Ephorate of Prehistoric and Classical
    Antiquities (Pella and Emathia, Museums of Aegae, Beroia and Pella).
Dr Elena Kountouri, Archaeologist, Head of the secretariat of the Central
    Archaeological Council of Greece.
Professor Sophia Kremydi, Associate Researcher in the Research Centre for
    Greek and Roman Antiquity, National Hellenic Research Foundation.
Mr Robin Lane Fox, Ancient historian, Tutor and Fellow at New College,
    University of Oxford.
Dr Maria Lilimpaki-Akamati, Emeritus Director of Antiquities, former
    Director of the 17th Ephorate of Prehistoric and Classical Antiquities.
Dr Jonathan Musgrave, University Senior Research Fellow, Centre for
    Comparative and Clinical Anatomy, University of Bristol.
Professor John Prag, Honorary Professor in the Manchester Museum
    and Professor Emeritus of Classics in the University of Manchester.
Professor Chrysoula Saatsoglou-Paliadeli, Member of the European Parliament
    and Professor of Classical Archaeology, Aristotle University of Thessaloniki
    and Director of the University of Thessaloniki Vergina excavations.
Dr Susan Walker, Keeper of Antiquities, Ashmolean Museum,
    University of Oxford.

We thank especially:

H.E. Dr David Landsman OBE, Manolis Achladianakis, Professor Ioannis N.
Akamatis, Dr David Berry, Dr Olympia Bobou, Suzanna Choulia-Kapeloni,
Vangelis Chrysostomou, Dr Kristina Glicksman, Ioannes Graekos,
Dr Jack Green, Helen Hovey, Niki Kakoulidou, Agatha Kalisperas, Panagiotis
Kamatakis, Elena Kavoukopoulou, Eva Kontogoulidou, Dr Nancy Kyriakou,
Dr Maria Lagogianni, Harikleia Lanara, Mr Robin Lane Fox, Professor Irene
Lemos, Dimitris Papoudas, Ilaria Perzia, Sadie Pickup, Dr Stella Skaltsa,
Dr Victoria Solomonidis, Dr Maria Stamatopoulou, Jennifer and Arthur
Stephens, Anna Tsamakda, Dr Maria Tsibidou-Avloniti and Professor John
Wilkes

Foreword

Dr Christopher Brown CBE
Director, Ashmolean Museum

It is a special pleasure to host the exhibition *Heracles to Alexander the Great* in collaboration with the Hellenic Ministry of Culture and Tourism and the 17th Ephorate of Prehistoric and Classical Antiquities and I would like to thank in particular Dr Angeliki Kottaridi, who has been very generous with her time, expertise and knowledge. We owe the privilege of showing such a marvellous collection of artefacts dating from about 1300 BC to 300 BC to the reputation of the University of Oxford as a centre for the study of ancient Greece and notably Macedonia.

This catalogue provides you with a record of these treasures, which have been excavated since the 1950s in northern Greece, at a village now called Vergina, an hour's drive from Thessaloniki. Vergina is the location of the ancient royal capital of Aegae, the seat of the Temenids – the dynasty of Alexander the Great. In the 1970s the distinguished archaeologist Manolis Andronikos found the undisturbed tomb of Philip II here, and subsequent excavations brought several more royal tombs to light, many of which belong to women of the court. Vergina is one of the UNESCO world heritage sites, the third most visited in Greece and only a visit to the site and the museum will give you an understanding of its scale. Our exhibition offers a different experience of Vergina from that of a visit to the palace and tombs, showing to a large public fragile objects, many of which have not been seen before. The gold, silver and bronze jewellery dazzle our modern eyes as do the weapons, the exceptional bronze and silver vessels, the terracotta figurines, and sculptures. They also allow us to understand more about who these kings and queens were and how they lived. They put Alexander the Great and his family as well as the royal capital in clearer perspective, permitting us to understand better the kingdom of Macedon.

The exhibition and associated collaborations extend beyond the walls of the Ashmolean Museum: the University's Faculty of Classics is hosting a special seminar programme and, in this way, the museum can truly be an open door to the University's research and teaching, with all the visual pleasures of the display. The exhibition also provides an expanded context for our permanent collections, which are well known to our visitors.

I would like to thank the editors and authors of the catalogue, the designers of *London Atelier* for making the exhibition a visual delight and all the staff at the Hellenic Ministry of Culture and Tourism, at the Museum of the Royal Tombs of Aegae as well as at the Ashmolean Museum who have been working behind the scenes to realise this remarkable project.

Foreword

Dr Maria Andreadaki-Vlazaki
General Director of Antiquities and Culture Heritage
Hellenic Ministry of Culture and Tourism

From 7 April to 29 August 2011 the Ashmolean Museum of the University of Oxford will showcase the exhibition *Heracles to Alexander the Great: Treasures from the Royal Capital of Macedon, a Hellenic Kingdom in the Age of Democracy.* The exhibition is under the aegis of the Prime Minister of the Hellenic Republic. It is a collaboration between the Ministry of Culture and Tourism – 17th Ephorate of Prehistoric and Classical Antiquities and the Ashmolean Museum. The 552 antiquities that will be displayed in this exhibition come, almost in their entirety, from the Museum of the Royal Tombs at Aegae. The vast majority of the objects have not been shown to the public before. Most of them come from the excavations of the last twenty years conducted at Aegae both by the Aristotle University of Thessaloniki and the 17th Ephorate of Antiquities.

The objects on display are treated primarily as bearers of important historical information as it emerges from the archaeological context. The main aim of the exhibition is to present to the visitor the development of the kingdom of Macedon from its early beginnings, sometime at the end of the Late Bronze Age and the beginning of the Early Iron Age, to the time of Alexander IV, son of Alexander the Great and last of his generation; to show the development from the time when the kingdom of Macedon was one of many Greek peripheral tribal states, while in Athens and many other city-states democracy was being established, to the time of Philip II and Alexander the Great. Father and son, Philip and Alexander changed the ancient world with their leadership, paving the way for the Hellenistic *koinē* that made Greek culture the property of people across the known ancient world.

According to Herodotus, in the middle of the 7th century BC, Perdiccas, a Dorian from Argos, became king of the Macedonians, establishing the dynasty of the Temenids. These rulers, descendants of Heracles and Zeus, governed Macedon for three and a half centuries; having Aegae as their ancestral centre, they ruled over the rich land that was to take from them its name. From the time of the Persian wars, the Macedonian kingdom partook actively in the common political developments as well as the institutions that united the Greek world.

The exhibition places emphasis on the Macedonian kings and queens as well as the people of their immediate environment through royal offerings, finds from the city, the palace and predominantly the tombs of Aegae, which show a great peak and wealth during the Archaic and Classical periods. The death of the Temenids was accompanied by heroic honours and funeral games and it was associated with magnificent funeral pyres, which bring to mind the descriptions of the *Iliad*; while the bodies of the queens were wrapped in purple and gold.

During the time of Archelaos, and especially in the time of Philip II, old legends acquired new dimensions. Philip sought ideological support for his policy in the circles of artists and intellectuals he invited to his court. His son, Alexander, established a glorious new Hellenistic world. The wonderful wall paintings of the royal tombs and the marvellous gold and ivory couches are grandiose artistic products of this period. The architecture of the palace of Aegae encapsulates the entire Classical tradition and paves the way for a new era. With this exhibition monuments and artefacts will be presented to the wider audience and the academic community, and will shed light onto the crucial years of the creation and establishment of the Macedonian kingdom and underline in a clear and unequivocal way the identity and development of the Macedonians. We hope that this truly interesting material will promote scientific research and will constitute a starting-point for scientific dialogue, without being presented in an introvert academic manner. On the contrary, the aim is to achieve a lively and expressive presentation of the material on display.

We thank the Minister of Culture and Tourism, Mr Pavlos Yeroulanos, for supporting this ambitious effort; the Director of the Ashmolean Museum, Dr Christopher Brown, and his colleagues for the organization and hospitality of the exhibition and the excellent collaboration; the Director of the 17th Ephorate of Prehistoric and Classical Antiquities and lead curator of the exhibition, Dr Angeliki Kottaridi, as well as the staff of the Ephorate for their valuable help. We also thank the academic colleagues and excavators of the Aristotle University of Thessaloniki and especially the Director of the University excavations at Vergina, Professor Chrysoula Saatsoglou-Paliadeli, because with their participation in the exhibition they contribute, to the extent possible, to a more complete presentation of Aegae. After all, the long archaeological research of the Aristotle University of Thessaloniki along with the continuous work of the 17th Ephorate are the main contributors towards the better understanding and promotion of Aegae. We are also grateful to the Directorate of Museums, Exhibitions and Educational Programs of the Hellenic Ministry of Culture and Tourism and especially the Director, Dr M. Lagogianni, and Mrs H. Lanara for their constant support in the preparation of this exhibition. The Greek embassy in London and especially His Excellency the ambassador Mr Aristidis Sandis and the Minister Councillor for Cultural Affairs, Dr Victoria Solomonidis, showed great interest and unstinting support in the materialization of this exhibition.

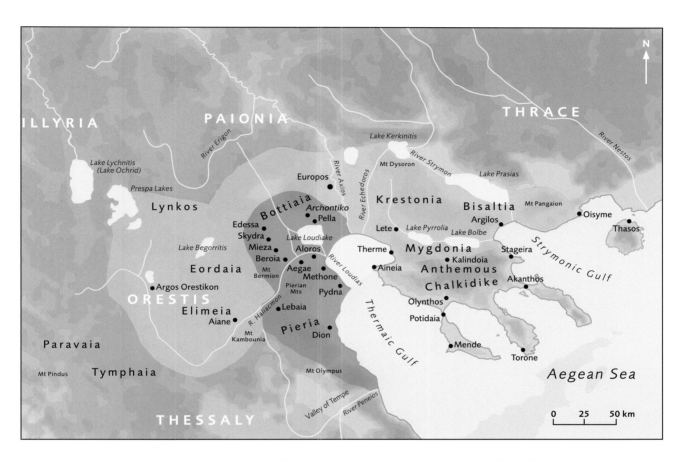

Map 1: The kingdom of Macedon in the late 6th century BC (in red)
and during the reign of Alexander I (498–454 BC) (in yellow).

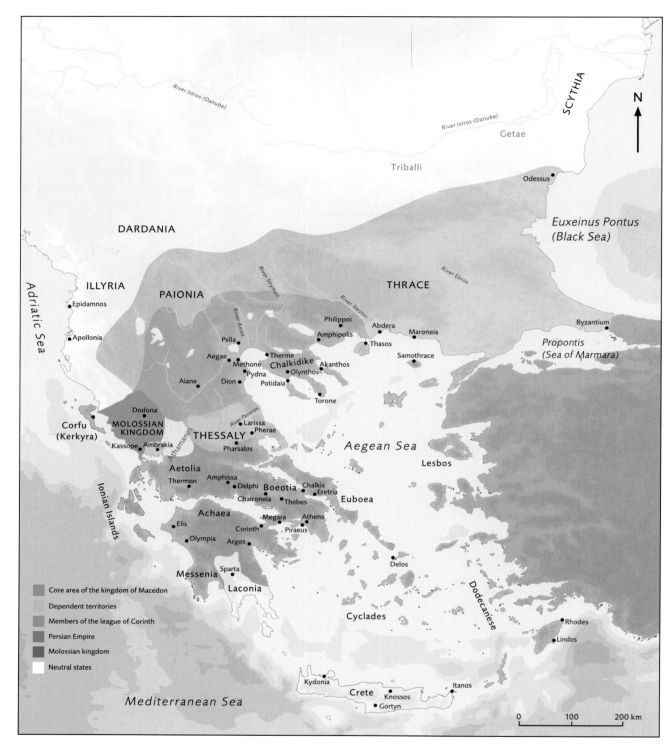

Map 2: The kingdom of Macedon during the reign of Philip II (360/359–336 BC).

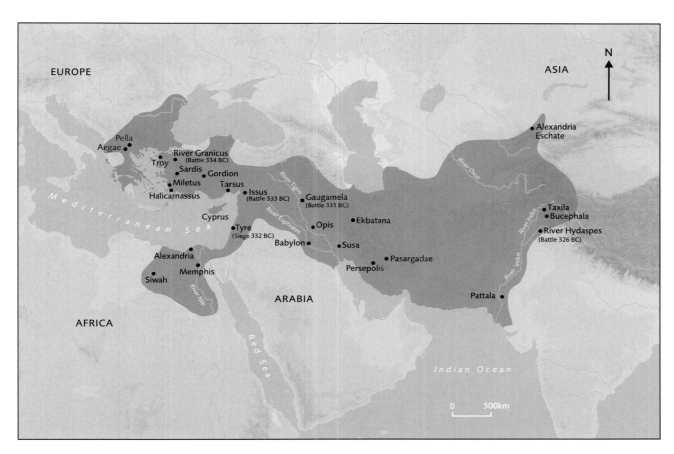

Map 3: The conquests of Alexander the Great.

1 The Legend of Macedon: a Hellenic kingdom in the age of democracy

Angeliki Kottaridi

> 'Thyia bore Zeus, who loves thunders, two sons that dwelt in Pieria and Olympus—Magnes and Makedon, the horse lover.'
>
> Hesiod, Fr. 3 West-Merkelbach

Thus, in poetic fashion, within a mythical genealogy as befits archaic thought, Hesiod, a Boeotian living around 700 BC, defines the tribal identity and the connections of the Macedonians, placing them in real geographical space, undoubtedly echoing the knowledge and perceptions of his audience.

Zeus, as the almighty god, is the father of gods and men; yet it is the mother, Thyia, who offers a clue to the identity of her sons: daughter of Deukalion and Pyrrha and sister of Hellen – who gave his name to the Hellenes (the Greeks) – she belongs to the first generation after the legendary deluge. Her name, which derives from the verb 'thyo' (sacrifice), connects her directly with the main religious act of sacrifice and reveals her hieratic role. Thyia is the archetypical high-priestess of Dionysus from whom the maenads – the female fervent followers of the god of wine – are also named 'Thyiads'. The religious activity of Thyia and of the Thyiads was centred on the tradition of Delphi – yet it also recalls the special connection of the women of Macedonia, particularly the members of the royal family, with the god of ecstasy.

The close blood relationship of the mother with the eponymous hero of the Hellenes underlines the connection of her sons with the Greek line of descent, while the fraternal relationship between Magnes and Makedon highlights the special connection between the two homonymous northern Greek tribes in the eyes of the rest of the Greek world.

The Magnetes were to give their name to eastern Thessaly (known to this day as Magnesia). The Macedonians in the time of Hesiod are already located in Pieria and Olympus, that is to the south of the River Haliacmon, in the land of Makedonis (*makedonida ge*) of Herodotus. The root 'mak-', from which the adjective 'makedon' or 'makednos' derives, is interpreted as 'long, tall' (e.g. *makedne aigeiros* in Homer is the tall poplar). It is associated with the homonymous tribe (Macedonians) that settled in the mountainous plateaux of Pindus, Olympus and the Pierian mountains, while the adjective

Fig. 1 The gold *larnax* of Philip II

'hippiocharmes' (fighting on horseback or chariot fighter) denotes the close connection of the Macedonians with horses, paving the way for the decisive role of the Macedonian cavalry across the ages.

At the beginning of the fifth century BC, Hellanikos (*FrGrHist* 4, ap. 74) believed that Makedon was son of Aeolos, and in this respect grandchild of Hellen. Herodotus, in less poetic fashion, insists on identifying the Macedonians with the Dorians. Anyway the fact is that the Macedonians remained for centuries an archaic, conservative tribe. Isolated in their self-sufficiency – which was reinforced by the abundance of goats, wooded mountains and fertile plains – and, in the absence of ports and islands, not being obliged to turn to trade or to open themselves up to the world by founding colonies, the Macedonians, like the rest of the northern and northern-west Hellenic tribes, such as the Molossoi, Orestes, Eordoi, Elimiotes, did not participate in the social and political developments of the south that led to democracy. For this reason, down to the fourth century BC they preserved the institutions, customs and traditions typical of Homeric society.

As happened with the Messenians and the Spartans, the Macedonians retained the monarchy as their main characteristic until the end of their existence as an independent state. Following the ancient model the king was the 'head' of his people. The name Karanos (from the Greek word 'kara', meaning head) attributed to a legendary royal forefather, who was probably not introduced into Macedonian dynastic legend before the fourth century BC, denotes exactly this. Probably this name was nothing else than the traditional title for the Macedonian king.

As recorded by Herodotus (8.137–8), about the middle of the seventh century BC, when the old hierarchy collapsed in southern Greece and new forms of power emerged, Perdiccas, a Dorian from Argos, descendant of royals, was forced, under the pressure of political developments, to seek a better fate in the remote northern regions. There he managed to become king of the Macedonians, establishing the Temenid dynasty that was to rule for three and a half centuries and offer to world history two of its most fascinating heroes, Philip II and Alexander the Great.

Scions of Temenos – an offspring of Heracles, who, like Agamemnon, was king of Argos – the Macedonian rulers, blood descendants of Zeus himself, continued the tradition of the 'Zeus-born' / 'Zeus-nurtured' kings of the Homeric poems and incarnated the heroic archetype. Upon their death, they received heroic honours: their bodies, together with substantial offerings, were 'consumed' in magnificent fires that recall those described in the *Iliad* – and let us not forget the funeral games that continue to take place until the end of the fourth century BC.

The names of the Temenid rulers signify in eloquent manner the virtues that the Macedonian king should possess: he should be intelligent, like the founder of the dynasty, *Perdiccas* (a name derived from 'perdika', meaning partridge in Greek, which was considered the cleverest of all birds); swift as the wind, like *Argaeos* (from the Greek word 'argos', meaning fast); and *Aeropos* – 'he who has

Fig. 2 Heracles – detail from a silver jar (*oinochoe*) found in the tomb of Philip II. The Macedonian king was a descendant of Heracles

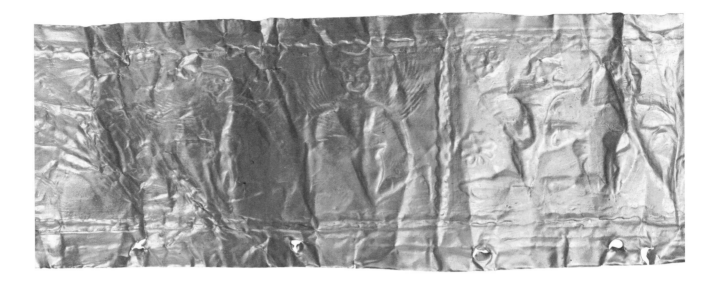

the appearance of the wind'. He should also be a great rider, like *Philippos* – 'he who loves horses'; and strong, like *Alcetas* (from the Greek word 'alke', meaning power). He must also be a leader, *Archelaos* ('he who leads his people'), but above all he is the guardian and defender of his people, *Amyntas* (from the Greek word 'amyna', defence) and *Alexandros* (from the verb 'alexomai', to defend). The illustrious results of their fathers' actions and political intentions are often suggested in the names of the royal daughters, such as *Stratonice*, 'the victory of the troops' (daughter of Alexander I); *Cleopatra*, 'the glory of the country'; *Thessalonice*, 'victory over the Thessalians'; and *Europe*, three daughters of Philip II (for Philip's 'European' ambitions see further below).

Leader and defender, first in battle and first in the hunt, guarantor of law and order, carrier of divine blessings, sacred and sacrosanct, the Temenid ruler is the tangible manifestation of the power and stability of the state; a genuine fatherly master of his folk. When he dies, his people become orphans. For life to continue normally, without chaos prevailing, his substitute must be nominated immediately; that man of his tribe who has all the prerequisites and the approval 'by acclamation' of the 'armed' Macedonians. The primary duty of the

Fig. 3 Perseus being pursued by the two Gorgons (Stheno and Euryale) after having killed their sister, Medusa. To the right, Theseus is slaying the Minotaur. Detail from the gold diadem of the Lady of Aegae (Cat. no. 328)

[4] ANGELIKI KOTTARIDI

Fig. 4 The blinding of
Polyphemus by Odysseus and
his companions, detail from
the gold diadem of the Lady of
Aegae (Cat. no. 328)

new sovereign is to bury his predecessor with every honour, thus legitimating his own power (fig. 1).

A symbolic persona, the monarch was essentially deprived of private life. His residence was constantly the centre of religious, political, military and even intellectual authority. In other words, the royal palace functioned as a political agora as well as a sacred acropolis in a democratic city-state. The luxury and splendour of royal possessions were a barometer of the strength of the kingdom's economy, essential elements for the prestige of the king and his kingdom. The same is true of the palaces of the epic heroes, with whom – as a genuine descendant of Heracles – the Macedonian king was on a level, at least in the eyes of his people (fig. 2).

In the golden diadem and strips that decorate the funeral garb of the Lady of Aegae, the labours of Dionysus, Heracles, Perseus, Theseus, and Odysseus are narrated, as are the funeral games in honour of Pelias; the queen of Amyntas I descends into Hades and the underworld escorted by gods, heroes and demons (figs. 3–4). The young Alexander, probably her son, excelled in the games at Olympia, reaching the finishing line at the same time as the winner. The same person, as a king in 479 BC, after his victory against the retreating Persians, made his presence noticeable in an equally impressive way by dedicating his golden statue to the sanctuary of Delphi (Herodotus 7.121.2). Among the statues of generals and the dedications of cities, the image of the Heraclid king is not only the most valuable, but, because of its rich materials, is also the one most closely related to the image of Apollo himself. The monumental octadrachm of Alexander I (495–452 BC) shows a beardless rider wearing a *chlamys* and a *petasos*. Escorted by his little dog, holding two spears in his left hand, the aristocratic hunter, perhaps the king himself, rides serenely and with full self-control, incarnating in this image the prototype of the absolute nobleman (fig. 5). Along the same lines, the famous poets Pindar (Fr. 120, 121 Snell) and Bacchylides (Fr. 20 B Snell) take the opportunity to praise the bravery and generosity of the descendant of Heracles, whose charm enchants Herodotus as he tells the story of his excellence in the Greeks' battle against the Persians (Herodotus 5.18-21).

At the beginning of the fifth century, the *Hellanodikes* (judges of the Olympic games) investigated and approved the legend of the Temenids' royal house as an historic event. Although this decision may surprise us today, it continued to hold force even in the golden age of democracy, when a tendency for rationalisation and secularisation affected the ways in which the ancient Greeks perceived even their own gods. The 'father of History', Herodotus, eloquently tells the story of the coming of the Temenids to Macedonia and the excellence of their founder, Perdiccas I. Even the austere Thucydides (2.100), who does not hide his respect for Archelaos, considers a given fact the connection of the Macedonian royal family with Argos in the Peloponnese.

In the middle of the Peloponnesian war, in an attempt to save his kingdom from the military operations and dangers in which the two superpowers – Athens and Sparta – were entwined, Perdiccas II (454–413 BC) needed powerful help, which he found in the legendary founder, Heracles himself. The image of the bearded Heracles was struck on the coins of the king; on the reverse, Heracles' club – an ancient weapon and magical device to avert evil – is connected with the beaten wild boar, prey of the ancestral hero as well as symbol of the initiation of Macedonians from boyhood to adulthood.

An inscribed bronze tripod, placed as an heirloom in the tomb of Philip II, was given in the fifth century to Perdiccas II or another member of the Macedonian royal family as a victory award in the games of the Argive Heraion and bears witness that the old legend regarding the Peloponnesian descent of the Temenids, reborn according to the new needs of the family, could still secure politically profitable connections and alliances with the Peloponnesian city of Argos (figs. 6–7).

During his reign – a true heyday for the kingdom of Macedon – Archelaos (413–399 BC), the most prominent *maecenas* (patron) of his time invites and hosts in his court with every honour the most significant intellectuals, poets and artists of Greece. They, in their turn, decide to enrich with their pens the legend of the Temenids.

Fig. 5 Rider wearing a *petasos*, escorted by his little dog

Fig. 6 (bottom) Tripod stand (with detail) from the tomb of Philip II – a prize at the games of the Argive Heraion and by the time of its deposition in the tomb of Philip, an heirloom (Cat. no. 90)

Fig. 7 (top) The inscription on the rim of the bronze tripod given to Perdiccas II or another member of the Macedonian royal family as a victory award in the games of the Argive Heraion. It reads 'I am from the games of the Argive Hera'

In 408 BC Euripides presented the tragedy *Archelaos*. The legend of the Temenids is 'taught' to the Athenian people. The heroic adventures, in the distant north, of the legendary Archelaos, son of Temenos, king of Argos, come to life on the stage of the Dionysiac theatre at Athens – a story not dissimilar to those of the famous heroes of Greek myth. As the Delphic oracle commanded, the mythical Archelaos followed a goat and became the first *oecist* (settler) and founder of Aegae (Hyginos, *Fabulae* 219.143–4). The head of this animal, a symbol of the Macedonian capital, appears on coins issued by the king (fig. 25), underlying its connection with Euripides' poetic drama.

Thanks to their value, small size, durability and wide distribution, coins are an excellent medium for the transmission of images, views, thoughts, and propaganda. Their impact is far-reaching since they act as symbols and signs of cities as well as of rulers. Heracles was the favourite hero of the ancient Greeks, a mortal son of a god who became immortal thanks to his virtue; a god close to the people, whose popularity increased steadily from the Geometric period to classical times. Heracles, the esteemed founder of the Temenids, appears on the coins of Perdiccas II and on those issued by his son, Archelaos, underlying in this respect the divine power of the Macedonian ruler (fig. 8).

Fig. 8 (top left) Head of *Heracles Patroos* wearing a lion's skin

Fig. 9 (top right) Head of Zeus Olympios wearing a laurel-wreath

Fig. 10 (lower left) Head of Apollo wearing a laurel-wreath

Fig. 11 (lower right) Head of *Heracles Patroos* wearing a lion's skin

[8] ANGELIKI KOTTARIDI

The head of Heracles, often accompanied by his attributes, was to become the trademark of royal labours in the difficult times ahead. On the coins of Amyntas III and Perdiccas III, Heracles the ancestral god (*Heracles Patroos*) becomes the guarantor of power, which is under threat; on the other side of the coin, the eagle that devours the snake is a clear omen, presaging victory for the Macedonians.

While the kingdom was facing serious difficulties, at a time when the Greek cities were fighting each other and democracy was proving incapable of stopping social degeneration, the idea of the enlightened ruler emerged within the intellectual circles with which the Macedonian court never broke relations. The philosopher Euphraios, tutor of Perdiccas III, brought the doctrines of his teacher Plato to Macedonia and, since mystical knowledge of Orphism was already popular there, the kingdom proved a fertile land for the reception of these new ideas.

After a terrible defeat that resulted in the death of Perdiccas III, in 360/359 BC the king's brother Philip II took over a decimated army and a state in the process of collapse. The young king, however, proved to be more than capable of dealing with the crisis: a man of great intelligence and resolve, an outstanding general and an excellent diplomat, Philip managed during the twenty-four years of his reign to transform Macedon into the leading power of his time.

Alongside his unbroken military and political struggles for power, Philip also emerged as a great patron of arts and letters, an enlightened sovereign according to the Platonic model, by gathering at his court the cream of artists and intellectuals. The new trends and currents that came into being in the circle of Philip II were transmitted by Alexander and formed the foundations of the brilliant new era of Hellenism.

Philip, himself a devotee of the ideas of the Pythagoreans, was able to weigh up the use of symbols and archetypes and to realise the immense power of myth – a privileged field, where according to ancient Greek reasoning, history and politics merged with the suggestive power of religion.

Invigorated by the new trends and currents, the ancient family legend became the foundation of a new expansion. As blood descendant of Zeus, Philip, concurrently king and high-priest, claimed the right to be the defender of traditional faith and worship. He easily managed to take under his protection the little known, until then, sanctuary of the Great Gods at Samothrace, which through his intervention swiftly became a site of panhellenic worship. Matters were more difficult with Delphi, the navel of Greece. Even there, however, his persistence was richly rewarded. At the end with the construction of the Philippeion, he left his everlasting mark even in Olympia, in the sacred Altis itself, next to the temple of Zeus.

On Philip's silver and gold coins, the most powerful monetary currency of the time, apart from ancestral Heracles and his attributes, appear the laurel-wreathed Delphic Apollo and Zeus, the almighty god of the ancient Greek pantheon (figs. 9–11). Alongside the young rider and the chariot, illustrating the victories of the Macedonian at Olympia, the divine relatives guarantee

Fig. 12 Philip II – fragment from one of the gold and
ivory funeral couches found in the tomb of Philip II.
Shown enlarged

Fig. 13 Side view

Fig. 14 Alexander III – fragment from one of the gold
and ivory funeral couches found in the tomb of Philip II.
Shown enlarged

Fig. 15 Philip on the reverse of a coin as a peaceful, unarmed rider

victory, legalise the ambitions and bless the choices of Philip. At times, in a clear move to illustrate his intentions, Philip himself appears on the reverse of the coins as a peaceful, unarmed rider, wearing the sacred diadem with his right hand raised in a friendly gesture (fig. 15).

In 346 BC, the Athenian politician Isocrates called upon Philip, as a genuine descendant of Heracles, to prove himself equal to his great ancestor, by bringing peace and unity to the Greeks and Hellenic law and culture to the barbarians. The invitation of this elderly and eminent politician obviously struck a chord with the king, who mobilized sculptors, painters, architects, poets, actors and philosophers in order to support and illustrate his vision.

Finds from Pella, the new Macedonian metropolis which probably expanded under Philip's new plans, and the celebrated discoveries at Aegae offer us a glimpse of this activity. Covering an area of 12,500 square metres, the palace of Philip II at Aegae is the largest and, together with the Parthenon at Athens, the most important building of classical Greece. The palace became the manifesto of political thought of the new era. Perfectly combining functionality with mathematical precision in its planning and in geometric clarity of form, this unique building gives substance to the divine harmony of the Pythagorean doctrines. The number φ, the ratio of beauty is the 'common denominator' that runs through all its details and connects its parts to a whole, expressing the golden mean that marks the presence of God in the Platonic universe.

Incorporated into the palace is a *tholos*, a round building dedicated, according to the inscriptions found there, to the worship of ancestral Heracles (*Ηρακλής πατρώος*). The paintings that once adorned the palace have not survived. Yet the extraordinary mosaic with its narrative scene impresses the viewer: above a sea of grey-blue pebbles a galloping bull can be seen; the bull is surrounded by *erotes* (*cupids*) riding sea monsters. Although the centre of the mosaic is now destroyed, we identify the scene: the abduction of Europe by Zeus transformed into a bull. Philip's last child, born in 336 BC was named Europe, while the historian Theopompus, a contemporary of the king, declared that: 'Europe has never produced such a man as Philip son of Amyntas' (*FrGrHist* 115). All this cannot be mere coincidence. Could Philip – king of the Macedonians, elected leader of the Greeks and conqueror of the Balkans – have perceived himself as leader of Europe on the eve of his expedition to Asia? This seems very likely. What we can be more certain about is that the legendary representations, the heroic battle scenes, images of gods and heroes, mythological beasts, sea creatures and mermaids, satyrs and maenads (figs. 213, 219 and 223), became part of everyday life at the Macedonian court.

On the other hand, at the back of the marble throne that was to become the eternal seat of the Queen Mother Eurydice, a painting, bathed by the light of the Elysian Fields, was depicted. In this unique picture, the rulers of the World Beyond appear with peace and splendour in an unexpected composition expressing the inescapable fate of mortals (fig. 16).

Even more radical, sealed by tragic tension and passion, is the artistic expression of death's pain in the tomb of the young wife of Philip II. Here, the

Fig. 16 The marble throne and eternal seat of the Queen Mother Eurydice

half-naked Maiden, prey in the hands of Hades, becomes the highest symbol of divine and human passion (fig. 252). Demeter, the mother, petrified by pain, unable to save her child, even though a goddess, expresses the submission to the omnipotent law (fig. 170). And the three white-dressed Fates, the daughters of Necessity (Anagke), present for one time only the Platonic myth of destiny. Testimony of passion and at the same time of promise of salvation for the initiated and chosen ones, the presence of Persephone in the tombs of two royal women confirms the heroic dimension that the crossing to the World Beyond prescribes for members of the royal family.

In 338 BC, after the victory at Chaironeia, Philip became the undeniable leader of Hellas. At the end of the battle Philip made two moves of immense political importance. First he decided not to go after, punish or humiliate his enemies, thus revealing his intention to lead his kingdom and all Greeks with the wisdom, benevolence and justice befitting a truly enlightened ruler. Secondly he ordered the construction of an elaborate *tholos* within the sanctuary of Olympia and next to the temple of Zeus. In the Philippeion he placed five gold and ivory statues, creations of the famous artist Leochares. Apart from Philip himself, these portrait-statues represented his son and successor Alexander (cf. figs. 12–14), his wife Olympias, his father Amyntas and his mother Eurydice.

The shape of the Philippeion (typical of buildings destined for hero worship), the material used for the portraits (until that time exclusively reserved for divine figures), and, more importantly, its placement at the heart of Olympia (the most celebrated panhellenic sanctuary) next to the most sacred temple of the king of Gods leaves no doubts as to the message Philip was trying to convey. The Heraclid ruler is not simply using here an old myth to justify his political ambitions, a practice very common among the Greek city-states; an offspring of a divine bloodline, *aristos* (noble) by blood, chosen as the initiated one, enlightened and victorious, through his labours, he is claiming for himself and his bloodline a place in their natural environment – which is none other than that of heroes and immortals. Thus, Philip becomes the hero and at the same time the creator of a new myth: his own.

Among numerous other objects found in the tomb of Philip II was an exquisite suit of armour – the fine creation of an artist-armourer, equal to the mythical armour of Achilles (fig. 17). The iron helmet, which would have originally shone like silver, is similar to that which, according to the ancient sources, Alexander wore in the battle at Gaugamela. On the front of the helmet is a relief bust of Athena (fig. 18). The cuirass strengthened with iron and almost impenetrable was outwardly lined with fine cloth, perhaps purple-dyed. It recalls the traditional image of the hoplite cuirass (fig. 19). The same is true for the large, round, gold and ivory shield, the size and shape of which recalls earlier weapons.

While the form of royal armour stayed quite intentionally within the limits of classical tradition, its embellishment, intricate construction and

Fig. 17 (opposite) The royal
armour of Philip II

Fig. 18 (above) Detail of the
helmet of Philip II

ornamentation surpassed everything else known. Sturdy gold strips wrap and decorate the cuirass, keeping in place the various layers of materials such as textile, iron and leather. The heavy gold bosses take the shape of lions' heads, ancient symbols of power, discrete allusion to the first labour of Heracles. To the right, where the warrior is unprotected, a golden strip decorated with the figure of Athena was attached (fig. 19). Companion and guardian of all Greek heroes, the daughter of Zeus comes to protect her relative. Obviously, it is not a coincidence that the goddess is here shown in the type of *Parthenos* (maiden), the famous statue created by Pheidias almost a century earlier in Athens – the only difference is that instead of a *Nike* (goddess of victory), she is holding a spear, always ready for new battles.

Heraldic lions appear in the silver gilded strips that keep the *ochanon* in place at the back of the shield (fig. 20). In between the small miniature shields and ivy leaves appears the club of Heracles, an archetypical weapon, the winning instrument against the beasts, an amulet and a testimony for the constant presence of the great forefather. Yet the most interesting element here are the *Nikes* (Victories) which are coming flying to crown the owner of the shield with victory bands (fig. 21). These winged figures wear the heavy *peplos*

THE LEGEND OF MACEDON [17]

Fig. 19 (above) The cuirass of King Philip II –
it recalls the traditional image of the hoplite
linen cuirass

(right) Side view of the cuirass of Philip II –
the golden plate at the bottom right hand side
depicts Athena

Fig. 20 (right) Heraldic lions decorating the inside of the ceremonial shield of Philip II

Fig. 21 (below) A winged *Nike* arriving to crown the owner of the shield, Philip II

cloth wrapped around their waists. Their hair is tied, forming a characteristic pony-tail at the top of the head. A bronze head of the fifth century BC from the Athenian Agora is said to suggest the image of *Nike* that Athena *Parthenos* once held in her hand. This head is very similar to those of the *Nikes* adorning the inside of Philip's shield. Similarities in proportions and dress as well as body posture can also be found between the *Nikes* on Philip's shield and the Nike of Athena of the Varvakeion – a humble Roman copy of the famous Pheidian creation. This allusion to the famous statue may not be accidental, but another political statement.

The front of the shield is remarkable: inside an impressive meander pattern of ivory, glass and gold, similar to that in one of the mosaics at the palace, we find a relief of the highest artistic quality. Ivory indicates the representative character of the object, offering a clear impression that this shield was a parade weapon rather than a piece of defensive armour used in battle. What is even more important is the image at the centre of the shield: on a rocky outcrop of the gilded background a Greek warrior is giving the fatal blow to an Amazon who is falling between his legs. The unexpected clash of their bodies which form a closed unit and the intensity and passion of the last glance can all be clearly seen in this representation despite the worn condition of the materials. It is a scene that recalls the tragic and predestined embracement of Achilles and Penthesileia – at the very moment of the latter's death (fig. 22).

This is also a typical Amazonomachy scene where the masculine element – the Greek hero – represents the civilised state, rational order and the rule of law. This element subdues the wild feminine element represented by the Amazon, who incarnates the dangerous power of the irrational – the barbarian creature of a world beyond borders, outside law and order.

Amazonomachy was one of the main subjects chosen by Greek cities for the metopes and friezes of their temples, through which they celebrated their victory against the Persians. It appears here as the emblem on the shield of

Fig. 22. (opposite) A Greek warrior and a defeated Amazon form the emblem on the ceremonial shield of Philip II

Fig. 23. (above) The golden wreath of King Philip II

the ruler, to whom Athena *Parthenos* sends from the Parthenon her winged Victories, since he is now the sole protector and defender of Greece.

Despite the fact that it is almost impossible to prove this suggestion beyond dispute, I have the strong feeling that this armour, onto which in a modest yet tangible way the basic themes of the panhellenic legend co-exist in a harmonious composition, was the parade armour used by Philip at the congress of Corinth in the winter of 338/337 BC, when he was elected ruler of all Greeks, and general commander, *autocrator* (sole possessor of power) in the war against the Persians.

How far did Philip go with the creation of his own personal myth? Until the end …

In the summer of 336 BC the oracle given to the ruler said: 'The bull is garlanded. All is done. The sacrificer is ready.' (fig. 23) Refusing to take the ominous message into consideration, the king celebrated at Aegae his omnipotence. The procession entered the theatre bearing twelve statues of the gods and a thirteenth of the king himself. Philip, who was placing his image on a par with those of the gods, followed alone; the golden wreath on his head, dressed in white, on foot and unarmed. Before he reached the orchestra he met his fate.

Fig. 24. (opposite) The
Ashmolean Heracles, having
successfully killed the
Erymanthian boar – Roman
copy of a Greek original
(Cat. no. 1)

Fig. 25. (below) Zeus Olympios
seated on a throne. The goat-
head in the field possibly refers
to the city of Aegae. Early
tetradrachm of Alexander III

Stricken by the assassin's knife he fell dead before the eyes of the spectators, dyeing the earth with his blood.

Now we can imagine what that elegant image of the king's last procession was like: not an idealised depiction but a true portrait, with the ravages of time and the wounds of the battle scored on his face. Philip, who turned chaos into order and weakness into strength, who yoked cities to his chariot and achieved the hitherto unachievable – to be acknowledged ruler of all the Greeks – was truly an extraordinary man, and he knew it. Himself the model and the ideal, he did not need to appear handsome. In his circle the realistic portrait was born.

Similar to the stories of the great dramatic heroes, Philip's personal drama ended in the theatre at Aegae. Alexander declares himself king of Macedon and, following the political legacy of his father, he is elected king of the Macedonians, and by the city-states, ruler of the Greeks. As Commander-in-Chief of the army and representative of all the Greeks, in the spring of 334 BC he celebrated at Aegae, with feasts and sacrifices to the gods, the beginning of his great campaign, which renewed the old conflict between West and East. However, at the end, through his political actions as a world ruler he managed to overcome antithesis and paved the way to the most creative synthesis and co-existence of cultures that the world had ever encountered.

Son of Philip and Olympias, descendant of Heracles and Achilles, Alexander carried in his blood the most precious extract of the panhellenic myth. Honouring his heroic legacy, he will yearn to overcome all obstacles, to transcend all precedents, to reach the end of the world, even further than Heracles (fig. 24), even farther than Dionysus had done. In addition to his forefather, Heracles, Zeus and Athena were further guarantors of his victory, and they appear on Alexander's coins in the type of Pheidias's famous statues (fig. 25).

Pupil of Aristotle, initiated in the ideas of Plato and Pythagoras, surrounded by historians, geographers, architects, mathematicians, and philosophers, Alexander will turn the campaign that aimed for the conquest of the world into an epopee for the conquest of knowledge. The seed which was sown in the school at Mieza was to yield rich fruits in the courts of the successors (*Diadochoi*), with the pinnacle being the famous Museum of Alexandria: the world's first university.

An undefeatable warrior and at the same time an inspired visionary, Alexander proved ready to respect and accept 'others' to the degree that he provoked his own people. By sacrificing in honour of their gods, by respecting their customs and honouring their traditions, Alexander conquered the hearts of his subjects and became a hero in the legends of the peoples of the world. Thanks to Alexander, Hellenic civilization reaches the Far East and is transformed into Hellenistic culture; the Hellenistic 'koiné' becomes a point of reference for peoples ranging from Europe to Egypt and India. A new perception of the world is born, having as its reference axis not isolated nations but the *oecumene*.

Disseminated across three continents (Map 3), the inexhaustible reserve of Hellenistic culture became the starting point for dialogue, a source of ideas and ideologies, the matrix of the new world which gave birth to the Roman and Byzantine Empires; it left its mark on Indian art and Arabic science and formulated the modern perception of the world.

As centres of commerce and intercultural exchange, the Hellenistic cities at the extremities of Africa and Asia set the network of the routes of civilisation for the Hellenistic *oecumene* (fig. 26). Alexander himself the sole invincible, horn-bearing god (Zul Karnein) haunts Arabic manuscripts and Persian miniatures; fights ghosts and monsters in order to be lifted in glory in the cathedrals of Europe and to reappear dauntless in the photographic palimpsests of Andy Warhol and the epic battles of Oliver Stone, keeping the legend always alive; keeping forever his unprecedented charm and beauty which transcend the limits of space and time.

Fig. 26. Diademed head of Alexander the Great with horn of Ammon from a silver coin of Lysimachos, King of Macedon, Thrace and Asia Minor (306–281 BC)

2   Macedon, c.650–336 BC

Robin Lane Fox

The Macedonians lived under the same political system uninterruptedly for some five hundred years. Nowadays we admire the ancient Greeks for their invention of democracy, but even among the Athenians democracy lasted much less long. Macedon's system was monarchy, the most stable form of government in Greek history. It persisted from *c.*650 BC to 167 BC and only stopped because the Romans abolished it.[1]

Why did it establish such deep roots? Were the Macedonians 'unpolitical' and mostly living outside urban settlements? Were they perhaps not 'really Greeks'? Were they only consumers, but never producers, of Greek culture? Modern students of archaic Greek history usually omit Macedonians as 'beyond the fringe', except for the few mentions of their king in Herodotus' account of the Persian wars in 480/79 BC and Thucydides' descriptions of the bewildering changes of alliance by their king Perdiccas II in the first four books of his *History of the Peloponnesian War* (431–424 BC). Instead, Macedonians burst dramatically onto the stage of history-teaching and essay-writing with the accession of Philip II, father of Alexander the Great, in 360/59 BC as if from a 'failed state'. The Macedonians' subsequent conquest from the Danube to southern Greece, Lake Ohrid to (eventually) north-west India can then be told as the biggest surprise of all ancient history.

There are still plenty of surprises in Macedon's success, but at least three decades of widespread, intensive archaeological research have complicated the old picture of Macedon as an isolated compound of forests, swampy plains and mountains. The identification of Vergina as Aegae, the kings' dynastic centre, has, since October 1977, the moment when Manolis Andronikos' great work began to uncover the royal tombs, led to the most rewarding excavations in the Greek world.

Both of the great Greek historians, Herodotus and Thucydides, appear to have visited the Macedonian court. They agree on the number of previous Macedonian kings and, if we follow them, we can date the Macedonians' awareness of their monarchy's history back to *c.*650 BC. The kings presented their first ancestors as migrants from Greek Argos in the southern Peloponnese, but legendary 'kinships' and genealogies were rife in the Greek world: the neighbouring king of Epirus claimed a fictitious descent from the mythical Greek Aeacus. Macedon's first kings were members of a family called 'Argaedai', whence, no doubt, their supposed link with the similar-sounding Argos. The historicity of this link is accepted nowadays only by a minority of scholars.

Careful research into surviving words, personal-names and month-names of the Macedonians has established that the 'Macedonian tongue' spoken even by Cleopatra in Egypt in the 40s and 30s BC, was a dialect of Greek, probably close to north-western Greek. It suggests an origin there for the royal family. Later sources testify to 'Argos Orestikon', a settlement in the north-west of the kingdom, up near the Pindus mountains: perhaps the 'Argeadai' originated there and came south-east. In the 440s/430s BC Herodotus was told a superb tale of three royal brothers, supposedly exiled from southern 'Argos', who entered Macedon's lowland plains. The route of the three, he claims, ran from 'Illyria' down the River Haliacmon to a settlement called Lebaia, recently located by excavation near modern Daskion, north-west of Velvendos. A fine folk-tale follows, by which the three pioneering brothers escape from Lebaia, cross the river and enter lowland Macedon, the fabled 'Garden of Midas', where Herodotus even comments on the 'sixty-petalled' roses. Here, they founded the line of the 'Argive' – Argead kings. To this day, it is awe-inspiring to retrace their route.

Behind this story may lie the fact of a new clan's arrival, speaking north-west Greek and perhaps landing a migrant group of herdsmen who had previously practised transhumance in the Pindus mountains. They came down the Haliacmon valley and then conquered or won over the various peoples whom they found already in residence in and around 'lowland Macedon'. Thucydides tells us of seven such peoples, from the Eordoi (west of Mount Bermion) to the Almopians (north of the future site of Pella), Pierians, Bottiaeans, Bisaltians and others to the east. Few, if any, of these people were Greek-speakers already, but like the Greek kings on Cyprus some five centuries earlier, the incoming Macedonians under their Argeadai spread their Greek language as rulers. They encountered a small settlement at Aegae–Vergina which they duly made their own. They conquered coastal Pieria and founded Dion, making it another religious centre for their subjects. Between *c.*650 and 550 BC they gained huge territory, an achievement ignored in modern history books of archaic Greece, which focus, instead, on the Greek 'tyrants' in the *poleis* and little islands of the south-east and the Aegean.

The kings ruled with an entourage of companions, or *hetairoi*, who in turn probably had links with local settlements in their kingdom. Their subjects were organised, it seems, around 'hearths' (the *pyrokauseis* of later evidence) but already in the lowlands several townships were formed, such as Beroia, Edessa and perhaps already Mieza. From the start, a 'Homeric' ethos of valour and prowess prevailed, lived out by warrior-males in battles and in hunts against the teeming wildlife of their local forests and river-valleys. A Macedonian could not recline at dinner unless he had killed a wild boar without using a net. Lions, bears and stags also tested a man's mettle. He could wear a belt only if he had killed an enemy in combat. This culture of male prowess was to characterise Macedon throughout its history, extending to the kings' dining and drinking parties, where reputations, too, were made and lost.

The growing kingdom had three main components by c.520 BC: the cantons of Upper Macedon to the west and north-west of Aegae, whose people were grouped in villages as members of *ethne* dominated by local ruling families; the lowland Macedonian plain; to the east and south-east, the 'Chalkidic' lands and adjacent territories. Here, Greek settlements had already proliferated for quite other reasons. Part of the inland territory had been inhabited by Thracians; importantly, too, the coastline had become dotted with many *polis*-settlements of Greeks from the Aegean and elsewhere, especially by Euboeans, one of whose home settlements, Chalkis, gave its name to 'Chalkidike'. Already in the tenth century BC contact between Euboea's important settlement at Lefkandi and the coastline in, and adjoining, Chalkidike is archaeologically attested. One attraction was the local river-gold, arguably the gold which was then used in Lefkandi's remarkable 'Dark Age' jewellery. In the late 730s BC, another Euboean *polis*, Eretria, founded Methone on the coast only some 20 miles east of Aegae. Excavations have shown typical Euboean pottery reaching Vergina's site even earlier in the century: Methone itself is typified by Euboean goods and many related precious imports. By 730s BC Euboeans were already literate, being inventors, and users of their alphabet. They were on the Macedonian kings' doorstep, a morning's journey from Vergina.

Nonetheless, until 550–510 BC, the actions of the inland Macedonian kings are unknown to us. In or near Chalkidike we know only that the aspiring Athenian tyrant Pisistratus made contacts at a settlement, Rhaikelos, which is as yet unlocated in Chalkidike. His interest, once again, was precious metal for the funding of his tyrannical aims. In c.513 BC, the expanding power of the Persian king Darius suddenly illuminates the kingdom. Macedon's king, Amyntas I, submitted to Persia. Envoys were sent and according to Herodotus, were gallantly murdered by Amyntas's son, Alexander, while the Persians were harassing Macedonian women during a royal banquet. The tale is probably apologetic and exaggerated. No Persian reprisals are known for such 'murders'. Instead, King Amyntas married off his daughter, Alexander's sister, to the son of the most prominent Persian general. The truth was that Macedon, the future 'avenger' under Alexander the Great of the previous Persian sacrilege, medised between c.513 and 479 BC.

Herodotus' stories about Alexander I, Amyntas' successor, reflect the actions of a king who was at best playing a double game during the Persian war in Greece. Many scholars credit the growth of Alexander's kingdom to Persian support and campaigning. For Herodotus, however, the frontier of the kingdom, even in 513 BC, lay just east of Mount Dysoron, now located by inscriptional evidence as beyond the River Strymon, almost as far east as Philip II's future Philippi. Has Herodotus projected back in time the enlarged frontier of Macedon in his own age? Many think so, but in *c*.507 BC Amyntas, Alexander's father, had been able to offer the exiled son of Pisistratus, the Athenian tyrant Hippias, lands at Anthemus, or modern Galatista, in the 'Chalkidic' zone. It is therefore wrong to limit sixth-century Macedon only to the plains round Aegae and Beroia. By 510 BC the kingdom may already have been bigger than historians now imagine (cf. Map 1). In the poetic *Catalogue of Women*, its eponym, Macedon, is presented as a son of Zeus and Thyia (linked with the god Dionysus). Homer had mentioned Pieria and Emathia as place-names, but had said nothing about the people 'beyond Olympus'. Now, Macedonians were linked to a Greek mythical genealogy. Accusations that their kings were 'barbarians' were henceforward the ignorant or insulting comments of enemies or misinformed outsiders in the south. The recent excavations at Aiane (centre of the local kingdom of Elimeia) and Pentavrysos (the probable centre of Orestis) show that fine Greek pottery and even Greek sculptures had been arriving at Upper Macedonian sites by *c*.500 BC. The 'golden burial' of the lady (Amyntas's queen?) at Aegae and the remarkable terracotta heads in another lady's grave there *c*.480 BC are evidence that Macedonians at the court were also surrounded by gifted craftsmen, working in a Greek style. I accept the clear ancient statement that Aegae, within daily view of Mount Olympus, had a festival called 'Olympia', obviously for Zeus. It may have been a yearly rallying-point for the king and his increasing number of subjects.

When Persian armies retreated in defeat in 479 BC, Alexander I prospered. During the war, he had helped, he said, to protect the medising Greek cities of Boeotia. Afterwards he was honoured with a praise-poem, or encomium, by the great Theban poet Pindar. He put up a golden statue of himself at Delphi, supposedly from spoils taken from the Persians. It is the earliest attested Greek portrait-statue. He had even been allowed, after a dispute, to compete in the Olympic Games (perhaps as early as the 490s BC), a mark of his acceptably Greek pedigree. A fine poem by Bacchylides, 'a golden wing from the Muses', connects drinking-parties in his presence with displays of gold and ivory, with trading abroad and young men's flighty thoughts of far-flung rule and conquest. There is a hint here that the young Alexander, too, might be over-ambitious.

From the mid-460s BC Alexander had to compete on his eastern frontier with the rising power of the Athenians and their allies. They, too, were attracted by the local silver mines and soon allied themselves with Berge, an inland polis which lay strikingly far from the coast up the River Strymon. In the mid-460s BC we first hear allegations, often to be repeated that an Athenian leader (in this case, Cimon) had been bribed by a Macedonian king. Alexander's revenues were vastly increased by his own exploitation of silver-mines near Lake Prasias and his silver coins give the best hint of his new vigour. We see a horseman, surely the king himself, mounted on a superbly formed horse (perhaps improved by Persian bloodlines, retained since 479 BC), armed with two hunting spears and accompanied by a small dog (probably, a 'Melitaean' breed) (fig. 5). Later sources allege that an Alexander, in my view Alexander I, even forced through an infantry reform, creating centralised royal 'foot companions' beside the old companion nobles and newer companion cavalrymen who had also been wooed with this honorific title. If Alexander reformed the infantry, there is no sign of them in the next century of Macedonian history. Perhaps he was cited only as a plausible 'founder' by later generations, Philip and Alexander's men. On his death, probably in the mid- to later 450s BC, the kingdom was torn apart.

King Alexander had been polygamous, a practice known in Greece among only a few previous ruling 'tyrants'. Herodotus thought wrongly that the royal succession passed by primogeniture: one modern theory is that it passed by porphyrogeniture, to the first prince born to a Macedonian king during his actual reign. The historical reality seems to be that no rule prevailed, that polygamy complicated the range of candidates and that companion nobles probably made or broke the chances of aspiring Argead family candidates. Succession struggles became endemic, and for centuries Macedonian kings were plagued by matrimonial intrigue and 'second-wife syndrome'.

Perdiccas II emerged as Alexander's successor, the king best known from Thucydides (who perhaps met him) and from an Athenian comic poet's quip that from Perdiccas' Macedon Athenians received only 'ship-loads of lies'. In fact Perdiccas has to keep changing his allegiances in order to hang on to his kingdom. One of his brothers rebelled against him; so did a highland prince. Perdiccas allied himself first with the dominant Athenians (to whom the Greek cities in Chalkidike were paying a yearly tribute) and then with the Spartan army led north by the audacious Brasidas in 424 BC. In response to the Athenian pressure in the later 430s BC and their foundation of a settlement, Brea, in western Chalkidike, Perdiccas encouraged the neighbouring Chalkidians to form a Chalkidian League, centred in the city of Olynthos. It was such a good idea that its power then returned to haunt him and his successors.

In 413 BC Archelaos succeeded him, a king more effective than the previous seven, according to Thucydides, who once again may have gone up to the royal court. Archelaos developed roads, built new strong points and distributed arms to his subject-soldiers. As the Athenian power diminished locally, he preferred to side with them. Above all, he intensified the kings' tradition of cultural patronage. He started a 'festival of the Muses' at Dion, near the slopes of Mount Olympus. It was he, not his successor, who developed the site of Pella. The fine artist Zeuxis was summoned to decorate his palace there. Two talented visitors stand out amongst his guests, the great sculptor Callimachus and the poet Euripides. Callimachus' presence at Aegae has been confirmed by a funerary verse-inscription and by clear signs of the local impact of his craftsmanship and skills. A rare word in the verse-inscription suggests that it may even have been composed for him by Euripides himself. The ageing Euripides was Archelaos' great catch. He even wrote a play, the *Archelaos*, about a legendary royal ancestor, invented in Archelaos' honour. Above all, it was in Macedon that he wrote his late masterpiece, the *Bacchae*, verses of which imply that it was to be performed at Pella itself. Macedon had various cults of Dionysus, including those for groups of young women who worshipped him in rites on the mountains. The historian-psychologist George Devereux has observed that the *Bacchae*'s scenes of ecstatic possession follow a plausible, near-clinical pattern, so much so that Euripides may have seen the ecstatic state and its therapy, probably in Macedon. Macedonians may not have written plays or sculpted statues, but they cannot be classed as ignorant 'consumers': their king was a very shrewd patron of the top contemporary talent. The great modern commentator on the *Bacchae*, E. R. Dodds, considered that the play was unlikely to have been performed in Macedon because its ideas were too intellectual and 'contemporary' for a Macedonian public. In fact it is excellent evidence for what a Macedonian court-audience in *c*.406 BC could enjoy. They would also have enjoyed Euripides' *Iphigenia at Aulis* and its able characterisation of Achilles, the future role model of Alexander the Great. However, Euripides left the play unfinished when he died in Macedon. He was honoured with a tomb at Arethusa out in the eastern 'Chalkidic' territories.

With the eclipse of Athens's empire in 404 BC Macedon ought to have prospered once again. Instead, the kingdom nearly fell apart. Archelaos' death from a plot while out hunting in 399 BC ushered in six years of succession problems with no fewer than five kings, only the last of whom, Amyntas III, survived for a long reign. Even so, in 393/2 BC, Illyrian tribes nearly drove the new king Amyntas out; in the late 380s BC, Macedon's creation, the Chalkidian League, invaded the lowlands and nearly did the same. Amyntas only survived with the help of a Spartan army. His one success was marriage to Eurydice, one of his two wives, who was a solid link with her home canton in Upper Macedon and proved an admirably resourceful protectress of her children and kingdom's interests. Like Archelaos, Amyntas at least re-founded the lowland coastal city of Pydna: in return, the citizens honoured him with a shrine in his lifetime, an 'Amyntaion', for honours 'equal to the gods'. Amyntas did not necessarily impose this cult, but it was the first such temple-cult for a living Greek ruler. Only in Macedon did Greek kings interrelate with autonomous Greek cities, the breeding-ground for such divine honours.

After a long but turbulent reign, Amyntas III died in 369 BC, apparently peacefully (a rarity in Macedonian history). His sons Alexander II and (initially with a regency) Perdiccas III succeeded him, but the former was quickly murdered in 368 BC and the latter died in 360 BC in a battle against the Illyrians in the north-west. Under Amyntas, first Sparta, then Athens had become essential allies: in 369/8 BC under Alexander II and his successor, the Thebans, too, became arbiters of the Macedonian succession and even took two sets of Macedonian hostages, eighty in all, back home to their city. From 368 to 365 BC, one hostage was Amyntas' third son, Philip. The kings' traditional patronage of external Greek talent continued (Aristotle's father came as court-doctor; a student of Plato, Euphraios, taught at Perdiccas' court) but for forty years the kingdom was basically a casualty of its neighbours.

From 360 to 336 BC Philip turned it round. He is the greatest kingdom-builder in ancient history, a man who designed a new model army with new tactics and balanced weaponry, who introduced Attic *koinē* Greek as his official diplomatic language, who struck the first Greek gold coins to have more than a local circulation, who resettled Macedonians in new sites across his kingdom, who extended Macedonian power from Lake Ohrid to the distant Black Sea and Danube, and who subjected the southern Greek powers in a new alliance with him, their leader, and then unveiled a grand ambition (Map 2): the invasion of the Persian Empire. He even increased massively his kingdom's horsepower by planned land-grants to horse-owners and horse-breeding initiatives. Many of Philip's innovations were crucial to the subsequent Hellenistic age and in every way he was a crucial model, and spur, to his son Alexander. His newly founded Philippi is a precursor of his son's many Alexandrias.

Unlike previous kings, Philip had seen life outside his home kingdom. As a boy he served as a hostage, first among the Illyrian tribes, then for three years at Thebes, the most innovative Greek military power of the 360s BC. The experience formed him in a new way. In a dazzling accession year he asserted himself against Macedonian rivals and then against foreign enemies on all four points of the compass. He initiated his new army; he moved fast and spoke well in public; he had the charm and energy of a young king aged 22 whereas Macedon's neighbours were all ruled by ageing dynasts. At first he pursued the traditional aims of previous Macedonian kings: a conquest of the Illyrians, involvement in neighbouring Thessaly, the capture of Amphipolis. Then, in 356 BC, he founded his new city of Philippi, and from 353 BC onwards became engaged, by Theban invitation, in the festering Sacred War in central Greece. Concluding it in 346 BC, he swore peace and alliance with the Athenians, although (in my view) he regarded it as only temporary. By then, perhaps even by the late 350s BC, I believe he had already conceived the grand design of invading Asia. First, he had to subdue his barbarian neighbours, the Illyrians and Thracians (in 341–339 BC). Then he had to deal with the Greek enemies whom his growing power and ambition had inevitably raised against him. He returned to win the decisive battle of Chaironeia in August 338 BC against southern Greek opposition, led by his former allies, the Athenians and Thebans. No Macedonian king had ever been so powerful, the master of all the Greek mainland and of Europe up to the River Danube (Map 2).

Philip was a master of political 'spin' and of vague promises which recipients unwisely over-interpreted. One-eyed after a wound in 355/4 BC, he was nonetheless praised by an Athenian visitor as handsome, seductively charming, a fine drinker, and a speaker with a good memory. Others were more hostile. The contemporary historian Theopompus centred a long history on Philip and began it by calling him 'such a man as Europe has absolutely never borne'. He then attacked Philip for his dissolute personal life, his extravagance and even the extreme homosexuality of his male 'companions'. In part, he mistook Philip's ostentatious 'culture of the gift' at court and the increasing gold and ivory splendour of his surroundings. Philip's gifts of gold, land and silver treasures bound Macedon's local leaders and neighbouring non-Greek tribes to his cause. He had to rule a Macedon which still differed from region to region. The cantons of upper Macedon, which he had reintegrated into his kingdom, were still largely under-urbanised. Each made up an *ethnos*, or tribe, led by a noble or a local royal house: most people's lives here still centred on villages. Lowland Macedon was populated with towns, administered by officials whose Macedonian names went back before Philip's reforms, *skoidos* (a judicial post), *tagos* or *peliganes*, the 'grey(-haired)' elderly local councillors. There were also 'overseers', *epistatai*, in the townships who were locally appointed for fixed periods. By contrast, the Chalkidic territories and adjoining conquests had mostly been populated with self-governing *poleis*, city-states with a long history of freedom. Philip drew this diversity together by giving local land to beneficiaries whom he resettled from elsewhere in the kingdom and turned into royal king's men of the future. His companions had strong local links too, and through the new magnet of service at his court and in his army they and their dependent communities could be unified to follow the king's demands. The kingdom rested on patronage, military success and the new riches of Philip's conquests. The productive gold and silver mines which he seized for the kingdom were crucial, especially the newly found gold mine at a 'hill of Dionysus' near his new city, Philippi. Philip's court became 'the place to be', and success and gifts entrenched loyalty to the kingship through the court based in Pella and Aegae.

Philip intensified the patronage of Greek talent from outside the kingdom, his predecessors' tradition. As the contemporary Isocrates told a Greek king on Cyprus, Greek culture 'tamed' those whom it benefited. It made them think; it gave them skills; it also enhanced the magnetic splendour of the lowland court. Significantly, Philip invented a corps of young Royal Pages, some of whom were from former highland families, and sent them with his growing son Alexander to be tutored by the great Aristotle beside the caves and lush green landscape near Mieza, still an enchanted site. Patronage of the best talent began early in his reign. Already in 360/59 BC (in my view) a statue of Attic marble (recently discovered at Aegae) was carved by the great Cephisodotos' workshop in Athens as a portrait-statue of Philip's mother, Eurydice, and sent up to her at court: she dedicated it to Eukleia, goddess of 'Fair Repute', in answer to the scandalous rumours of murder which her rivals were wickedly circulating against her. As Philip's power grew, the greatest painters, sculptors, jewellers, metal-workers and theatre-actors followed this same trail to Macedon from all over the Greek world. His culminating glory was his vast new palace above Aegae's theatre, excitingly restored to a date in his reign by Dr Angeliki Kottaridi and her team working there since 2007. At Olympia, Philip had also paid for a rounded building, his 'Philippeion', which was filled with gilded ivory statues of himself and four family-members. Conspicuously, it stood right inside Zeus' precinct, an unprecedented honour. At Olympia, Philip's central statue looked across to the nearby shrine of Zeus. In Macedon, on Aegae's hill, he was now ruling from a ceremonial palace, 12,500 metres square.

Fig. 27 Golden wreath with oak leaves and acorns and golden *larnax* – the container for the cremated remains of King Philip II

Fig. 28 (above) Silver cup (*kylix*) from the tomb of Philip II (Cat. no. 476)

Fig. 29 (opposite) Rider in battle – detail from one of the gold and ivory couches from the tomb of Philip II

His 'Philippeion' was made ready for the last Olympics before he and his army left for Asia. His palace at Aegae was ready to host Greek guests to his daughter's wedding in autumn 336 BC. By then the gold, ivory and marble of his court made the contemporary arts in Athens look decidedly provincial. On the day of the wedding celebrations for his daughter, Philip was murdered in public in Aegae's theatre, a victim (it was said) of court scandals. Some blamed a homosexual grievance; modern historians identify two other tensions, one of which Philip had tried to counter, the other of which was his own creation. In the murder and its aftermath there were signs of the local factions and loyalties within Macedon which Philip's court, royal army and land-grants had tried to break down. There was also matrimonial tension, centring on Philip's seventh wife, his first Macedonian bride, mother of a daughter and, days before, of a son. In his early forties Philip had upset his household.

The style of Philip's funeral testifies to 'Homeric' Macedon's new splendour (fig. 27). He was cremated in a specially built wooden 'house'; his bones were then deposed with silver vessels (fig. 28), fine ivory couches (fig. 29), much weaponry and his great royal shield in the back chamber of Aegae's royal 'Tomb II'. No text or inscription attests this tomb as his, but the occupant was a king in his mid-forties (as the bones testify) and a woman (in her mid- to late twenties) was also cremated and laid in the front chamber. There are only two royal candidates, Philip II or the half-wit Philip III, his son, who was murdered at Aegae in October 317 BC. Philip III has been championed by some,

Fig. 30 (opposite) Above the
door of the tomb of Philip II his
son Alexander, the new king, is
represented

Fig. 31 (right) Line drawing of
the same scene

but he is now seen to be excluded by the fact of the great cremation (he was
reburied at Aegae after he had been dead and rotting in the ground for several
months and unfit for such a cremation). He is also at odds with the subject of
the tomb's painting (it shows Alexander and Philip II hunting with able-bodied
royal pages, not a scene for the defective Philip III) (figs. 247–250). The age of
the accompanying female also does not fit the woman buried with him (she
was his valiant wife, Philip II's granddaughter, and was killed when only 18–19
years old). Nothing in, or about, the great Tomb is inconsistent archaeologically with a dating to 336 BC, the date of Philip II's death. He alone fits the fact
of the cremation and admirably suits the subject of the accompanying painting, which shows himself (one-eyed in profile) hunting a lion with the Pages,
his own creation.

Above the door of this tomb Alexander is represented, the new king who
paid for this masterpiece (figs. 30–31). With him, the Macedonians were to
go east beyond even Philip's immediate dreams. But Alexander remained a
Macedonian in large measure, and it is to Macedon that his own formation
must be traced and assessed in a contemporary context, not just in terms

of modern moral values and priorities. Even in Asia, thoughts of this green homeland accompanied him and his men. It was to Aegae that his body was intended to return and it was to Macedon that his ageing successors, Antigonos and even 80-year-old Seleukos, aspired to return as conquerors. From coastal Syria to the River Euphrates and beyond, their Macedonians named the local landscapes and their new settlements after place-names in their former homeland. Their Macedonian upbringing never deserted them.

3   Royalty and Democracy: the case of Macedonia

Miltiades B. Hatzopoulos

The Athenians, like the Arcadians, were no more autochthonous than other Greek peoples, but, unlike the Thessalians or the Boeotians, who settled in their respective territories during the last centuries of the second millennium, they did not maintain any recollection of their Middle Bronze Age (2000–1600 BC) migration to their historical habitat. The Macedonians knew they were relative latecomers and their legends (or mythological tradition) situated their occupation of the Central Macedonian Plain seven generations before the time of Herodotus, roughly in the first decades of the seventh century BC.[1]

In fact, the Greek presence in what we today call Macedonia was significantly older and the Argead Macedonians, originally transhumant pastoralists, speakers of a north-western Greek dialect, who originated from the Pindus mountain chain and founded the Macedonian kingdom in Lower Macedonia (having conquered a Brygian town named Edessa, making it their capital, Aegae), were only the latest Greek-speaking group to appear in the region. Recent archaeological discoveries show that even in the Late Bronze Age (1600–1200 BC) the Mycenaean world extended well north of Mount Olympus and the Kambounian mountains, comprising at least the southern part of Macedonia. Abundant Mycenaean pottery, both imported and locally produced, weapons, pins, brooches and syllabic script have been discovered in tombs at Orestis, Elimeia and Pieria. Elements of the Achaean dialect of this early Greek-speaking stratum emerge in later inscriptions from these areas, while an early Greek presence of a different origin is also traceable on the shores of the Thermaic Gulf and in the Chalkidic peninsula, which were eventually incorporated into the Macedonian kingdom. Recent excavations have brought to light there Late Mycenaean period settlements of Ionian Greeks hailing from Euboea, whom Herodotus would later call the *Chalkidikon genos*.

These newcomers from the Pindus mountain chain merged with earlier Greek speakers, founding several principalities in the Macedonian uplands. Thucydides (2.99.2) mentions the kingdoms of the Lynkestai and the Elimiotai 'and other peoples of the highlands', who were subject to the kings of Lower Macedonia, but had their own kings. Among the omitted names of peoples

[39]

Fig. 32 Goats near Aegae in a snowy landscape

who might have figured are the Orestai, the Tymphaioi and Paravaioi, and perhaps the Derriopes. We know that the Lynkestian kings claimed descent from the Bacchiads of Corinth and the Orestai from Orestes himself, but neither could compete with the kings of the Argead Macedonians, who called themselves Temenids and claimed lineage to Heracles as the great-great-grandfather of Perdiccas, the founder of their kingdom. It is perhaps thanks to this association that they were recognised as the suzerains of the lesser Macedonian princedoms.

The ancient literary sources on Macedonian institutions are far from straightforward, often expressing the personal prejudices of their authors. It is unclear if Macedonia was a unitary state of the *ethnos* (people) or a federation of *poleis* (city-states). Pseudo-Skylax, a geographer writing in the mid-fourth century BC, uses the term *ethnos* to qualify the Macedonians, but at the same time lists a series of Macedonian *poleis*, thus employing a term which elsewhere in his work designates the other form of independent states known in Greece. The Macedonian form of government is also contentious: was it an absolute monarchy or a democratic kingship? The second-century BC historian Polybius denounces the inexperience of Macedonians in democratic government, but elsewhere draws attention to the 'egalitarian' relationship between the king and ordinary Macedonians, who are never described as subjects, but as citizens. The ignorance, prejudice and sometimes even hostility to which statements in the ancient authors bear witness have left the field free for subjective modern constructions, some of which show admiration and others denunciation of ancient Macedonian institutions, for reasons that have to be sought in the personality of the individual writers. In contrast, increasing evidence provided by the archaeological, epigraphic and numismatic record in recent years allows us to form a less subjective opinion.

Macedonia was – and still is – to the Greeks of the south an exotic country. The traveller who penetrates the Valley of Tempe to enter Pieria discovers a land that in scale, if not nature, is completely different. He is greeted by the permanent snows of Mount Olympus, the highest mountain in Greece (2,917m). Straight roads, bordered by tall poplars, lead him across vast grasslands, watered by perennial rivers, whose banks are grazed not only by goats and sheep (fig. 32), but also cows and buffalo. Except for a strip along the coast, he will not see any olive trees. As he ascends to the high plateaux, he encounters forests of oak, beech and even birch. Although the lion and the wild ox, once the favourite trophies of royal hunts, no longer inhabit the hills, the deer, the lynx, the wolf and the bear still resist the attacks of hunters. Over the vast stretches of lakes Prespa and Vegorritis fly swans, storks and pelicans, while in their depth swarm freshwater fish.[2]

Macedonia, along with Thessaly and Epirus, belongs unquestionably to a distinctive unit, legitimately called 'northern Greece', but one that should not obliterate another division between western and eastern (or Aegean) Greece cutting down the peninsula along the Pindus range from as far north as the lake district to as far south as the Gulf of Corinth. Lower Macedonia shares with Thessaly the vast plains and wide temperature variations. On the other hand, they both contrast with the strongly folded limestone mountain ranges of Epirus, between which the valleys are tightly squeezed. The Upper Macedonian districts of Orestis and Tymphaia also form transitional areas between Epirus on the one hand and Lower Macedonia and Thessaly on the other. In this respect Macedonia, with its two constituent parts, occupies an intermediate position between Thessaly and Epirus, reflected in its dialect, economic and social life, and political institutions. Macedonia, with an important pastoral economy in the uplands and extensive farming in the plains, falls between the Epirote and the Thessalian model. Unlike the latter, it provides little evidence for the existence of a servile population. Significantly, there is no trace either of aristocrats of baronial status comparable to the Thessalian model, or serfs bound to the land. Large domains did exist, especially in the conquered territories outside Macedonia proper, seemingly lent or leased to members of the owner's family, or tenants, rather than being directly exploited with the help of servile or helot manpower. The hearth, applicable to their ancestor's transhumant past, retains the name *pyrokausis* (camp fire), generally comprising a couple with their unmarried children, possibly some poor relatives and servants. Slavery was of the Homeric rather than of the chattel type. Manumitted slaves remained with the family of their previous owners, or were given assistance towards acquiring their own establishment. Another vestige of transhumant pastoralism was that women, who had to fend for themselves during the menfolk's prolonged absences, had acquired the possibility to engage in legal transactions without the presence of a *kyrios* (the male guardian); if widowed, women could also act as heads of family and guardians of their underage children, and within the royal family as regents.

Geographic conditions and economic activities largely determined the extent and pattern of settlement. The uplands of Upper Macedonia, like those of Epirus and most of western Greece, were until the fourth century essentially faithful to the *kome*, the open, unfortified village. In contrast, the plains of Lower Macedonia, like those of Thessaly, experienced urban life from the end of the sixth century at the latest.

This disparity is also reflected in the economic, social and political conditions. Transhumant pastoralism, common for centuries for both the Argead Macedonians and their cousins of the Upper Macedonian princedoms, is incompatible with the autarky and self-centredness of the Greek *polis*. Even until a few decades ago, herdsmen, before moving great distances from plain to mountain in the spring and upon their return in autumn, held gatherings and celebrated festivals, thus maintaining a sense of community. These gatherings gradually created common religious centres, such as Dion in Macedonia, which evolved around the cult of Zeus Olympios. Regular assemblies, called *apellai* were held on these occasions, which among other things designated the *basileus*, the part-hereditary and part-elective Head of State. This sense of community was enhanced by the part-real and part-constructed memory of the common origin of the group, the *ethnos*, which after the collapse of the Mycenaean world had conquered and appropriated the land.

Although the Macedonian kingdom appears from its inception as the state of an *ethnos*, of a people – albeit centred around a *polis*, or capital, Aegae – its expansion led to the inclusion of other communities that, from the end of the sixth century at the latest, are qualified in the extant literary sources by the term *polis*. This development of sedentary life and the rise of urban centres soon became the focal point for economic, social and political activities in the kingdom of Lower Macedonia, altering the traditional relations between local institutions and those of the whole *ethnos*. The cities acquired proper institutions, in particular a board of executive magistrates called *tagoi* (ordainers) and councils composed of elders named *peliganes* (grey-haired, *i.e.* elders), providing a layer of local administration between the gatherings of the popular assemblies.

By the final years of the fifth century there are clear signs of conflict between the king and the cities of Lower Macedonia. Some cities detached themselves from the kingdom, either joining as autonomous units other political formations such as the Athenian Confederation, or in an attempt to achieve independent status. The movement was to intensify during the first half of the fourth century under the impulse of the Chalkidian League, nearly leading to the disintegration of the common institutions of the Macedonian ethnic state.

For this period, the sources provide sparse information about political life in the cities and only glimpses of the central authorities at work. The mainspring of power seems to be the king, but he was nevertheless obliged to govern according to the ancestral custom, the *nomos* of the Macedonians. These restrictions regulated his relations with the *ethnos*, and above all the other members of the dynasty and with his Companions (*hetairoi*) – those few dozen who formed his entourage, without whose support he would have been unable

Fig. 33 The hieratic diadem of
King Philip II (Cat. no. 87)

to rule effectively. The common people made only rare appearances as a last resort, punishing a king's failures by dismissing him. The predominant role of the king derived from his position as political, military and religious leader of the Argead Macedonians, but also his capacities as suzerain of the kings of Upper Macedonia and master of the conquered cities and territories not yet colonised by the Macedonians and integrated into Macedonia proper, the revenues of which accrued to the royal chest (fig. 33).

As Aristotle observed, 'royalties are preserved by bringing them into a more moderate form; for the fewer powers the kings have, the longer time the office in its entirety must last, for they themselves become less despotic and more equal to their subjects in temper, and their subjects envy them less' (Aristotle, *Politics* 5.1313a). We know from epigraphic evidence that in the late fifth century the Molossian king Tharypas, anticipating Aristotle's advice, introduced reforms creating a contractual kingship based on the mutual observance of the traditional *nomos*. His Macedonian contemporary Archelaos (413–399 BC) was also a reformer king, with his efforts cut short by his assassination in 399 BC. The ancient authors insist on his building activities and military reforms. However, Archelaos was also known to have reorganised the Olympic festival at Dion in honour of Zeus Olympios and the Muses. Given that this was a festival later attested as one of the two occasions of the biannual meeting of the Macedonian assembly and delegates of the cities, it is not impossible that this reorganisation had an institutional significance. From the early decades of the fourth century, Macedonians begin to be identified by a city ethnic, implying reorganisation into local political units.

ROYALTY AND DEMOCRACY [43]

The great instability punctuated by the civil wars and foreign invasions following Archelaos' assassination left the task of radically transforming Macedonia to another reformer king, Philip II (360–336 BC). The presence in the Old Kingdom of cities such as Pydna and Pella, each jealous of its autonomy and ready to rebel and secede, along with the annexation of formerly independent city-states in the New Territories east of the River Axios, such as Amphipolis and Apollonia, necessitated a reorganisation of the Macedonian state on the basis of the *polis*. The autonomy of the existing cities was formally recognised. In the indigenous hinterland of the New Territories, new cities were founded by Macedonian colonists or created by the federation of villages based around a market town called *metropolis*. In Upper Macedonia the former semi-independent *ethne* of the Elimiotai, the Orestai, the Lynkestai and the Tymphaioi-Paravaioi, were granted *polis* status. Thus in Macedonia proper, each local political unit had its own citizenship (*politeia*), legislation (*nomoi*), and governing body (*ekklesia, boule, archontes*) headed by an *epistates* and an eponymous magistrate, the priest of Asclepius. Philip, who was elected as hereditary Head of State of Thessaly, recognised the advantages of its regional organisation into four districts governed by an equal number of tetrarchs. He introduced it in Macedonia, creating four districts, each with its local capital (Amphipolis, Thessalonice, Pella, Heraclea?), where assemblies could be held and taxes collected. This reform combined the advantages of decentralisation in a country that Philip's conquests had more than trebled (Map 2), with a better control of the autonomous cities through the *strategoi* who were probably appointed to head each district.

The king was surrounded by a *synedrion* (council) of Companions, friends and army generals, which took political decisions with him. The most important questions were formally submitted for approval by the Assembly of the Macedonian citizen-soldiers, which was able to pass judgement on capital offences and acclaim the new king. Thus by the end of the third quarter of the fourth century BC, besides the Head of State and the Common Assembly, the two traditional organs of the Macedonian ethnic state, there existed scores of autonomous communities who sent their delegates to the festivals, coinciding with the meetings of the Common Assembly, but without being organically integrated into them. This new order lasted until the Roman conquest of Macedonia in 168 BC.

The Macedonian 'constitution' as it evolved under the reign of Philip II, shared a number of features with the 'constitutions' of pre-republican Thessaly and Epirus, which set the three northern ethnic states apart from their cognates in the south, such as the Achaean and the Aetolian federations. The salient feature was the paramount position of a Head of State – not with an annual mandate but life tenure – theoretically elective, but in practice hereditary. In internal affairs the local communities were usually left to their own devices, once the Common Assembly had appointed or – more usually acclaimed – the Head of State. This implied conferral on him of the traditional prerogatives to mobilise and command the army and freely dispose of the 'federal' revenues,

Fig. 34 Gold discs found in the tomb of a member of the royal family of the Temenids (Cat. no. 60)

so that he was in effect able to pursue the foreign policy of his choice. The control of war and diplomacy (through the declaration of war and the ratification of treaties), usually listed among the traditional rights of the Common Assembly, inevitably became illusory. Once the army was mobilised under the orders of a prestigious commander-in-chief, the actual decision on the declaration of war was bound by mere formality, with no assembly likely to challenge an advantageous treaty contracted by a victorious chief. In case of failure, of course, the Head of State could always be deposed, as happened several times, but this action was an extreme means of popular control. A Macedonian king would appear to an Athenian politician not only as a supreme commander in war, master of all sacrifices, and judge in law-suits (at an appellate court), according to the classical definition of heroic kingship by Aristotle (Aristotle, *Politics* 3.1285b), but also as 'sole master of his own policy, open or secret, at once general, absolute ruler and treasurer' (Demosthenes, *First Olynthiac* 1.4-5 on Philip II) (fig. 34).

Another shared feature of the three northern monarchical *ethne*, in contradistinction to the southern republican ones, was the absence of a *synedrion*, a standing organ of representative government reflecting the relative importance of the constituent local communities and enabling them to make their voice heard. The only *synedrion* in Macedonia under the Argead and the Antigonid kings is not a proper organ of the *ethnos*, but a consultative body composed of the king's companions or friends – a court nobility recruited among city elites. Such interpenetration of the political personnel at the central and the local level made up for the absence of genuine representative *synedria*. It is also true that delegates from the local communities might join this Privy Council on certain occasions, but even this did not make them equivalent to the genuine *synedria* with the proportional representation of the southern republican *ethne*. It is only after the abolition of kingship by the Romans that Macedonia acquired such a deliberative body.

In the absence of a genuine *synedrion* integrating local political units into central government, what were the relations between central and local governments in Macedonia under the kings? The evidence that enables us to view such relationships in action consists of the letters (*epistolai*) and ordinances (*diagrammata*) emanating from the Head of State, the real holder of central authority. Some twenty-eight letters and eight *diagrammata* from the central Macedonian authorities offer us a varied and instructive picture of the relations between central and local authorities. There was a clear distinction between a reserved domain (army and court) where central authorities possessed a discretionary power to legislate, and other government matters in which the royal will could manifest itself only if mediatised through local authority. In military affairs the king as commander-in-chief had a direct relationship with the Macedonians under his command, who were paid and often equipped by him. Thus army regulations were decided, probably in Council (*synedrion*), but by the king's sole authority, acquiring force of law largely without any intervention from local authorities. Therefore there was no mention of an addressee and the order for publication was included in a clause of the text of the *diagramma* itself.

The king could also request from the local authorities the publication of all sorts of information or rulings made by him, either in the form of letters or of ordinances. The latter were transmitted by a covering letter to the competent authorities of the local communities, who, according to the scope and content of the documents, took the appropriate steps for publication.

Letters from the central authorities, accompanying extracts of ordinances, might name a single person, the *epistates*, or the city authorities as their addressee. The occasional use of the second person plural leaves little doubt that even in the former case the chief magistrate figures in his representative capacity and the whole community is the real addressee. The explicit mention of the city authorities in royal letters is usually an indication that the request of the central authorities could not be satisfied by a simple executive decision by the chief magistrate, but required legislative action by all the deliberative organs (magistrates, Council, Assembly) of the community.

On the other hand, as we learn by over 25 civic legislative documents discovered to date, local legislation and decisions on local matters (laws concerning education or taxation, decrees honouring citizens and foreigners) lay entirely within the competence of the local authorities. Even if we suspect that they were prompted by royal initiative, these local authorities could even take decisions that theoretically had a bearing on foreign policy, such as the granting of citizenship, proxeny and decisions relating to security in time of war or peace.

This unstable equilibrium between the Head of State, the *ethnos* and the local political units it comprised, in order to last, it required all the stature the heroic dynasties could provide and exceptionally capable personalities such as the Temenids (and later the Antigonids). The unfailing loyalty of the Macedonians to their institutions highlights that it would have continued had it not been brutally destroyed by the Romans in 168/167 BC. The reforms of Philip V and Perseus during the first third of the second century which granted more autonomy to districts and local political units exemplified by the replacement of the single *epistates* by boards of two politarchs and the end of the royal monopoly of minting, signified the creation of a political system more integrated and respectful of the composite nature of the state. The Macedonian kingdom in its final phase, could indeed claim its place among the autonomous peoples and the democratic cities of Greece.

4 Aegae: 160 years of archaeological research

Yannis Galanakis

'Under these Macedonian monuments ... it is not just some ancient remains that await to be excavated; it is the life and history of people that will be discovered.'

Léon Heuzey commenting on what may lie under the great tumulus (Heuzey and Daumet 1876, 233–4)

Tucked away from the Macedonian plain, Aegae is situated on the northern slopes of the Pierian mountains, immediately to the south of River Haliacmon in northern Greece (fig. 35). From the acropolis and the palace site one has an excellent view over the plain. In antiquity, when the coastline was situated further inland (15km away instead of 25km today), the sea would have been clearly visible.

In the early age of archaeological exploration in Greece, Léon Heuzey (1831–1922), a 24-year-old member of the French Archaeological School in Athens, set off to explore two relatively rugged regions: Macedonia in 1855–56, still part of the Ottoman Empire, and Acarnania in western Greece in 1856–57. In both areas he is justifiably considered an archaeological pioneer. It was during his first trip in 1855 that, with the help of a local guide, he saw the ruins on the hill of Agia Triada, between the hamlets of Koutles and Barbes and near the village of Palatitza (Palatitsia), which he immediately identified as a palace. At first he dated the palace to the age of the *Diadochoi* (the Successors of Alexander the Great) but following his 1861 small-scale excavation there, he re-dated it to the reign of Archelaos I (413–399 BC).[1]

Heuzey was so struck by the beauty of the site and the importance of the ruins that he later called it 'Pompeii of Macedonia'. In 1858 he was appointed by Emperor Napoleon III to lead an expedition, which presented a first-class opportunity for Heuzey to explore the archaeology of Macedonia in more detail. In 1861 he conducted excavations in the east wing of the palace near Palatitsia, while on the plain he excavated a Macedonian tomb. Objects and architectural fragments from these excavations were taken to the Louvre.

Heuzey identified the ruins near Palatitsia as belonging to the ancient Balla, an association unquestioned for almost a century. In his richly illustrated publication *Mission Archéologique de Macédoine*, written with the architect

Fig. 35 River Haliacmon

Honoré Daumet (1826–1911) and published in 1876, Heuzey set the foundations for the more systematic exploration of the ruins near Palatitsia and of Macedonia as a whole.

After the annexation of Macedonia to Greece in 1912, archaeologists turned their attention to this area anew, but not to the ruins near Palatitsia.[2] The year 1922 saw the exchange of populations between Greece and Turkey – refugees from the Caucasus and Pontus settled in the area of Koutles and Barbes (by that time abandoned). The new settlement was named Vergina, after a queen in a local fairytale; according to a version of this story, in times of danger the queen of Beroia (also known as Vergia or Vergina) could escape into safety via an underground passage to Palatitsia.

In 1937 Konstantinos Rhomaios (1874–1966), professor at the Aristotle University of Thessaloniki, became the first after Heuzey to explore the site in a systematic manner, following the discovery of a tomb now named after him ('the Rhomaios tomb') (fig. 36). For four seasons Rhomaios and a team of students, among them Manolis Andronikos from 1938, excavated the tomb and brought to light part of the palace. In 1940 the Italian invasion of Greece and the Second World War brought the archaeological work at the site to a halt. After the war, Rhomaios, as emeritus professor, briefly continued his work at Vergina alongside the Ephor (superintendent) of Antiquities for the region, Charalambos Makaronas (1905–1977).

Of all the excavators, Andronikos (1919–1992) would be the one to link his name inextricably with the archaeology of the site (fig. 43). He first visited Vergina as an 18-year-old undergraduate student. In 1951 he conducted small-scale excavations under the auspices of the Hellenic Archaeological Service. Between 1952 and 1961, over seven seasons, he excavated 32 burial mounds in the tumuli cemetery mainly under the auspices of the Athens Archaeological Society (fig. 37).[3] Andronikos's excavations of the tumuli were published as a monograph in 1969, the same year when another Macedonian tomb, one of the latest examples dated to around 200 BC, came to light in the Bloukas plot, in the northern outskirts of the village. From 1960 to 1962, 75 tumuli were excavated by Photios Petsas (1918–2003) as part of salvage works, undertaken during the construction of the new road linking Palatitsia with Vergina. Four more mounds were excavated by Aikaterini Rhomiopoulou in 1980.

Charalambos Makaronas conducted small-scale excavations at the palace between 1954 and 1956. Between 1959 and 1974, Andronikos and Georgios Bakalakis resumed and continued Rhomaios's excavations at the palace, with the support of the University of Thessaloniki. The site became an important fieldwork school for numerous Thessaloniki archaeology students. The preliminary publication of the palace in 1961 by Andronikos, Bakalakis, Makaronas and Moutsopoulos complemented the work of Heuzey and Rhomaios. The excavators agreed with Rhomaios's interpretation, that the palace was probably built some time during the reign of Antigonos Gonatas (276–239 BC) and was used as a royal resort.

Until 1968 the scholarly community followed Heuzey's identification of the site near Vergina with the little-known ancient Macedonian town of Balla. In that year Nicholas Hammond (1907–2001) first suggested that the ancient capital of the Macedonian kingdom was not located at Edessa as previously thought, but at Vergina. He based his idea both on textual and archaeological evidence, mainly the presence of a palace. At first, his interpretation was not welcomed by the academic community, though Robin Lane Fox came, independently, to the same conclusion in 1970. By 1976 Manolis Andronikos was also convinced that Vergina was indeed the site of the royal capital, Aegae.[4] Using this hypothesis, Andronikos concluded that the great tumulus (110m in diameter × 15m in height, the largest in the region) could only conceal royal graves.

By 1952 Andronikos had already established that the mound was man-made and, following additional work on the great tumulus during 1962–63, he became convinced that whatever tomb was concealed under this mound was not to be found inside but rather underground. As this excavation would require more time and substantial effort, Andronikos decided to wait until his work at the palace was over. In 1976, with the palace excavation completed, he turned his attention on the excavation of the great tumulus.

In October 1977 Andronikos started to reveal under the great tumulus tomb I with the wall painting showing the abduction of Persephone by Hades, and the unlooted Tomb II with its astonishing hunting frieze on the façade. This tomb is now identified as that of Philip II and dated to 336 BC. The tomb was provided with a rich assemblage, while the impressive remains of the funeral pyre were placed on top of the tomb's roof. In the subsequent year another intact tomb, Tomb III or the 'tomb of the Prince' (now thought to be that of Alexander IV and dated to c.310 BC) came to light.[5]

Andronikos's discoveries caused a worldwide sensation, not least because of their archaeological importance: exquisite jewellery, silverware, worked gold (fig. 38) and ivory, arms and armour, bronze and ceramic vessels, painted *stelai* (tomb markers) and friezes, all added an important chapter to the archaeology of ancient Macedonia. Similar to the discoveries at Mycenae and Knossos, those at Aegae became an archaeological milestone and helped refocus the world's archaeological attention on Macedonia. Until that point, it was the early (Neolithic and Bronze Age) archaeology of the region that had attracted the most interest, compared with the marginal role of classical Greek archaeology (predominantly explored by the Hellenic Archaeological Service and the Aristotle University of Thessaloniki).

In 1982, the acropolis and the terraces below the palace were investigated, revealing the theatre of Aegae (for a plan of the site see fig. 172). In 1981–82 more Macedonian tombs, near the tomb excavated by Heuzey, were discovered in the Bella plot, dated to the third century BC (three Macedonian tombs and a cist tomb). In 1982, systematic investigations also began on the fourth-century BC sanctuary of Eukleia, the goddess of Fair Repute, by Professor Saatsoglou-Paliadeli of the University of Thessaloniki, alongside excavations of a cist grave near the village of Palatitsia (excavated in 1984–85) and more importantly the theatre (under the supervision of Professor Stella Drougou) where Philip II was assassinated. Between 1983 and 1987 work continued at the theatre, the Eukleia sanctuary, the acropolis and the fortification walls (the latter two investigated by Professor P. Faklaris of the University of Thessaloniki), while a large public building to the NW of the Eukleia sanctuary also began to be uncovered (investigated by Dr A. Kottaridi, assistant of Professor Andronikos at that time). In 1987, only a few metres to the east of the 'Rhomaios tomb', another Macedonian tomb was discovered, the 'tomb of the throne', dated to around 340 BC: it preserves an Ionic façade at the back wall of the chamber and impressive painted decoration (fig. 42) as well as an astonishing marble and gold-gilded painted throne depicting the couple of the underworld (Hades and Persephone) riding a four-horse chariot (fig. 92). The tomb has been identified as the resting place

Fig. 36 (below) The marble throne inside the 'tomb of Rhomaios'

Fig. 37 (above) The burial of a woman with bronze jewellery from the tumuli cemetery at Aegae

of Eurydice, queen and mother of three kings and grandmother of Alexander the Great. Another Macedonian tomb with an Ionic façade, much deprived of its original building material and dated to the late fourth century BC, was discovered next to the New Cultural Centre (now Vergina's Municipal Hall), raising the number of Macedonian tombs at Aegae to a dozen; the largest concentration of such tombs from any other known Macedonian site.

In 1988, the Lady of Aegae, a late archaic burial (c.500 BC) bedecked in gold from head to toe, was excavated by Andronikos and Angeliki Kottaridi (fig. 39). The following year, four more burials dated between 480–420 BC were excavated in the same cluster (now known as the cluster of the queens: see 8. Kottaridi, this volume). These burials yielded impressive assemblages that included lifesize clay male and female heads and a fine group of white-ground Attic *lekythoi* painted with vivid colours (figs. 40–41). In 1990, the discovery of another tomb in the Queens' cluster dating to around 350–325 BC produced a fine group of terracotta figurines, while excavations by Professor Stella Drougou of the University of Thessaloniki begun at the Metroon, the sanctuary of the mother of the gods. Concurrently, new and impressive discoveries were made at the sanctuary of Eukleia (see 14. Saatsoglou-Paliadeli, this volume).

Following Andronikos's death in 1992, excavations at Aegae were continued by his students and university colleagues. Work resumed at the sanctuary of Eukleia, the Metroon, the acropolis, the fortification walls, and more tombs

continued to be excavated, especially in the area of the modern village, providing important information on the sixth and fifth centuries BC. A Hellenistic house, discovered in 1980 and excavated in 1989 was re-studied in 1992–93 by Bettina Tsigarida. At the same time a new shelter was built over the tombs found under the great tumulus. In 1996 the 'Archaeological site of Aigai (modern-day Vergina)' was inscribed as a world heritage site by UNESCO and a year later the spectacular museum of the royal tombs prepared by Kottaridi opened its gates to the visitors, making Aegae the most popular tourist destination in northern Greece.

A reinvestigation by Professor Stella Drougou during 1998–99 of the tomb excavated by Heuzey in 1861 led to the discovery of another, rather 'idiosyncratic', Macedonian tomb nearby ('Heuzey tomb α' with an entrance from the side but covered with a flat roof). On the north-east side of this new tomb a small cist tomb was explored in 1999 ('Heuzey tomb β'). Although the tomb excavated by Heuzey and 'tomb α' were found looted, the small cist ('tomb β') was intact, containing a large number of objects within an area of only 1.47sq.m.: the cremated remains of a man furnished with weapons, metal *symposion* vessels (a calyx-krater with relief decoration, kantharoi, situla, among others), and clay vases, dated to around 320–310 BC. This discovery helped establish the sequence of use in this area of the necropolis, with the Heuzey cluster predating the tombs at the Bella farm.

Excavations in the last twenty years by Angeliki Kottaridi and her team under the auspices of the 17th Ephorate of Prehistoric and Classical Antiquities

Fig. 38 (above) Gold Medusa – originally attached to the linen cuirass of King Philip II. Medusa heads were popular evil averting devices in antiquity (Cat. no. 91)

Fig. 39 (opposite top) The Lady of Aegae bedecked in gold during excavation

Fig. 40 (opposite bottom) The group of fine white-ground Attic *lekythoi* as found

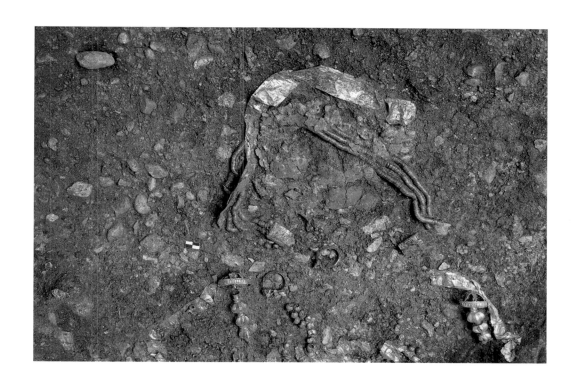

Fig. 41 (opposite) Detail from an Attic white-ground *lekythos* decorated with vivid colours – these vessels brought to the Macedonians the fruits of painting, an art they were to bring to perfection (Cat. no. 245)

Fig. 42 (above) Detail from the tomb of Eurydice's painted interior

have added an important chapter to the history of the site. More than a thousand tombs, many of which are dated to the sixth and fifth centuries BC have been investigated in the necropolis of Aegae (see 8. Kottaridi, this volume). At the same time, the archaeological investigation extended to the broader area of Aegae in the region outside the *asty*. As a result several settlements, necropoleis, forts, farmsteds, and small local cemeteries were discovered. One of the most important results of this activity was the discovery and systematic exploration of the NW section of the city wall of Aegae, where remains of earlier phases of this wall were also preserved (see 11. Kottaridi, this volume).

In 2000 a tile stamped with a goat's head was found in Goultidis's field near the north part of the city walls, while in 2001 another similar tile was discovered in the Metroon. These tiles, along with the palace, the royal graves and the dedications to *Heracles Patroos* found in the tholos and by Queen Eurydice to Eukleia, are considered further evidence for the site's identification with Aegae, which is now almost unanimously accepted.

Between 2003 and 2005 the elongated mound (43.75 x 24.75m) was investigated by Saatsoglou-Paliadeli and her team of the University of Thessaloniki. First considered by Andronikos in 1981, the excavation revealed three tombs; a pit grave at the centre of the mound and two cist graves in the north and south section of the mound. The tombs, dating to the second half of the fourth century BC, were looted twice: during the Gallic invasion (third century BC) and during the Roman conquest (in the second century BC). Nevertheless, the few finds retrieved from these burials suggest that they belonged to members of the elite. A stone-built structure, erected near the elongated mound, is identified as a *heroon* (a shrine dedicated to a hero) or funerary monument, similar to the structure found under the great tumulus. Among the most notable finds was a marble volute *krater*.

More surprises awaited the team of the Eukleia sanctuary excavations led by Professor Saatsoglou-Paliadeli. In 2008 a bronze vessel (*pyxis*) was discovered which concealed a unique golden pyxis. The latter held the cremated remains

Fig. 43 Manolis Andronikos
(1919–1992)

of a man along with a gold wreath (see 14. Saatsoglou-Paliadeli, this volume).

Prior to the recent restoration project at the palace, only the tholos (the round structure near the eastern main entrance) had been re-investigated in 1999 and during 2003–06 by Saatsoglou-Paliadeli. Since 2007 Kottaridi and her team have been working on the restoration of the palace, a major undertaking that involves considerable archaeological work. The fruits of their labours are already very promising: important new evidence has come to light regarding the date as well as the construction and appearance of this imposing structure (see Appendix, this volume).[6]

With work at the palace in full flow, one can only reiterate Heuzey's hope that many more scholars will continue their engagement with the archaeology of Macedonia and Aegae in particular. For Heuzey, Rhomaios and Andronikos (fig. 43), 'a certain honour will remain as [they] were the first [each for his own reason] to attract with perseverance the travellers and scholars' attention to this site'.[7]

5 The Mycenaean presence in Macedonia: new evidence from the region of Emathia

Elena Kountouri

The most dominant subjects of study in Late Bronze Age research in Macedonia are the relationship between this region and southern Greece, the influence of Mycenaean civilisation and the extent of Mycenaean presence in the area.[1] Macedonia is generally regarded as having been outside the core of the Mycenaean world, yet influenced by it to a considerable degree, especially during the twelfth and eleventh centuries BC. The impact of Mycenaean civilisation is best witnessed in the coastal and more easily accessible sites in Macedonia. It is interpreted by scholars either as a result of commercial contacts or as a physical presence of Mycenaeans in the region in the form of prosperous commercial stations or even of permanent settlements or colonies, perhaps for the sourcing of timber and woodlands and the control of copper and gold deposits.

The first traces of contact between Macedonia and the Mycenaean world are observed in the early Mycenaean period with the presence of imported pottery (seventeenth–fifteenth centuries BC) at Torone in Chalkidike and in the toumbas (man-made tells) at Kalamaria and Olynthos as well as in the form of a gold ornament found in the settlement at Kastanas. This ornament resembles similar examples from Grave Circle B at Mycenae, and perhaps originates from the same source. This early penetration of Mycenaean products in Macedonia should be interptreted as coincidental and a result of exchange networks that were in operation between neighbouring regions and which took advantage of the natural access routes created by the fertile plains and the large, navigable rivers of Axios, Strymon and Haliacmon that run through this region.

It is within this framework of exchanges and contacts that the two swords (BM 1040-1041), fine examples of Mycenaean metallurgy and now in the Museum at Aegae, should be interpreted. They were handed to the museum at Aegae as chance finds, having been found in the region of Sphekia on the western slopes of the Pierian mountains. These swords are also the only available evidence for Mycenaean presence in the plateau of Sphekia, which is situated next to the main, diachronic land route that connects Macedonia

Fig. 44 Late Bronze Age swords from the area of Sphekia near Aegae (Cat. nos. 3–4)

with southern Greece. According to some scholars, the early date, quality and quantity of these finds, together with the geographical significance of this area, suggest that it was here in the narrow valley of the Haliacmon, between the villages of Sphekia and Rizomata, that the ancestral cradle of the Macedonians should be located – Lebaia, according to Herodotus.

The bronze sword BM 1041 (fig. 44, bottom) was cast and beaten to form a long and narrow blade, which reveals the work of a highly skilled craftsman. Along the entire length of the blade is a high strong midrib, decorated with an incised double running spiral.[2] This sword resembles Aegean 'type A' and 'type B' swords, especially in the structurally weak short and thin tang, which could prove fatal for the warrior in battle. Yet it is difficult to classify it as it appears to constitute a variant or an outgrowth, in other words a transitional type between the two known types. It recalls 'type A' swords in the shape of the long and narrow blade, which becomes sharper towards the tip; in the high strong midrib; in the disproportionately short and thin tang in comparison with the length of the two-edged blade; and in the size of the hole for the attachment of the handle which would have also occupied part of the blade (the midrib extends to the beginning of the tang). In contrast to 'type A' swords, the shoulders of BM 1041 are not arched, but have shallow indentations, resembling in this respect the wide squared shoulders of 'type B' swords, the sides of which, when bent, form projecting quillons. The rather short length of the blade is also closer to 'type B' swords than to 'type A', which are characterised by long blades.

Sword BM 1041 belongs to a group described as a variation of 'type A' swords.[3] These swords have convex shoulders without ricasso and equipped with two rivet holes and a short tang with one rivet hole. All these rivet holes help keep the attached handle, made of perishable materials, in place. Very few swords of this type are known from the Mycenaean world. They date to 1450–1375 BC and come from tombs at Zapher Papoura (Crete), Nichoria in Messenia (south-west Peloponnese), Katarrachtis in Achaea (north-west Peloponnese), Kalkani at Mycenae (Argolid), Andronianoi in Euboea, perhaps Aulis in central Greece and Staphylos on Skopelos.

BM 1041 is morphologically closer to the sword found in Tomb 44 at Zapher Papoura near Knossos and the sword from the Nichoria Minnesota Messenia Expedition tholos, with which it also shares the double running spirals. Typologically it bears a closer resemblance to the sword from Zapher Papoura, having the same cross-section and being almost identical in length (the Zapher Papoura sword measuring 0.53m and the Sphekia sword 0.523m). The only difference between the two swords is the number of rivet holes for the attachment of the handle, as both the Zapher Papoura and Nichoria swords have three holes, two on either side of the shoulders and one on the tang. The common morphological features of these three swords (Sphekia, Zapher Papoura and Nichoria) appear to suggest that they may have been products of the same bronze workshop.

The incised decoration on the blade may provide us with a hint as to the place of manufacture. This elaborate spiral decoration, often gilded, is common on the handles and blades of 'type A' swords from Grave Circles A and B at Mycenae, the Minoan origin of which is considered certain. Similar decoration with spirals in two or three rows is also attested in blades of horned and cruciform swords, the weapons par excellence of the military aristocracy of Knossos and the Argolid. These regions have been put forward as the place of origin for these swords, with Knossos and the palace workshops constituting the most probable candidate given that most known examples, often with elaborate hilts and blades, have come to light from tombs in the area of Knossos.

Unfortunately, the exact findspot and context of the Sphekia sword is not known. Based on the examples from Zapher Papoura, Nichoria and Kalkani at Mycenae, a date to around 1400–1375 BC looks probable for the manufacture of the Sphekia sword. However, one cannot exclude the possibility that, despite the date of manufacture, the sword may have ended up in Macedonia much later either as an heirloom or as an antique object (even as loot).

The other bronze sword, BM 1040 (fig. 44, top), belongs to the category of Mycenaean horned swords.[4] These swords appeared in the Aegean world around 1450–1400 BC and continued to be manufactured until about 1350 BC. According to Nancy Sandars they are also of Minoan origin, although other scholars are of the opinion that the sturdiness of this sword suggests a Mycenaean inspiration.

The double-edged horned swords have a flat blade with high midrib, a full-flanged tang and projecting quillons on the shoulder which look like 'horns'. The tang offers better grip, while the quillons protect the warrior's hand.[5] Numerous swords of this type are known from a number of sites and regions: Crete, the Aegean islands, the south-east Peloponnese, Elis, Phocis, Attica and Thessaly. Their distribution highlights regional 'military aristocracies' in the core areas of the Mycenaean world (the Peloponnese and central Greece) as well as Crete and the Dodecanese. A few isolated swords that have come to light in Macedonia, Epirus and Albania probably belonged to members of the local elite, independent from the palatial military aristocracy of the Mycenaean centres. The closest parallel to the horned sword from Sphekia comes from Tomb 188 at Nea Ionia at Volos (Thessaly), dating to 1450–1375 BC. Although the Nea Ionia example is longer (73cm) than the Sphekia sword (47cm) and despite the differences in the number of rivet holes, it is possible that they are both the product of the same bronze workshop (situated either in the Argolid, Knossos or the Volos area in eastern Thessaly). Other similar swords from Knossos, Katakali near Grevena, Thessaly and Albania also suggest a date to 1450–1375 BC. As with BM 1041, one cannot exclude the possibility that this sword reached Macedonia later than its time of manufacture.

Long-bladed swords are ideal weapons for close combat, and the available iconographic evidence suggests that they formed part of the warrior's kit. Their good performance in battle and the value of the metal itself gave both the swords and their owners a certain social status. Their often rich decoration appears to highlight further the importance of possessing such a sword.

The presence of both swords in the periphery of the Mycenaean world, away from the palatial centres, may perhaps have added to the social status of their owners. Unfortunately, the lack of information about the original site of deposition of these two swords prevents us from drawing firm conclusions. Swords are normally found in individual burials ('warrior' burials), hoards and sanctuaries. For the Sphekia swords we can tentatively suggest that they may have come from a burial. From the rest of Macedonia the other eight known Mycenaean swords and daggers come from graves (four examples) or constitute chance finds. Three swords and a dagger from the known corpus belong to the horned type, two are cruciform, while one each belongs to types 'G' (also horned, i.e. with projecting quillons) and 'F' (with squared shoulders and strong midrib with incisions). The distribution of these swords from the region of Olympus to the Pierian mountains and western Macedonia (Grevena and Aiane) appears to highlight the way through which these examples reached Macedonia, that is, via Thessaly and the natural corridors (e.g. the middle valley of the River Haliacmon or the land passes via the Pierian mountains towards central Macedonia), probably excluding the possibility that they may have reached this region via Epirus and the Adriatic coast, as has been suggested in the past by some scholars.

The two spearheads BM 1042 and BM 1043 (fig. 45) constitute chance finds delivered to the museum at Aegae. They are also said to have come from the area of Sphekia. Their morphological characteristics render them unique and distance them from typical spears of the Mycenaean world. The spear, used in Crete from the end of the Middle Bronze Age (1800–1700 BC), was known in many variant forms throughout the Mycenaean period. From the available iconographic evidence on tomb markers (*stelai*), inlaid daggers, seals, ornaments and wall paintings, it is evident that spears were used in hunting and warfare as long-reaching thrusting weapons.

The lack of a slit on the spear socket suggests that these particular spearheads

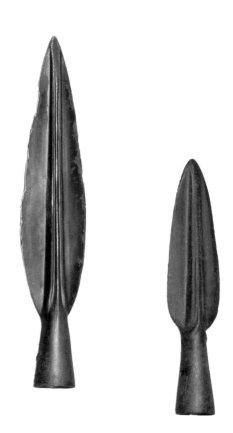

Fig. 45 Late Bronze Age spearheads from the area of Sphekia near Aegae (Cat. nos. 5–6)

were constructed in one piece, with the pouring of the metal in a mould. The only parallels in the Greek world with regard to the relief decoration on the blade are the examples from Polemistra near Aiane (Kozani) and a blade on display in the Volos Museum with an unknown provenance.[6] The distribution of typologically similar examples includes the tumuli (burial mounds) and hoards of bronzes in Albania, Croatia, Hungary, Poland and Romania. They were particularly popular between the cultures around the broader area of the Ukranian Carpathian mountains, where their manufacturing workshops should perhaps be sought.

These examples date to around 1350–1200 BC, while they are still sporadically attested around 1200–1000 BC. The findspot and context of the Sphekia spearheads is not known. Tentatively, we could venture a dating to the period between 1350 and 1200 BC, which coincides with the widest spread of the Mycenaean world from the west to the east Mediterranean and the Black Sea, in search of raw materials for bronzeworking. The presence of four such spearheads with relief lines in areas within or near Thessaly, the coast of which is considered as a stop-over on the way to the Dardanelles and the Black Sea, could suggest that the Sphekia and Aiane spears arrived there via Thessaly rather than the land routes of the Balkan penninsula. The two spearheads from Sphekia also constitute a remarkable quantitative and qualitative addition to the few known examples of Mycenaean metal working from Macedonia (e.g. Vardino, Leivadia and Polemistra near Aiane, Galatini near Kozani, Katakali near Grevena and Spathes on the western slopes of Mount Olympus). To these examples one must add the three spearheads in the Boston Museum of Fine Arts, with a possible provenance from Macedonia. Apart from the flame-shaped spear from Galatini (Snodgrass 'type B') with a central European origin and a few comparanda, the rest belong to types 'A' and 'C' of Snodgrass and have many parallels in the Mycenaean world, where they originated.

The clay, wheel-made Mycenaean-type *alabastra* (containers for aromatic oil or a more viscous substance, perhaps to anoint the body of the deceased) were handed to the Aegae Museum from Metochi, a village 3km to the west of Vergina (ΒΠ 3716, ΒΠ 3717, ΒΠ 3718, ΒΠ 3719 and ΒΠ 4722). They were found in 1951 during the construction of a local road inside a burial pithos and were delivered to the guard of Vergina, P. Pavlidis. They are all small (7.4–8.6cm in height and 7–8cm base diameter) and of local manufacture. They are painted in a brown or brown-red colour of a matt appearance, which associates them more with the local handmade matt-painted tradition rather than with Mycenaean ceramics. They are decorated with bands and lines.

In ΒΠ 3717 (fig. 46, top left) the repetition of the 'cross-hatched triangles' motif under the handles is worth commenting on: this is a characteristic idiosyncracy of the south-west Peloponnese, dating to 1400–1300 BC. The presence

of this feature on the Metochi vessel appears to constitute an interesting anachronism. On the underside of the base there are concentric circles, a decorative tradition commonly attested in southern Greece from 1400 BC onwards. The use of certain decorative patterns, such as the zigzag on BΠ 4722 (fig. 46, bottom right) and the concentric circles on the shoulder of BΠ 3719 find many parallels in southern Greece (e.g. Aigina and Achaea, dating to around 1200–1150 BC). The best parallel example for BΠ 3719 (fig. 46, bottom left), especially with regard to the rim, is a cylindrical *alabastron* from Kastanas in Macedonia,[7] which appears to confirm a date for this object to 1200–1150 BC. The vertical lozenges arranged as a chain on the shoulder of BΠ 3716 find a close parallel to an amphoriskos from Thessaly, usually dated to 1150–1100 BC. The 'net triangle' motif on the shoulder of BΠ 3717 (fig. 46, top left) is also dated to that period or perhaps a little later (1100–1050 BC), although one should not exclude the possibility that this is a motif adopted and adapted from the repertoire of the local handmade matt-painted pottery of Macedonia. All four *alabastra* may then be dated within the period 1200–1100 BC. Rather unusual is the survival of the rounded *alabastron* in Macedonia after 1200–1150 BC, in contrast to southern Greece where, based on the available evidence, this shape disappears. BΠ 3718 (fig. 46, top right) also has an unusual shape combining

Fig. 46 Mycenaean *alabastra* (aromatic-oil containers) (Cat. nos. 8–11)

features of the rounded and cylindrical *alabastron*, being closer to the latter rather than the former. It is decorated with a rather clumsy net pattern, attested in southern Greece from 1400 to 1100 BC. In Macedonia it is attested on similar vessels between 1300 and 1150 BC (e.g. at Assiros, Perivolaki and Kastanas). Based on the other *alabastra* a dating for this vessel between 1200 and 1100 BC looks secure.

Generally speaking, the presence of Mycenaean-looking vessels from the broader area of Aegae is compatible with the overall pattern of distribution of Mycenaean pottery in Macedonia. Imported Mycenaean pottery appears sporadically during 1375–1200 BC, while in the following period (1200–1050 BC) local ceramics are directly influenced by those in southern Greece, leading to adaptations and imitations. The production of this local pottery continues into the protogeometric period (1050–900 BC), with the local workshops introducing only a few innovations known from this period in other regions.

Two Mycenaean-type *alabastra*, unpainted and with an angular outline and rather careless construction, were found by Manolis Andronikos in burial mounds Δ and N at Vergina (Aegae) – the one from mound N is on display in this exhibition: ΒΠ 3031 (fig. 47). They were dated by the excavator to around 1000 BC,[8] though an earlier date for their manufacture should be taken into consideration (1100–1000 BC). Their presence within the finds from the burials under the mounds is problematic and has been interpreted

Fig. 47 Mycenaean-type *alabastron* from the tumuli cemetery at Aegae (Cat. no. 12)

either as a survival of the shape in this particular region (well after the end of the Mycenaean period), or as a reuse of earlier objects within the funerary assemblage of later graves (as antiques or heirlooms). The case of these two *alabastra* is not unique: something similar is observed at Phiki near Trikala in western Thessaly, where a similar-looking *alabastron* was deposited alongside pots dating to 1000–950 BC. This particular shape is otherwise well attested in Macedonia.[9] In many cases *alabastra* were found in tombs and were probably used in a similar way to that of southern Greece. In this respect, the inhabitants of this region adopted not only the Mycenaean wheel-made painted ceramics but also the practices associated with them.

Emathia, where Aegae is situated, was an important region throughout the Bronze Age since it constituted the connecting link between the coastal area of the Thermaic Gulf and Pieria with the areas of western Macedonia and Thessaly. The discovery of products of Mycenaean bronze-working and of local imitations of Mycenaean ceramics from Sphekia, Metochi and Aegae is unfortunately fragmentary at present and does not answer important research questions of the Late Bronze Age in Macedonia regarding the permanent presence of Mycenaeans in the area either as colonists or most likely through the establishment of a Mycenaean socio-economic configuration similar to that in operation in southern Greece.

Nevertheless, these finds constitute important evidence for the relations of this area with the southern Greek core during the Mycenaean period. Mycenaean swords, objects of status, appear to suggest the existence of a local elite, which may have been in contact with regions to the south. The spears could have reached this area through the commercial networks mentioned above; alternatively, they may constitute evidence for the presence of visitors in the region from the Mycenaean world or Central Europe, perhaps in search of raw materials (timber, copper and gold) or even as mercenaries. Finally, the Mycenaean-looking pottery suggests the penetration of a way of life from southern Greece into this area, possibly through neighbouring Pieria and Thessaly, where the Mycenaean presence is dynamic. The continuation of excavation and archaeological work in the region, as well as scientific analysis, is necessary for broadening our knowledge of Mycenaean presence in the area and understanding the complex social networks in operation from around 1400 to 1000 BC.

6 Trade and exchange in the Macedonian court

Ioannes Graekos

The notion of an isolated and primitive *ethnos* for the Macedonians, living on the periphery of the Greek world, is now largely disputed because of the amount of recent archaeological data, mostly concerning the early stages of Macedonian history.

The evolution of the Macedonian state and its institutions over time should be understood more through terms of spatial expansion rather than terms of temporal sequence relating to different types of administration or regime. The kings of Macedonia were members of a single royal family, the Temenids, originating from Heracles and Zeus. This fact was never challenged. Their birthplace, located at Aegae and the nearby mountains, was always the centre of that state and a constant reference for all Macedonians, concerning their myths, royal legacies, history and identity. In Macedonia, a Homeric type of royal authority, settlement and economy based on the land was for a long time a vivid reality rather than a poetic or traditional perception.[1]

The landscape of the old Kingdom and core of the state, with its abundance of natural resources (wooded mountains, big rivers, fertile plains, mineral deposits), provided the inhabitants with the necessary means for a self-sufficient agricultural and pastoral life.[2] At the same time Μακεδονίς γη (the land of Macedonia) was part of an ancient network of exchange, trade and communication. The sea and the colonial world of the Thermaic Gulf were not far away. Mountainous passages to Upper Macedonia or Thessaly had long been used for the movements of cattle or military campaigns. Crossing rivers eastwards was a venture for possessing and exploiting more land and resources.

Although the first known historical written sources mentioning Macedonia are dated to the fifth century BC, the place was always 'exposed to all the political and economic currents and cultural influences of the Aegean world'.[3] From the Late Bronze Age to Hellenistic times the chief artistic styles, representative artefacts, technology for the production of pottery, metal objects, clay figurines and other plastic arts, such as jewellery, are represented and well attested in old and recent archaeological finds. Mycenaean or Mycenaean-type pottery is

found in many sites across Macedonia, including the tumuli cemetery between the modern villages of Vergina and Palatitsia, the place where Aegae, the royal capital of the kingdom of Macedon, was founded in the seventh century BC. At the same cemetery, protogeometric pottery, the first common artistic style known after the collapse of the Mycenaean world, is also found in a number of graves, mostly in the form of cups, decorated with pendant semicircles and other geometrical patterns (fig. 48).

The image of a grave excavated, royal or not, 'rich' or 'poor', provides through its contents a clear view of the historic, economic, ideological and social background of Macedonian society in every period of time. Next to the local products, such as pottery in traditional shapes, easily recognisable imports from the major centres of the Aegean highlight the dual character of Macedonian society – traditional and at the same time open to external cultural currents. This image will be a constant feature in the Macedonian burial context until Hellenistic times.

Until recently, archaeological evidence of the Archaic period in Macedonia derived mostly from the burial context. Research into cemeteries distributed in the old Kingdom (Aegae, Beroia, Mieza) shed light into burial practices as well

Fig. 48 (above) Protogeometric bowl (*skyphos*) decorated with pendant semicircles (Cat. no. 443)

Fig. 49 (below) Protocorinthian *aryballoi* (aromatic-oil containers)

as the organisation of space and early settlement patterns. It seems that until the end of the fifth century – or even the middle of the fourth century BC – populations in the Macedonian land mainly settled in villages (*kata komas*), not in walled cities.

From the second half of the sixth century BC, goods traded from the great production centres of south and eastern Greece became very popular in local markets. Most typical are the small Corinthian perfume jars (fig. 49), Athenian black-figure vases and Ionian cups (fig. 50). The northern Aegean soon aroused the interest of the southern city-states, primarily because of its inexhaustible natural resources. The Macedonian land produced abundant wood for building ships and metal for minting coins – the basic means for conducting trade in the Aegean. Macedonia was also famous for horse and cattle breeding, animals of burden suitable for conducting trade overland. Euboea, Athens, Corinth and the islands founded colonies or *emporia* (trading places, markets) along the coasts of the Thermaic Gulf, and in eastern Macedonia and Thrace and the nearby islands. For example, Potidaia, a Corinthian colony founded on the Chalkidic peninsula in the seventh century BC, produced clay pots that were widely distributed in the Macedonian market and are often found in tombs as burial offerings. Closer to Macedonia, Methone and Pydna on the western coast of the Thermaic Gulf, were city-states with harbours (Map 1).

At the end of the archaic period (late sixth century–early fifth century BC) Macedonia came under the control and administration of an external power for almost thirty years. The Persian presence in Macedonia was marked by two major facts relating to the way Macedonians communicated with their immediate surroundings and the rest of the world. An 'international' road system, available for moving people and vehicles on a great scale, was established by the Persians as they invaded Europe. At the same time, Macedonia and nearby

Fig. 50 Clay black-figure cup from Chios, with a representation of a lion (Cat. no. 487)

Fig. 51 Clay figurines from Samos: a *kouros*, a seated goddess and twin belly-demons (Cat. nos. 189, 191, 42)

regions were entering the monetary economy. The early coinage of the northern Aegean appeared in two basic versions: 'heavy', for tax payments to the Great King and the state; and 'light', for internal circulation.[4] In Macedonia the first silver issues were minted by King Alexander I. For the first time in local history a king's portrait was depicted on coins and thus widely distributed. It is also the first time a Macedon king partakes in the affairs of southern Greek city-states. From that moment on the Macedonian state would be seeking to expand its boundaries and looking for new sources of affluence. In the same period, next to Attic products a general 'Eastern or Ionian colour' would be recognised in a large range of artefacts found mostly in graves. Popular eastern Greek sculpture types were distributed on a large scale in the form of clay figurines, thanks to the technique of mould-making (fig. 51). Not only were artefacts transported from Asia Minor, but also the technology for producing them in local workshops. Glass (fig. 53), ivory, and alabaster were all imported and used mainly in the production of prestigious goods (fig. 52). The use of aromatic oils, largely imported, continued uninterruptedly throughout this period (figs. 54 and 56).

After the Persian wars, trade was predominantly with Athens. For almost a century the Macedonian kingdom would suffer from dynastic instability, frequent wars and a relative economic immobility. The northern Aegean would once again be the theatre of competitive operations between local and foreign powers. In the same period new cities appeared and others were totally

Fig. 52 Ostrich eggs with painted decoration used as aromatic-oil containers (Cat. nos. 237–38)

Fig. 53 (left) Glass perfume vessel (Cat. no. 383)

Fig. 54 Perfume vessel in the shape of the head of Adonis (Cat. no. 401)

re-formed, such as Olynthos, which developed into a significant trade centre. The Athenian hegemony aimed to expand its interests and political influence. In 431 BC Amphipolis was founded as an Athenian colony at a strategic location, close to the River Strymon. Archelaos, king of Macedonia from 413 to 399 BC, tried to re-form urban and rural space by building roads and city walls. He also invited to his court the great artists of his time, such as Euripides. The city of Pella located closer to the sea flourished and became Macedonia's most prominent city in the fourth century BC and thereafter.

Macedonia continued to export its best products, including timber for ship-building. It also attempted to expand its eastern boundaries in order to attain more land and mineral resources. In the first half of the fourth century BC it is highly likely that immigrants from southern Greece may have organised local workshops, since Athenian and Athenian-type pottery became popular throughout Macedonia (fig. 55).

After the unification of the kingdom and the transformation of the old cities into prestigious and powerful political centres under Philip II (360/359–336 BC), local workshops would elaborate their own technical and artistic character. In Macedonia, the production of high-quality artefacts in metal, clay, stone and many other materials became more systematic because of the new political status quo and the increasing input of wealth coming from the newly spear-conquered lands.

The royal tombs at Aegae contain the acme of almost every art and craft known at that time: architecture, painting, sculpture, metalwork (fig. 57), weaponry, jewellery, pottery and textiles. Soon Hellenistic art would be the expression of a newly expanding world, conceived as a political programme and realised as a cultural reality in the Macedonian court.

Fig. 57 A silver *amphora* from the tomb of Philip II

7 War and Hunting: the world of the Macedonian king and his companions

Ioannes Graekos

Fig. 58 Iron knife with curved blade (Cat. no. 28)

'But the boy, happening to have a knife on him, said "We accept what you give, O king" and drew a line around the sunlight on the floor with his knife; which done, he gathered up the sunlight into the fold of his garment three times and went away, he and his companions ... Now there is a river in that land to which the descendants of these men from Argos make sacrifice as their deliverer. The river, when the Temenids had crossed over, rose in such a spate that the horsemen could not cross through it. The brothers came to another land of Macedonia ... When they had acquired possession of this land, they issued forth from it and began to subdue the rest of Macedonia as well.' [1]

This myth of Macedonian royalty, first cited by Herodotus (7.137–138), is a reflection of the pastoral early stages of Macedonian history and of the emergence of the Macedonian institutional state. Members of a wanderer hero's family, the three Heraclids (sons of Heracles) from Argos, travelled from southern to northern Greece until they settled at a king's house, pasturing his flocks, at a place called Lebaia, in the Pierian mountains. Expelled from there by the king, Gauanes, Aeropos and Perdiccas took sunlight as repayment for their service, crossed the River Haliacmon and found themselves on Mount Bermion, a place where roses blossomed by themselves and strange creatures, such as Silenus, intermingled with archetypical human beings, including King Midas. The three Temenids established their own royal power by moving from a king's place to another king's place, separated from each other by a big river. This movement will always represent the essence of the Macedonian state: from myth to history the expansion of that state is marked by the crossing of a big river.

In this myth, the boy Perdiccas, first king of Macedon, by defining space with a *machaira* (an iron knife) and dividing sunlight into pieces, initiates the starting point of Macedonian history (fig. 58). Macedonian territory will be the land whose boundaries are defined by a spear. The Macedonian era starts

when the first king took daylight and divided it into countable parts: a celestial or solar symbol became the emblem of Macedonian royal power (figs. 59–60). Perdiccas' act is both religious and political, enacted by a young man in the role of an adolescent hunter. The young shepherd's gesture is the *aition* (the first cause) of three of the main offices taken by the king of Macedon in historical times: hunter, warrior and high-priest.

Sacrificial sites were marked by a circle segregating the place, the participants and the animal to be killed. The act of sacrifice included dividing up the parts of the slaughtered domestic animal, then the cooking and consumption of those parts.[2] As a breeder of domestic animals, Perdiccas drew a circle with his knife and took three parts of daylight. Aristotle has highlighted that, according to Pythagorean logic, number three symbolised perfection or completion and was specially applied to religious practice (Aristotle, *On the Heavens* 268a).

Moving from Lebaia, a place where everyday activities in its king's humble house involved a circular perception of time, to Mount Bermion, a miraculous place of no- or pre-time, the Temenids established the linear time of their dynasty and its legacies. The Greek perception of an annual period of time, as expressed by local calendars, is mainly religious, with twelve lunar months, whose names derived either from gods celebrated at a particular time or festivals held by the community. Almost all aspects of personal and communal life (hunting, agriculture, war, disease, death and birth) are connected with a certain religious activity. Everyday and political events are experienced through participation in specific religious ceremonies. Sacrificing to the gods was the king's first duty each morning (Plutarch, *Alexander* 23.2). The Macedonian calendar contained the months *Dios, Apellaios, Audonaios, Peritios, Dystros, Xandikos, Artemisios, Daisios, Panemos, Loos, Gorpiaios* and *Hyperberetaios*. The first month's name derives from Zeus, forefather of all Macedonians, and was very common in the Greek poleis, being attested since Mycenaean times. Zeus' descendants, the kings of Macedon, directed every religious act in their role as high-priests, mediating between the divine and human worlds. *Heracles Patroos*, the ancestral 'father Heracles', was the heroic figure worshipped in traditional royal manner at the palace of Aegae as the ancestor of all Macedonians. Knowledge of the *patrooa hiera* (ancestral rites) was passed on from generation to generation by royal succession (Athenaeus, *The Deipnosophists* 14.659f-660a). Any important event concerning the royal house or state affairs involved a sacrifice by the king. At his daughter's wedding, Philip 'held magnificent sacrifices to the gods' (Diodorus Siculus, *Library of World History* 16.91.4). Alexander sacrificed to Zeus Olympios at Dion, the city sacred for all Macedonians, before his military campaign (Arrian, *Anabasis* 1.11.1). Macedonians also made offerings to river gods, retaining the memory of their first ancestors who established the authority of their royal power, as attested in the passage mentioned at the beginning. As Perdiccas' descendants, the Macedonian kings would perform an initiation ritual to define urban space at the foundation of a new city (Quintus Curtius Rufus, *History of Alexander* 4.8.6).

The gilded diadem, decorated in imitation of a band, was found next to the iron helmet at Philip's tomb and is the most significant symbol of royal political and religious authority (fig. 33). Macedonian kings are often depicted on royal coinage wearing a similar band, representing the sacred insignia of priesthood.

The *machaira* was not only a sacrificial instrument but a weapon specially attached to young boys during their *ephebeia*, the period of ritual transition from childhood to manhood (Plutarch, *Lycurgus* 28). *Ephebeia* was the civic institution whereby adolescents were prepared for taking on the status of adults. This particular rite of passage helped young boys achieve the level of a political subject, chief of their families, and thus able to bear weapons as soldiers. Similar rites were celebrated in Crete, Sparta and Athens. In Macedonia the entry of young males to the army was celebrated in the month of *Xandikos*.[3]

During the *ephebeia*, hunting and war are closely related as complementary activities, with arms used on both occasions. It was considered that the achievement of killing an animal or an enemy provided access to the community of adult men. There was a long tradition in Macedonian society for a group of armoured men – each member a *hetairos* (companion) – to accompany the king. In local royal tradition, ancestral Heracles was the exemplary hunter, just as hunting was the quintessential heroic activity. This is why heroic hunting insignia (lion skin and club) are often depicted on royal coinage as symbols of the king's authority.[4] The cult of Heracles *Kynagidas* (leader of the hunters to the woods) in the Macedonian *poleis* is one of the earliest attested and widespread cults,[5] and closely related with young groups of hunters (*kynegoi*). Participation is organised by the *poleis*, hunting in the royal woods signifying an elevation to the status of king's companion and offering a privileged contact with the heroic past and the political present.

Fig. 61 (below) Ivory boar from the footstool of the gold and ivory funeral couch associated with Philip II (Cat. no. 485). Shown enlarged

Fig. 62 (opposite) Combat scene once decorating the shield of a warrior (Cat. no. 61). Shown enlarged

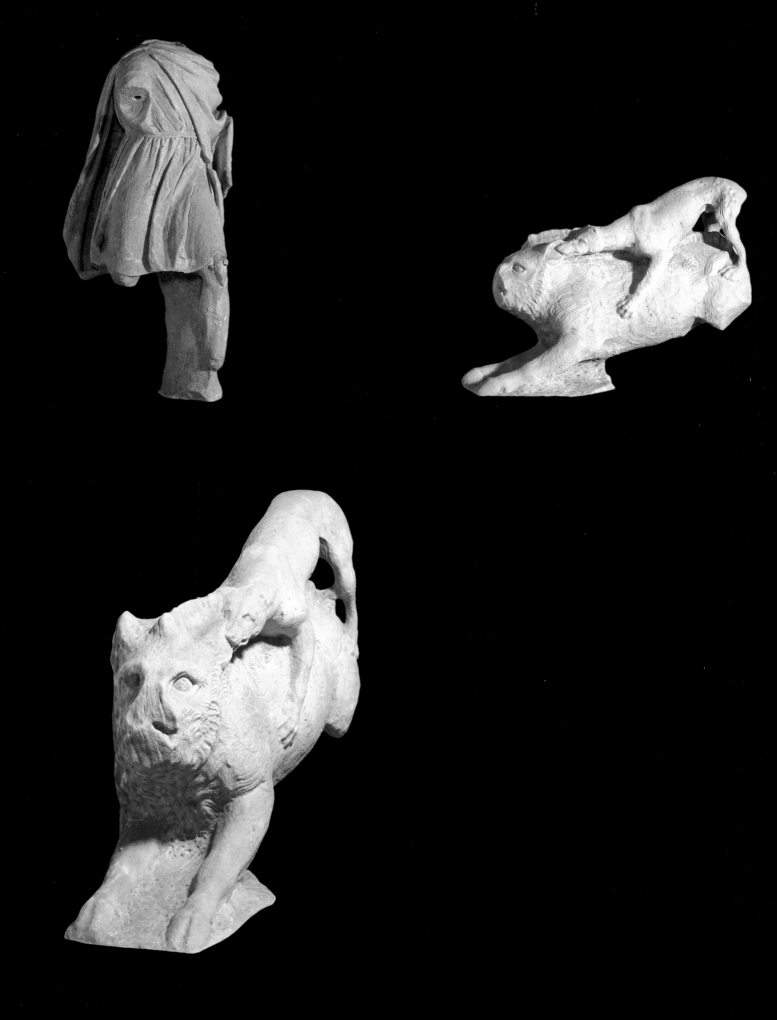

Managing weapons for the purposes of hunting was perhaps the first opportunity for young boys to experience warfare and killing. To return with his prey was a heroic achievement, qualifying the hunter to participate in royal symposia and therefore state affairs. It is said that Cassander was not permitted to recline as other men at symposia because he did not kill a boar without using a hunting net (Athenaeus, *The Deipnosophists* 1.31.6-12) (fig. 61). In the Greek *poleis* hunting was both a private and a collective activity, a social medium incorporating unstructured space and wild nature, with set boundaries and definite identities. Hunting and war were a constant reference to the origin of the Macedonian state, but were also the means by which the Macedonian royal house and society were structured in historical times (fig. 62). The institution of royal Pages was the Macedonian version of *ephebeia*, found elsewhere in Greece: selected young boys were prepared to act as the king's armoured companions. In other major political institutions in Macedonia, such as the *gymnasium*, attested by inscriptions,[6] the main concern of the young boys' education was physical training and instruction in arms (fig. 63).

The king's death is a crucial political moment. His burial is a major religious ceremony where all the royal insignia are displayed. For centuries the kings of Macedon were members of a single family.[7] The hereditary monarchy was never challenged (Thucydides 1.13.1). Narratives about the royal succession, divine or human, are structured by the themes of conflict, dominance of the mightiest or fittest, sovereignty in a new status quo. Zeus' divine power was established after he had defeated his predecessor, his father Kronos; and it was as Zeus' descendants, through Heracles, that the Temenids claimed their royal authority. In the Derveni papyrus – a religious text probably written after the middle of the fourth century BC and found charred in a Macedonian burial context – the main idea is that the final establishment of Zeus' divine power to the world (*kosmos*) is based on the mixture of pre-existing archetypical elements.[8]

The unification of the Macedonian kingdom by Philip II was also based on re-composing, re-defining and mixing pre-existing elements: the people and the land. His new political *kosmos* was the Macedonian state based equally on the king and his people. As his son, Alexander, put it in his famous speech at Opis (Arrian, *Anabasis* 9.9.2):

Philip took you over when you were helpless vagabonds, mostly clothed in skins, feeding a few animals on the mountains and engaged in their defence in unsuccessful fighting with Illyrians, Triballians and the neighbouring Thracians. He gave you clothes to wear instead of skins, he brought you down from the mountains to the plains; he made you a match in battle for the barbarians on your borders, so that you no longer trusted for your safety to the strength of your positions so much as to your natural courage. He made you city dwellers and established the order that comes from good laws and customs.[9]

The great painting of the royal hunting scene (*thereios graphe*) depicted on the façade of Philip's monumental tomb at Aegae, far from being simply a decorative device or illustrative of a theme close to royal court is essentially a visual statement of what the Macedonian state was and represented in 336 BC. Some 5.56m in length and 1.16m in height, it depicts ten human figures, three horses, nine dogs and six quarry, situated in a sacred wood, creating a climactic hunting scene divided into six episodes (figs. 247–48).[10] All the male participants except one are of Perdiccas' age: young, beardless, naked or half-naked. Their age and distinguished status represent the dynamics of the royal institution: hunters by mythical origin, soldiers under political will. The representation of various kinds of hunted animals juxtaposed with the hunters creates a hierarchical scheme. The scene culminates around the lion, the royal prey. More people with more weapons are engaged in this emblematic act, killing the animal, which signifies the heroic past of kingship. In the Macedonian context, the representation of royal hunting was a reminder of how the state was built: by transforming a rural and mountainous activity into a political programme, using weapons for killing animals to weapons for supporting the state. Portraits of Alexander and Philip can be seen in the faces of the young rider in the middle of the scene, ready to throw his spear, and the bearded man to the right, close to the lion (figs. 30–31, 249–50). Their presence in the frieze is emblematic of a prestigious royal succession from one generation to the next, expressed by the participation of both, the dead and the new king, in the same heroic activity. The painting's theme is not just one of royal hunting but of Macedonian kingship as expressed by one of its supreme institutions, hereditary authority religiously attached to a heroic past.

All ten human figures depicted represent the hierarchy of the state in its social, political and military order. In the right-hand corner a man is depicted wearing a *diphthera*, an animal skin, as described by Alexander in the passage cited above. This man holding a hunting-net is actually a Macedonian of the pre-Philippic era, now incorporated into the new political order.

Weaponry is a constant feature in Macedonian burials. The importance of arms and warfare to people living primarily on the mountains is not surprising. The early economy of the state was based on the household and related activities, and the head of the self-contained household was a senior male. Herodotus' description of the origins of Macedonian kingship illustrates the conditions sustaining pastoral life and everyday activities, including stock breeding and food preparation by women. The Early Iron Age cemetery at the necropolis of Aegae, comprising group burials within a single precinct and covered by a mound, represents the family structure of this early society. Similar burial customs are attested all over the mountains, where the actual events of the first Macedonian myths allegedly took place. In that early stage tumuli were the most monumental structures, distributed across the landscape and serving for these transient populations as a constant reference to the common past of their ancestors. Nomadic or semi-nomadic life is bound up with war and hunting. Bearing weapons was not only a display of social status but

Fig. 64 Swords from Aegae
(Cat. nos. 13, 14, 56)

an everyday necessity. 'For in ancient times all Hellenes carried weapons' (Thucydides 1.6.1). Defending your family and livestock, hunting animals in the woods, performing sacrifices, even household activities, involved the use of knives, spears and swords. A Macedonian king representing himself as hunter, warrior and high-priest is showing that his authority derives straight from the starting-point of local history.

The earliest examples of metal weapons found on Macedonian soil are dated to the Late Bronze Age and are mainly swords (fig. 44). Although spearheads and javelins are known of the same date (fig. 45), offensive arms with a long double-edged blade qualified the man who could handle them as a warrior. Some time during the transitional period from the Late Bronze to the Early Iron Age the technology for producing arms changed: bronze weapons were progressively replaced by iron ones, while the types of swords remained more or less the same (fig. 64). Spearheads are also found in Early Iron Age burial contexts, but almost never with swords.

In the late archaic and early classical periods (sixth–fifth century BC) archaeological finds relating to warfare are more varied in form, shape and use (figs. 65–68). At the same time, defensive weaponry also makes its appearance – helmets occur in sets and identify a hoplite (fig. 69). Arms are now decorated with precious materials and placed in contexts such as funerary pyres, indicating a certain connection with heroic ideology (figs. 70–71). The one-edged iron *kopis* and the double-edged iron sword are the two main types of heavy weapon (fig. 72). The first was suitable for both warfare and everyday use. The swords, especially when decorated with ivory, silver or gold ornaments, are objects of prestige, denoting the extraordinary social and religious status of their owner (fig. 73). A Macedonian warrior's burial could be a Homeric image: the iron silver-studded sword found in the Temenids' burial cluster at Aegae recalls the typical epic description of a hero's weapon: 'and slung his silver-studded sword about his shoulders' (*Iliad* II.45). Macedonian funeral reliefs show the heroised dead wearing his sword on his shoulders. Spearheads are mostly found in pairs and probably likewise would have been carried. It is difficult to distinguish a thrusting from a throwing spear, especially when both are identical (figs. 74–75).[11] It is generally assumed that the smaller and lighter examples are best interpreted as javelins.

Different kinds of spears were used for hunting different animals and by different ranks of the military. Each weapon's weight, shape and manufacture, along with the length, weight and diameter of the wooden shaft, determined its use and effectiveness. Fighting or hunting from a close or a considerable distance was a matter of physical ability, skill and training. In the painted hunting scene on the façade of King Philip II's tomb, the distinction between long-distance and close combat spears (for hunting and fighting) is illuminating. The dead king is depicted holding a spear with a gilded shaft. Golden leaves and ornaments representing royal insignia (e.g. the club of Heracles, the winged Nike, etc.), often decorated the surface of weapons (fig. 21).

Fig. 65 Cup showing men at arms (Cat. no. 21)

Fig. 66 Corinthian *aryballos* showing warriors marching into battle (Cat. no. 34)

Fig. 67 Black-figure *krater* with warriors going to battle on a four-horse chariot (Cat. no. 54)

Fig. 68 Red-figure bowl showing the schooling of a horse (Cat. no. 82)

Fig. 69 (right) Helmet of the so-called
Illyrian type (Cat. no. 35)

Fig. 70 (bottom) Arms used in funeral
pyres indicate a connection with heroic
ideology

Fig. 71 Sword associated with the
cremation of a man (Cat. no. 47)

Fig. 72 *Kopis*-type swords used by the
Macedonian cavalry (Cat. nos. 55, 43)

Fig. 73 (left) Sword with ivory-lined hilt
(Cat. no. 26)

Fig. 74 (right) A spearhead from the
tomb of Alexander IV (Cat. no. 98)

Fig. 75 (opposite) Spear and javelin
points (Cat. nos. 22–25, 15–16, 67–69)

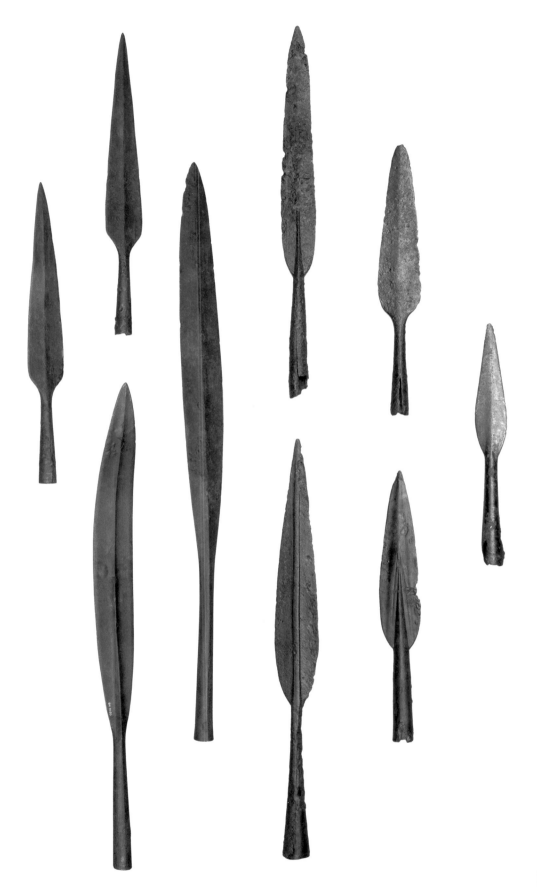

Fig. 76 The elaborate cover of a leather
quiver embossed with a scene showing the
capture of a city, from the tomb of Philip II

Fig. 77 Two Medusa heads originally attached to the linen cuirass of King Philip II to ward off evil (the one on the left: Cat. no. 91)

Fig. 78 (left) Pair of greaves from the tomb of Philip II (Cat. no. 93)

Fig. 79 (right) Sword from the tomb of Philip II (Cat. no. 97)

The possession of arms denotes their owner not only as a warrior but as a warrior of a certain social status. Even in the Early Iron Age (1000–700 BC) the distribution of weapons in burial contexts is interesting: as mentioned already, swords were never found together with spears – the king's grave at Aegae is the only occasion when all different kinds of weapons co-occur. In Philip's tomb one helmet, three cuirasses, four pairs of greaves (fig. 78), three gorgets (pectorals), three shields, a bow, at least seventy-four arrows and a quiver (fig. 76), four swords (fig. 79), thirteen spears and javelins, and valuable ornaments (fig. 77) were found.[12] Although bearing and handling arms, either for hunting or war, was the traditional education for a male Macedonian, it was not until Philip's time that the Macedonian phalanx became an almost unbeatable tactical formation for battle. Ever since, the *sarissa*, long pikes over 5 metres in length, became the emblem of Macedonian military power (fig. 80). As commander of the army the king was not only responsible for the soldiers' training but maintained a close relationship with each one, handling every kind of weapon and fighting from different positions on the battlefield, be it in cavalry or infantry. His most frequent military appearance was on horseback accompanied by the *hetairoi*, his royal companions. Macedonia was also 'a land of good and beautiful horses', according to Euripides (*Bacchae* 574).

The burial of the king and the coronation of his successor were religious ceremonies enacted in the presence of the army and the people. The dead king was buried in full armour, and his heir to the throne was pronounced king similarly clad. The continuity of royal authority was thus accomplished between these two heroic moments, which took place in close succession and served to connect the divine past with the divine future.

Fig. 80 *Sarissa* – the long pike of the Macedonian army and innovation of Philip II (spear point, middle part, and spearbutt) (Cat. no. 57)

8 Queens, princesses and high priestesses: the role of women at the Macedonian court

Angeliki Kottaridi

The Greek tribes of historical times are, in essence, patriarchal communities, and this also holds true for the Macedonians. Within the framework of this patriarchal structure the primary role of the woman, obedient as a daughter to her father and as a wife to her husband, is to give birth to legitimate heirs for her husband, thereby ensuring the continuity of his *oikos* (house) and the smooth transition of inherited wealth.

Hidden in the shadow of the women's quarters, excluded from the learning process, outcasts from the forefront of history, but nevertheless the main actresses in birth and death, ancient women are only named as mythical archetypes or as exceptions. This goes primarily for Athens, the democracy of rationalism, which condemned its women to deep silence. Yet it was apparently not always the case for Macedonia, which remains close to the Homeric traditions, whereby a woman could be a queen in her own realm (fig. 81).

Daughters in Macedonia grew up in their father's house and learnt from the older women all the tasks related to the running of the household. Education was for them an unnecessary luxury, something that, at least in earlier times, appears to have also applied to members of the royal family. For instance, even the powerful Queen Eurydice took up education later in life, being already the mother of adolescents, and celebrated this significant privilege by setting up a dedication in honour of the Muses.

Childhood officially came to an end for Macedonian girls at the age of 14. They were now considered ready to fulfil their roles as wives, with their fathers deciding on their future husbands, whom they then had to accompany to his household. Marriage and childbirth, which they often paid for with their own lives, were their most important moments. Between these they spent their days at home with much work and little entertainment, with poorer women also helping out in farming activities, even in animal husbandry when the household was short of manpower. In any case, their duties were multiple and crucial for everyday survival: women were responsible for the processing and the storage of foodstuffs, daily cooking, the grinding of cereals and the kneading and

Fig. 81 A woman looking at herself in a mirror (Cat. no. 420)

baking of bread – activities which, according to Herodotus, were undertaken in earlier times even by women of the royal family (8.137.2): 'Now the king's wife cooked their food for them, for in old times the ruling houses among men, and not the common people alone, were lacking in wealth.'

Women looked after the house, the babies, the children, the old men, the physically unfit as well as the dead who, like the gods, also wished to receive their offerings. They wove and spun the wool, they dyed the thread, they embroidered and knitted, they made clothes and bed sheets, rugs and carpets, sacks and bags. Like Helen, queen of Sparta in the *Odyssey*, the spinning of wool was for Macedonian queens their daily activity, marking their life and death. The Macedonian ladies took their spinning wheels with them to the grave, like the ladies of archaic Crete on the tombstones of Prinias; while Alexander the Great does not forget to praise the textiles of the women of his family.

Queens, ladies and ordinary Macedonian women, girls and wives spent hours in front of the loom weaving, spinning, plying, inch by inch, their own labours and desires, hours of joy and despair, making pretty clothes and dowry goods to adorn houses and warm hearts. Precious and humble, unadorned and gold-woven, a colourful, handmade universe of thread and dreams, now lost forever. Only a few traces have survived, which with their finesse and precision still amaze us. The unexpected gold-woven cloth from the *larnax* of Meda, allows us to dream of the beauty of these textiles that we will never be able to admire fully (fig. 82).

Aegae actually never became an extended town. Most people lived in the small settlements and villages surrounding the fortified city. The women of Aegae, as those of other Macedonian cities and settlements, retained a close relationship with nature, as often happens with traditional agro-pastoral communities. Girls and old women, maidens and wives went to the countryside in

Fig. 82. Alexander the Great praised the textiles of the women of his generation – this fine gold thread and purple piece of textile was used for wrapping the cremated remains of Queen Meda

Fig. 83. Dionysus – detail from a finely painted red-figure *lekythos* (Cat. no. 261)

order to wash clothes in the streams, bring water, gather greenery and bulbs, berries and wild fruits, flowers and branches to make wreaths for festivals and celebrations, and to collect herbs for making remedies and poisons. Knowledge of the mystical substances of plants, akin to medicine and witchcraft, traditionally belonged to women.

Public life, war and the exercise of power, athletics and education in letters and the arts were the privilege of men. In the Macedonians' official festivals, contests and banquets the presence of women was limited. However, there were a few exceptions. The festivals in honour of Demeter and her daughter Persephone were traditionally part of their realm. The same goes for the worship of Dionysus (fig. 83), with maenads fervently dancing in the forest, urging the earth to produce honey and milk, and wild women crowned by snakes and shredding their prey to pieces with their own bare hands. This vivid account of Euripides in his *Bacchae* resonates with the women of Aegae and their performances in the neighbouring Pierian mountains – rituals led by the queen herself, deeply rooted in the people's faith.

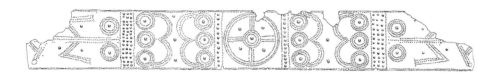

It is a well-known fact that Olympias, the mother of Alexander the Great, was a fervent and passionate follower of Bacchus. As suggested by the story regarding the dragon lying down beside the queen, but also by findings from the sanctuaries at Aegae, snakes had a prominent position in the religious life of the Macedonian metropolis and in the 'secret' realm of its women.

The archetypal relationship of virgin-woman-queen-priestess with the sacred dragon-guardian of knowledge – guardian of paradise, the embodiment of autochthony – is deeply embedded in ancient belief systems and rituals. It travels through the myth of the wise goddess-witch, Medea, and haunts the divine secret of the suffering Dionysus Zagreus. Hidden behind the shield of Athena *Parthenos*, it emerges tangible and unexpectedly vivid in the rituals of Macedon, connecting this frontier kingdom to the heart of the Aegean world.

Fig. 84 'Solar symbols' on the bronze diadem found with the burial of an Early Iron Age lady (Cat. no. 127)

When Argaeos was king of the Macedonians and Galauros was king of the Taulantii, the latter campaigned against Macedon. Argaeos, who had few soldiers, ordered the Macedonian virgins to present themselves from Mount Ereboia as the enemy advanced. They accordingly did so: and then many virgins came down from the mountain and made an appearance, brandishing their thyrsuses instead of spears and with wreaths concealing their faces. Galauros, thinking from afar that the virgins were men, was intimidated and ordered a retreat: the Taulantii fled, throwing away their arms and equipment. Argaeos, having thus obtained victory without battle, erected a temple to Bacchus Pseudanor and ordered the virgins, who were before called Klodones [branch-bearers] by the Macedonians, to be called Mimallones, because they imitated the men.

(Polyainos, *Strategems in War* 4.1.1)

Historical event or not, this narrative hints at the distinctiveness and determination of Macedonian women. It also recalls an attitude often found in regions under Dorian influence, such as Sparta. After all, if we are to believe Herodotus, Macedonians were closely related or were one and the same as the Dorians.

In democratic Athens, the *basilinna*, wife of the elected *archon basileus* (responsible for religious affairs and sacred law) had the privilege to play the leading part in the rites of the Sacred Marriage (*Hieros Gamos*), which was of paramount importance for the city and a crucial ritual for the life of any ancient community. At the centre of almost all mystical and public festivals, the Sacred Marriage was performed at many sites across Greece, from Samothrace to Eleusis and from Samos to Knossos. It would almost certainly have been performed in the kingdom of Macedon, where the old customs are kept alive more than anywhere else. Again, most of our evidence is centred on Olympias and her sacred marriage with Zeus, the fruit of which, according to an apocryphal tradition, was Alexander. Yet, Olympias is nothing but the culmination of a long tradition. Religious performance is the realm where aristocratic ladies, and especially the queens of Macedon, played an important role.

Bronze triple double axes, placed on top of wooden poles, are associated with sacrificial rituals and recall almost-forgotten archetypes of the Aegean world (fig. 86). Diadems with solar symbols, pendants and amulets of various shapes and forms 'words' of a lost symbolic language (fig. 84), four-spoked wheels, likely precursors of the magical apparatus that Pindar calls ιυγγα τετράκναμον (*iynx torquilla*), necessary for love spells (fig. 85) and the tiny bronze objects, something between a cauldron and a pendant, which may have contained residues of remedies and herbs are found in the graves of rich women of the Early Iron Age (1000–700 BC) (fig. 87). They bear witness to the fact that the aristocratic ladies and queens of Aegae had, until the seventh century BC, a power greater than that of their husbands: the privilege and commitment to communicate with the supernatural for the benefit of their people.

This tradition was followed by the Temenid women, as witnessed by the hieratic sceptre, adorned with ivory and amber, of the Lady of Aegae, which was found to the right of her body in a similar position to that of spears in the tombs of warriors. Placed inside a leather or wooden gilded casket, the iron spits that accompanied her to Hades, testify that the queen – wife of Amyntas I and perhaps mother of Alexander I – who died in her thirties early in the fifth century BC – along with the men of her family shared the privilege of partaking in the sacred dinners that followed the sacrifices to the gods. Next to the spits there was an iron model of a four-wheeled cart drawn by two wooden gold-covered animals – mules or oxen – recalling the story of the priestess of Argos whose sons, Kleobes and Biton, as an outward sign of respect and devotion pulled the cart the entire way so that their mother would not arrive late in the sacred procession. With their benevolent act the two brothers earned the bittersweet gift of the gods and died peacefully in their sleep. A symbolic object, the miniature cart (fig. 88) found in the tomb suggests that, as a high-priestess,

Fig. 85 Wheel-shaped disc
(Cat. no. 141)

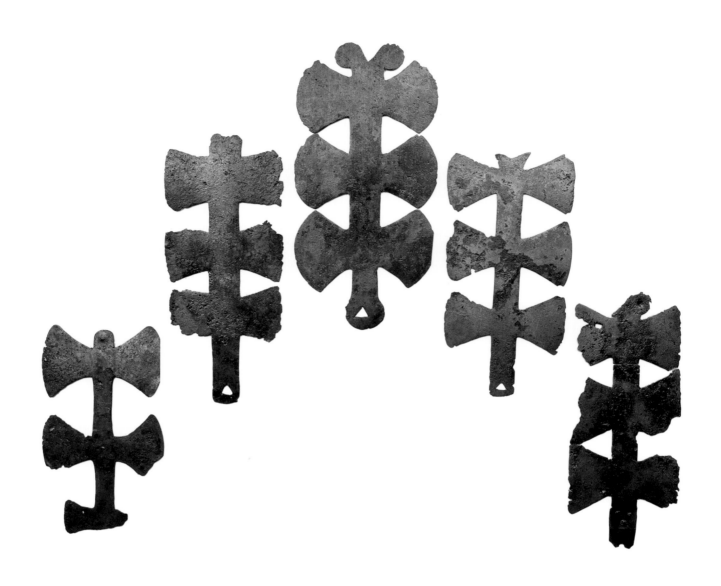

Fig. 86 Triple double axes – a symbol
of authority (Cat. nos. 128–29, 274–75, 309)

Fig. 87 Early Iron Age pendants – these tiny objects may have contained residues of remedies and herbs (Cat. nos. top [from left to right]: 136, 131, 134, 135; bottom [from left to right]: 138, 133, 130, 139, 132)

Fig. 88 Iron model of a four-wheeled cart originally covered with gold foil (Cat. no. 203)

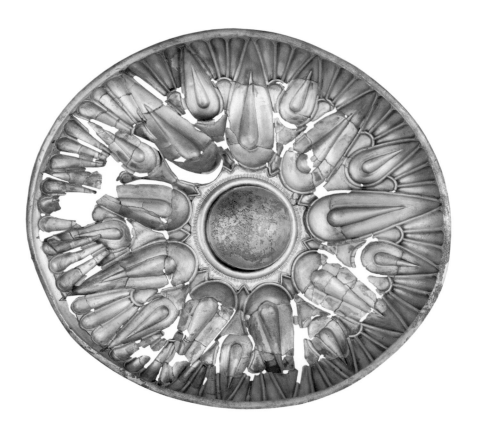

Fig. 89 Silver *omphalos phiale* from the Lady of Aegae – this type of vessel was preferred for making libations to the gods (Cat. no. 201)

the queen of Macedon, like the aristocratic ladies of neighbouring tribes whose graves held similar objects, had the right to appear in public and take part in ritual processions and ceremonies in honour of the gods, in which she officiated.

An inscribed silver gilt bowl (*omphalos phiale*), the preferred vessel for making libations to the gods (fig. 89), and the many other similar bronze bowls found in the tombs of the queens lend further weight to this hypothesis. A *patera*, a pan-shaped vessel, an official libation object similar to that used by the Macedonian king, was found in the tomb of one of the wives of Alexander I (fig. 90). Its elaborate handle depicts one of the few Macedonian *kouroi* that have come to light. In the same tomb more than 26 clay heads of wooden statues (*xoana*) were found – remains of an enigmatic ritual: they suggest a special relationship of the queen with the world of gods and demons and underline her connection to the Great Goddess (fig. 91).

The religious function of the queen, a tradition which derives from the remote heroic past, was renewed in the sacraments of the mystical cults that in classical times gained ardent devotees among the Macedonian court: Eurydice carries the god-bearing name of the wife of Orpheus, the first *mystes* (the initiated one) – and the symbolism of images on her funeral throne bears witness to her special relationship with the lady of the underworld (fig. 92). Her daughter-in-law, Olympias, initiated into the mysteries of the Great Gods of Samothrace, is well known for her devotion to

Fig. 90 (above) Handle from a pan-shaped vessel in the form of a nude man (*kouros*) with upraised arms. Traces of gold are still visible on the surface of the handle (Cat. no. 215)

Fig. 91 (right) Lifesize male and female clay heads – part of an enigmatic ritual, 26 lifesize clay heads were thrown into the tomb of a queen underlining her special relationship with the world of gods and demons (Cat. nos. 176, 173)

Fig. 92 The back of the marble
throne from the tomb of Queen
Eurydice showing the divine
couple of the underworld,
Hades and Persephone

Dionysus – the Mysteries' god par excellence – and was also a high-priestess of
the enigmatic 'agadistic' rituals – perhaps the mystic rituals of the royal family of the Argead Macedonians. These mystic rituals were probably similar to
those performed by the ancient family of Eumolpides in Attica or the aristocrats of Andania in Messenia. In the Hellenistic world, this tradition would
reach a peak with the Ptolemaic queens of Egypt: the Arsinoes, Berenices and
Cleopatras, who, apart from being high-priestesses, were also declared goddesses themselves.

Philip II's example is clear proof that the Temenids could have more than
one wife at the same time. The practice of polygamy was probably followed
to secure the fertility and the succession of the royal house, while simultane-
ously serving the aims of internal and external politics: to ratify alliances and
treaties and to obtain the friendship of powerful and potentially dangerous
neighbours. The male children of royal wives probably had, according to their
age and abilities, an equal chance of becoming kings. Yet it is likely that there
was a hierarchy among the wives, since one of them, probably the mother of
the successor, would execute the duties of high-priestess. It seems that these
outstanding women of the royal family were buried in a particular cluster: the
queens' cluster found in a prominent place above the necropolis of Aegae, next
to the north-western city gate. The rest – for example the two wives of Philip II,
Nikesipolis, the mother of Thessalonice, who probably died in childbirth in
the middle of the fourth century BC, and the Thracian princess Meda, who
followed her husband to the funeral pyre in 336 BC – were buried in the same
cluster or even in the same grave as their husbands.

Apart from their religious duties, the daughters and sisters of the Temenids
also had a role in public life, being an excellent means of establishing alliances
and relations that served military and political purposes. The marriage of
Stratonice, daughter of Alexander I, to Seuthes I of Thrace relieved her brother,
Perdiccas II – and hence Macedonia – from the threat of conquest by Sitalces,
king of the Odrysians. The Successors had an eye on the sisters of Alexander
the Great, Thessalonice and Cleopatra, knowing that marriage to one of them
would legitimate their claim to the throne.

Mothers and wives, daughters and sisters, bearers of the precious royal
seed and carriers of the sacred royal blood of a dynasty descending from the
gods – Temenid women, like the ancient mythical queens, were fully aware of
their descent and value and did not limit themselves to a passive role. While
in golden age Athens intellectuals debated the relationship of children to their
mothers and Aeschylus' judges acquitted Orestes of his matricide – since in
the Athenian democracy the son was related to his father, while the mother,
'foreigner to a foreigner', was simply a receptacle for hiding the seed until the
fruit became ripe – in the kingdom of Macedon the arcane acceptance of the
close relationship between mother and child was never called into dispute.
Indicative is the fact that the son of Gygaia, sister of Alexander I, and the Persian
official Boubaris, was named after his Macedonian grandfather, Amyntas. It
is not accidental that the deep and complex relationship between Alexander

the Great and his mother, Olympias, is the most impressive and characteristic example of the interdependence and mutual influence of mother and son that one finds throughout the history of ancient Greece.

Ambitious royal women were well aware that the ascent of their sons to the throne would solidify their own positions. When a king was under-age, the mother could hope that real power would end up in her own hands. With the exception of Olympias, who governed for a short period of time in the name of her grandchild, the most successful achiever in this respect was Queen Eurydice, widow of Amyntas III and mother of three kings; she succeeded in securing power for her under-age sons, trying at the same time to wield power herself. Her granddaughter, Thessalonice, and even her great-grandchild, Eurydice, made similar attempts, the latter losing, however, to Olympias.

It is worth remarking that these women set up dedications in their own name followed by their father's, rather than their husband's, name: 'Eurydice daughter of Sirras' or 'Queen Thessalonice daughter of Philip'.

Fig. 93 Steatite mould for making jewellery (Cat. no. 363)

With royal blood in their veins, Temenid women became symbols and bearers of power in the eyes of others. Having knowledge of their value and capabilities, they asserted their participation in the share of power and in the promotion of royal ideology. And while this was exceptional during the classical period, in the following centuries it became the norm. Pure-blooded Macedonians, the Arsinoes, Berenices and Cleopatras of the Hellenistic world, had a leading role on the stage of history. Their example was to be followed by others: the Greek Queen Thalassia, after the death of her husband, Hyspaosines, became regent for her underage son, reigning in the remote kingdom of the Characene in the Persian Gulf.

The emancipation of the women of the Hellenistic royal houses is a well-known fact. Their behaviour set an example not only for the aristocracy but also for people across their realms. Ideas rooted in the arcane beliefs of Macedonian society blossomed and yielded rich fruits by finding a fertile ground in the new world opened up by the conquests of Alexander the Great. In the open-minded societies of the Hellenistic world women obtained more rights and more power over themselves.

FASHION AT AEGAE AND THE ROYAL COURT OF MACEDON

The rich finds from the cemeteries of Olympus, Pieria and mountainous Makedonis and especially from the vast tumuli cemetery at Aegae help us obtain a complete picture of women's attire in the Macedonian kingdom during the first three centuries of the first millennium BC (1000–700 BC) (fig. 93).

The jewels made almost always of bronze – an alloy of copper whose yellow colour was reminiscent of gold – were quite rich and heavy, decorated with characteristic geometrical shapes. Similar, though simpler and more restrained than the jewellery found in the Balkans and the Italian peninsula, this jewellery finds its best parallels in Epirus, the Peloponnese and Doric Crete.

The dominant dress is the thick, woollen *peplos*, a plain dress fastened over the shoulder with simple pins so long that they could have easily been used as lethal weapons or heavy bronze brooches (*fibulae*). These brooches, originally bow-shaped (fig. 94), later acquire a figure-of-eight shape, incorporating the motif of concentric circles, cherished especially during the geometric period (900–700 BC) (fig. 95). Heavy bronze bracelets with one or more spirals adorned the arms (fig. 97); simple bronze rings, often decorated with figure-of-eight spirals, adorned the fingers (fig. 96); distinctive pendants, torques (collars) from thick bronze-twisted wire (fig. 98) and necklaces of cornelian (fig. 100), and heavy bronze beads (fig. 99) decorated the neck and décolleté.

The only gold jewellery during this time was the hair-ring made of thin wire, used to tie the curl that fell over the shoulders and back (fig. 102). The fine bow-shaped and figure-of-eight brooches found in the area of the head of the richest dead suggest that noble women wore intricate head coverings which, with the help of large bronze buttons, kept in place the bronze *fistulae* or *syringes* – coil-shaped ornaments that, like locks of blonde hair, framed the face with a warm golden shine. 'Deep girded', like the women of the Homeric

Fig. 94 Bow-shaped brooches used to fasten the heavy woolen *peplos* over the shoulder (Cat. nos. 343–47)

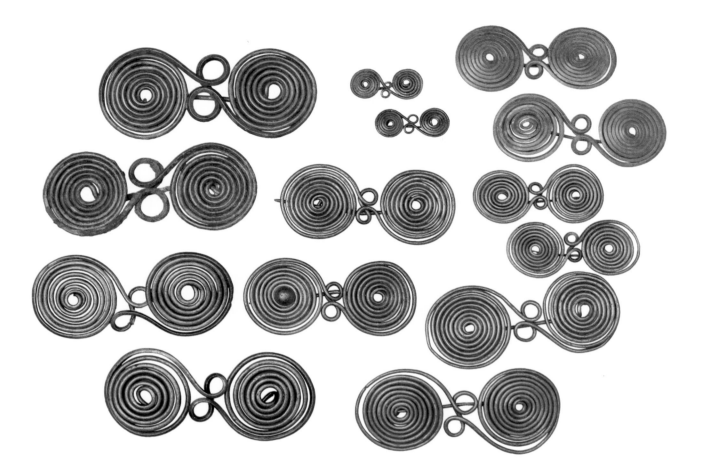

epics, the ladies of Aegae fastened around their waists impressive leather belts decorated with a series of small buttons and large shield-shaped ornaments (*omphalia*) (fig. 103), while a queen and high-priestess wore a tall bronze diadem decorated with solar symbols (fig. 84).

Thanks to the conservatism of Macedonian society, figure-of-eight brooches and necklaces made up of heavy bronze geometric beads continued to be produced until the end of the sixth century BC. Yet even in archaic times fashion was changing, along with forms, shapes and materials. The small, elegant, gold, silver and bronze bow-shaped brooches (figs. 104–105) often found on the shoulders and arms of buried women suggest that the thinly woven sleeved ionic tunic become increasingly popular, while the traditional woollen *peplos*, a heavy body-length garment fastened on the shoulders with small silver pins setting the arms free, became finer (fig. 106). Often both garments are worn together; one above the other. The most common coat was the *himation*, a large rectangular piece of fabric made of wool or linen, which covered the entire body and could even cover the head.

Jewellery, always cherished, became with time more elaborate and less bulky. Earrings appear at Aegae and soon become very popular. Expensive golden earrings with embossed decoration and elaborate ones decorated with

Fig. 95 (above) Figure-of-eight brooches (Cat. nos. 283, 306, 312, 349–52)

Fig. 96 (below) Finger ring with figure-of-eight decoration (Cat. no. 294)

Fig. 97 Heavy bronze bracelets with one or more spirals adorned the arms of the Early Iron Age ladies (Cat. nos. 272, 286, 300, 316, 356–61)

Fig. 98 Bronze collar (torque) (Cat. no. 291)

Fig. 99 Bronze necklace – despite its archaic date the beads allude to the
Geometric period underlining the conservatism that prevailed in the
Macedonian court (Cat. no. 403)

Fig. 100 Two cornelian necklaces that
accompanied an Early Iron Age lady to
the underworld (Cat. no. 277)

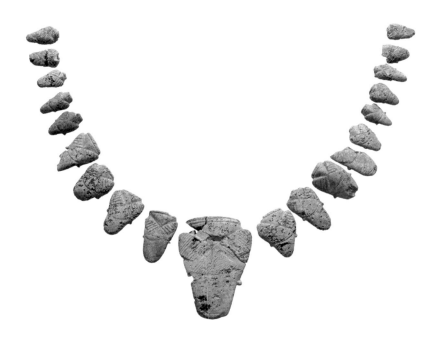

Fig. 101 Amber necklace – Baltic amber arrived at Aegae
most likely via the Po valley in Italy (Cat. no. 414)

filigree and granulation were destined for ladies of the court (figs. 116–17). More common and much simpler were the omega-shaped earrings (fig. 108), ending originally in snake heads and later lotus buds, usually silver and rarely in gold. There are also silver and bronze boat-shaped earrings (fig. 107), and plain silver rings. Twin gold and silver pins also became popular during the archaic and classical periods (fig. 109). Pendants, often in gold, were tiny and shaped like an *amphoriskos*, pyramid (fig. 114) or an acorn. Necklaces consisted of beads of gold (fig. 118), amber (fig. 101), glass, ivory and bronze (fig. 99). Silver and gold bracelets with one spiral only end up in snake-heads (fig. 110), as do several silver chains which were attached to the dress around the breasts (fig. 111). Finger-rings, in archaic times plain gold, from the classical period onwards acquired hollow bezels and were made of gold, silver, bronze and even iron; these finger-rings would have served as the signature of the bearer (fig. 81), similar to men's signet rings. Gold strips and ornaments adorned the clothes of aristocratic ladies (figs. 125–26).

In contrast to the commoners, whose ornaments were few and plain, royal and noble women descended to Hades bedecked in gold from head to toe (figs. 112–124), draped in purple, wearing shoes with gilded soles. Silver, and especially gold, was the material, granulation and filigree were the main techniques cherished by the ladies of the court. Yet stranger and more exquisite materials are also recorded. A queen who died shortly after the middle of the sixth century BC was buried with heavy iron dress pins that are best described as weapons rather than as pieces of jewellery (figs. 127–28); the intricately worked amber necklace that belonged to one of the wives of Alexander I is unique in the Greek world and may have been made in the Po valley or somewhere in south Italy (fig. 101).

Despite this wealth of materials, the jewellery at Aegae is characterised by a certain frugality and reserved standardization. This tendency is not limited to jewellery but can also be observed in other products of the Macedonian metalworking tradition at this time. The use of metals, especially the more precious ones, is always a good indicator of a state's economic situation and stability. It is certainly not accidental that Macedonian metalworking reached a peak during the reign of Philip II and Alexander the Great (360–323 BC), when Macedonian goldwork, in particular, flourished beyond measure. The talented goldsmiths were great artists who made every effort to meet the needs of the court, and with a unique dexterity enriched traditional forms and produced new elaborate designs. Similarly, with advanced technological knowledge, smiths created new alloys and used materials such as painted glass and precious stones in order to achieve a balanced polychromy with persuasively naturalistic figures, subdued to the harmony of geometry.

A superb example of their craftsmanship, the diadem of Meda adorned with flowers, bees and birds is one of the most remarkable pieces of ancient Greek jewellery to have come down to us, despite having endured the funeral pyre. The golden wreaths with their naturalistic forms are a characteristic product of the royal workshop. The golden oak wreath that followed Philip into the flames

Fig. 102 Gold rings for tying locks of hair over the shoulders (Cat. no. 278)

Fig. 103 Bronze *omphalia* (belt ornaments) (Cat. no. 302)

Fig. 105 Gold brooch ending in lion heads (Cat. no. 225). Shown enlarged

Fig. 104 Silver bow-shaped *fibulae* (brooches) (Cat. no. 416)

Fig. 107 Pair of gold earrings (Cat. no. 405)

Fig. 106 Silver pins
(Cat. nos. 411, 422, 424)

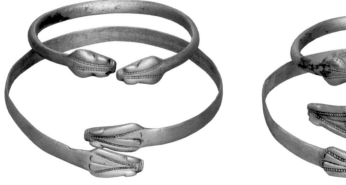

Fig. 110 Silver snake-headed bracelets (Cat. no. 421)

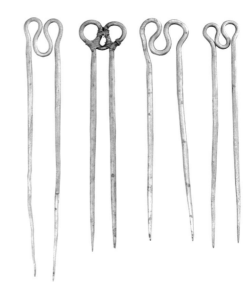

Fig. 109 Silver twin pins
(Cat. nos. 407–10)

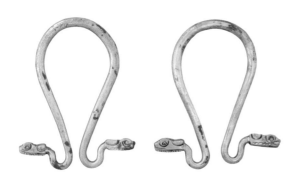

Fig. 108 Silver omega-shaped
earrings ending in snake-heads
(Cat. no. 413)

Fig. 111 Gold chains attached to the
dress around the breasts (Cat. no. 224).
Shown enlarged

Figs. 112–124: jewellery found with the Lady of Aegae – the flesh perished together with the textiles, the wood, and the leather, but the gold jewellery and strips remained intact

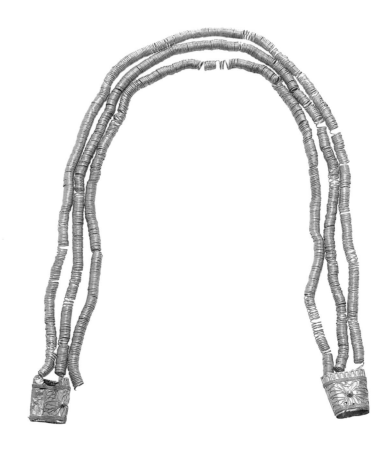

Fig. 114 Pyramid-shaped pendant lavishly decorated with granulation and a tiny narcissus flower at the apex (Cat. no. 332)

Fig. 112 Gold *syringes* (coil-shaped hair ornaments) – like locks of blonde hair framed the face of the Lady of Aegae (Cat. no. 329)

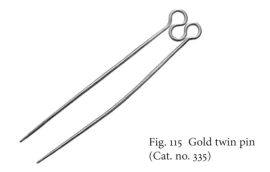

Fig. 113 Elegant gold bow-shaped brooches – often found near the shoulders and arms of women. They suggest that thinly woven ionic sleeved tunics became increasingly popular (Cat. no. 333)

Fig. 115 Gold twin pin (Cat. no. 335)

Fig. 117 The blossoming narcissus flower and the two close buds decorating the earrings of the Lady of Aegae (Cat. no. 330)

Fig. 116 Pair of intricately worked gold earrings (Cat. no. 330)

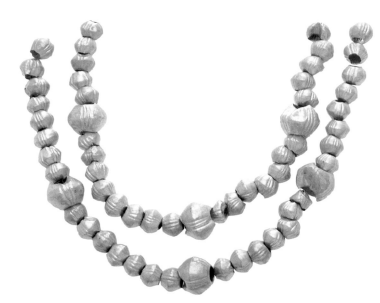

Fig. 118 Gold necklace adorning the lady's décolleté (Cat. no. 331)

Fig. 119 Gold terminals for securing a silver chain and a pair of cones decorated with filigree (Cat. no. 339)

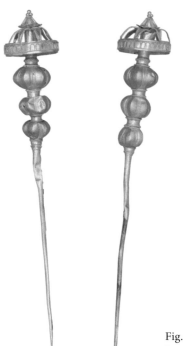

Fig. 121 Detail showing the blossoming flower crowning the head of the pin (Cat. no. 334)

Fig. 120 Large gold pins with impressive heads (Cat. no. 334)

Fig. 122 A silver and gold tubular object, perhaps a distaff (Cat. no. 412)

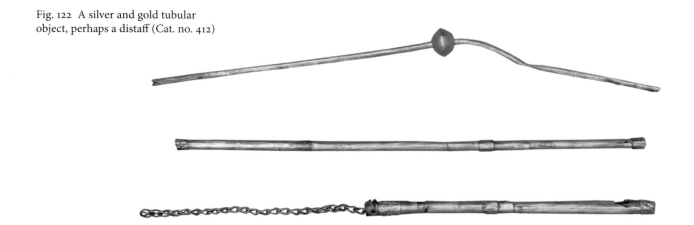

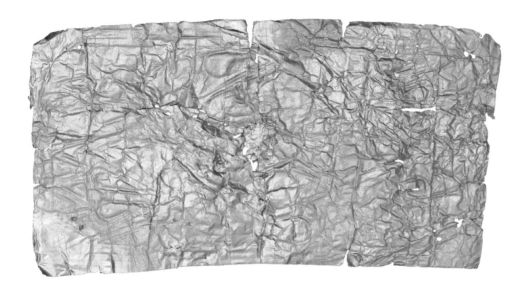

Fig. 123 A broad rectangular strip with repoussé
triangles and drop-shaped motifs – it was found
at the centre of the garment just below the waist
of the Lady of Aegae (Cat. no. 337)

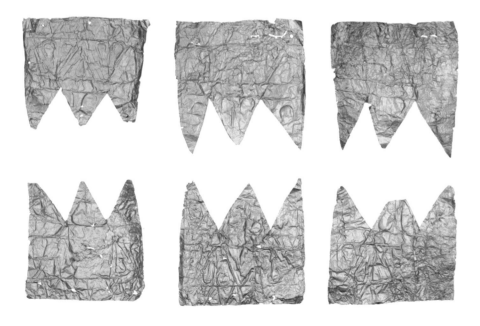

Fig. 124 Gold strips once adorning the overgarment
(*epiblema*) (Cat. no. 337)

Fig. 125 A gold disc (dress ornament) decorated with a Medusa head – found in the burial of an early queen (Cat. no. 218); gold roundels with embossed wild animals (Cat. no. 181)

Fig. 126 Gold roundels decorated with a star once stitched onto the funeral dress of the deceased (Cat. no. 251)

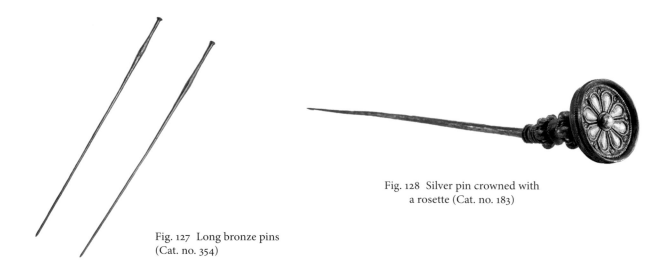

Fig. 127 Long bronze pins
(Cat. no. 354)

Fig. 128 Silver pin crowned with
a rosette (Cat. no. 183)

Fig. 129 The golden myrtle
wreath of Queen Meda
(Cat. no. 263)

of the pyre, perhaps the same that he was wearing in the hour of his 'triumph' when he was assassinated in the autumn of 336 BC, underlines the close relationship of the king and of his successors, who also wore similar wreaths with Zeus himself. Of similar quality is the charming myrtle wreath of Philip's wife Meda captured in its small branches the most blossoming moment of spring (fig. 129).

Despite the fact that in the tombs we have not yet found a single mirror, the women of Aegae were most likely vain and took great care of their appearance (fig. 81). Olive oil played a dominant role in hair and body care (fig. 131). Queens from the time of Perdiccas II onwards bought the sacred oil of the goddess Athena that was sold at the market by the winners of the Panathenaic games in Athens, as suggested by the Panathenaic *amphoras* found in their tombs and in the funeral pyre of Queen Eurydice. Along with oil, women used various ointments and creams and of course perfumes and aromatic oils from Corinth, eastern Ionia, Rhodes, Egypt and Phoenicia, often stored inside elaborate containers, the beauty of which vied with that of their contents. An iron *exaleiptron*, a container with bronze legs found in the tomb of the Lady of Aegae (fig. 130), large *alabastra* (fig. 132), egg-shell marble toiletry vessels (fig. 133) and ostrich eggs (fig. 52) – exotic prototypes of the elegant red-figure squat *lekythoi* (fig. 135–36) – suggest that personal hygiene and body care at the Macedonian court matched, in elaboration and luxury, that of Mycenae almost a millennium earlier. Even make-up was not unknown to the ladies at Aegae: minute ear-picks and tweezers, fine and elegant utensils and more importantly *pyxides* (fig. 134), cosmetic vessels containing white lead powder for whitening the skin, constitute the typical accoutrements of female toiletry and became, after death, along with jewellery, a good indicator for the archaeologist as to the sex of the deceased, especially useful at Aegae, where soil conditions hardly ever allow for the preservation of skeletal remains.

Fig. 130 Iron cosmetics container (*exaleiptron*) with an ornate bronze tripod base (Cat. no. 202)

Fig. 131 Clay perfume containers (*plemochoe* and e*xaleiptron*) (Cat. nos. 194, 377)

Fig. 132 Two large *alabastra* made of alabaster (Cat. nos. 236, 259)

Fig. 133 A group of two tall marble *lekythoi* (aromatic-oil containers) and a marble perfume container (Cat. nos. 233–35)

Fig. 134 Bronze *pyxis* (container)
with lid (Cat. no. 226)

Fig. 135 Attic red-figure *lekythos* with
Eros (Cat. no. 397)

Fig. 136 Clay Attic red figure *lekythos* showing a woman at her toilet, and clay perfume vessel (*askos*) decorated with griffins (Cat. nos. 241–42)

9   The occupants of Tomb II at Vergina: why Arrhidaios and Eurydice must be excluded

Jonathan Musgrave and John Prag

The examination of the skull from Tomb II at Vergina, ancient Aegae, that underpinned our now-famous facial reconstruction identified injuries, which demonstrated that the individual had been struck from above by a missile that must have blinded his right eye (fig. 137).[1] The ancient sources report that this was precisely the injury that Philip II suffered during the siege of Methone in 355–354 BC. Manolis Andronikos regarded this as cardinal evidence that the tomb is that of Philip II; the likely occupant of the outer chamber is then one of Philip's wives, Meda or Cleopatra. The bone evidence was fundamental to the argument, and it matched the literary, historical and archaeological sources relating to the nature of the tomb and the likely occupants of the other tombs.

Perhaps not surprisingly, the evidence was disputed and other candidates were put forward, notably Philip III Arrhidaios, Alexander the Great's half-brother and successor, and his wife Eurydice. The long-running debate was well summarised in 2008 by Miltiades Hatzopoulos in the journal *Tekmeria*. Most of the counter-arguments relate to the paintings in and on the tombs and to the historical events surrounding Philip II's death, but in 2000 Antonis Bartsiokas, Director of the Anaximandrian Institute of Human Evolution at Voula, published an article in *Science* in which he challenged our observations and conclusions. Using macrophotography to produce detailed close-up views of the frontal bone, he concluded that the skeleton belonged to Arrhidaios. Although rightly underlining the importance of the bone pathology, Bartsiokas's sweeping comments disregarded the historical sources.

He concentrated on two features of the face: a 'notch' on the superior margin of the right orbit and an associated 'pimple' which we had suggested might be attributable to trauma; and a probable healed fracture on the right cheek-bone associated with a nick in the right cheek-bone and maxilla at the anatomical landmark zygomaxillare. These are crucial to our identification of the remains, for they provided the evidence of the blinding injury to the right eye. According to Bartsiokas 'there is no evidence of healing at this suture' and what 'the skull shows is bone distortion owing partly to cremation and partly to a poor reconstruction of the facial skeleton'.[2]

That the face may have been incorrectly reconstructed was apparent when we studied it; and understanding this aspect was crucial to understanding the trauma to the skull. However, Bartsiokas also made a number of statements on the asymmetry of the face – he denies there was any – that we challenge. He supported his argument that this skeleton belonged to Arrhidaios by proposing that it had been cremated dry (degreased). The evidence he adduced for this claim is the pattern of the transverse fracture lines, especially on the long limb bones. Bones cremated with flesh on them are said to curve, but those burned dry are straight. He pointed to the left tibia and the right ulna in particular 'with [their] minimal warping and transverse cracking that is straight'. However we present ample evidence that the femora, right humerus, left ulna, both tibiae, and the cranial vault are markedly warped.[3] All this confirms that the man in the main chamber of Tomb II was burned as a fleshed cadaver. The bones from the antechamber have fracture lines proclaiming that this body too was burned with her flesh on.

Why is the dry versus flesh-covered argument so important? Arrhidaios was murdered and his wife Eurydice forced to commit suicide in the autumn of 317 BC. One of the arguments that Bartsiokas used in support of the identification of Arrhidaios as the occupant of the main chamber of Tomb II was his supposition that their bodies were fully skeletonised, degreased and dry when they were exhumed and reburied four to seventeen months later. However, if the occupant of the main chamber of Tomb II was murdered, buried, exhumed, cremated and given a state funeral within a four to seventeen-month period between early 316 and winter/spring 315 BC,[4] one might reasonably expect the bones from the antechamber to be qualitatively and quantitatively comparable. Here Bartsiokas failed to address the crucial question about what happened to the body of Eurydice during the months between her murder and final committal alongside Arrhidaios' remains.

Qualitatively these bones are comparable if one rejects Bartsiokas' claim that the bones from the main chamber were burnt 'degreased' and 'dry'. Quantitatively the comparison at first sight appears weaker. The larnax in the antechamber held 1,312g of miscellaneous fragments, but that in the main chamber accommodated an almost complete skeleton. Its weight has not been recorded, but the 379.13g of *miscellanea* too small to put on display offer a clue. If this collection represents 10 per cent, 12.5 per cent or 15 per cent of the whole skeleton, the latter's total cremated weight would be 3,791.30g, 3,033.04g or 2,527.53g respectively. These scores fall into the ranges of modern male and female 'cremains', as they are now called, recorded by Holck as 2,200–3,750g and by McKinley as 1,600–3,600g. The reason for the disparity can be found in Dr Angeliki Kottaridi's study of the pyre site, which revealed an impressively rich collection of offerings, and several hundred unfired mud bricks used for the construction of a small building inside which the body was burned, protecting it as if inside an oven.

We assume that the woman from the antechamber was cremated on an open pyre. That she was burned fleshed is not in doubt. The neck and proximal shaft

Fig. 137. Waxwork reconstruction of the head of the occupant of Tomb II – Philip II

of each femur, especially the left, show curved transverse fractures, as do several smaller limb-bone shaft fragments. For Bartsiokas this would presumably disqualify her from being identified as Arrhidaios' wife Eurydice as he believed her husband was cremated dry.

Have we any reason to believe that the bodies of Arrhidaios and Eurydice became fully skeletonised, degreased and dry during the months after their deaths? The ancient literary sources offer limited help. Diodorus Siculus (*Library of World History* 19.11) reports that Cassander buried the couple at Aegae (Vergina) 'as was the custom for royalty', together with Kynna, Eurydice's mother. Bartsiokas is silent on these historical details. Diodorus may give the fullest record of these events, but he was writing some 200 years after the event, and for the present discussion there is little to be gained in attempting once again to reconstruct the likely sequence of events as Cassander made his bid for power in 317 BC.

Nor can one write confidently about the condition of Arrhidaios' body at the time of the funeral ordered by Cassander in 316–315 BC. However, the evidence from human remains exhumed for forensic examination suggests that after six or even seventeen months in the ground Arrhidaios' body would still have had putrefying skin and muscle attached to his limb bones, and rotting viscera filling his thoracic, abdominal and pelvic cavities. He would have been far from dry and degreased. Above all, it is unlikely that the bodies of Arrhidaios and Eurydice were ever exhumed as rotting corpses for subsequent cremation at Aegae or elsewhere. It is unparalleled and incredible that corpses recovered in this way from their initial burial would have been secondarily cremated at their new resting-place. Their re-handling would have been seriously polluting for participants and grotesquely contrary to Greek beliefs about contact with decomposed corpses.

In short, Bartsiokas relies too much on his own specialised expertise and is thus too selective in his use of the evidence for his arguments to come together as a convincing case. From a study confined to just two regions of the face he draws wide-ranging conclusions that his evidence simply will not support. Other arguments in favour of Arrhidaios' candidacy, notably those based on the art-history of the tomb paintings, have been proposed. Attractive though these may appear to some scholars, we do not believe that they stand up to the cumulative historical evidence supported by bone pathology and taphonomy.

10 Burial customs and beliefs in the royal necropolis of Aegae

Angeliki Kottaridi

The vast necropolis of Aegae, the burial ground of the Macedonian kings, extends over the plain to the north of the ancient city, occupying an area of about two square kilometres or twenty hectares. In its core area 540 tumuli are still preserved. It is here that the main cemetery of the Early Iron Age was located (1100–700 BC). In the archaic period the necropolis expanded to the south and during the fifth and fourth century BC to the west and north-west, where in 336 BC Philip II was buried. From the last quarter of the fourth century BC, the tendency for expansion led to the east, through and beyond the old Early Iron Age cemetery. The horizontal expansion of the necropolis appears to be the general trend at Aegae. Its almost limitless spatial development, hampering even agriculture, is indicative of the underlying bonds of piety between the living and the dead, thus offering additional support with regard to continuity in Aegae's population.

The unprecedented looting of the necropolis of Aegae by the Gallic mercenaries of Pyrrhos in 276 BC (Plutarch, *Pyrrhos* 26.11-13) left intense marks everywhere. Although most of the burials are found looted, there are numerous finds that solidify the view that Aegae was the centre of the Macedonian kingdom until the end of the classical period.

So far more than 2,500 burials have been investigated. Most of them comprise earthen pits and rarely cists. The dimensions of these tombs vary according to the wealth and social position of their owner. Orientated radially towards the centre of the mound during the Early Iron Age, and along the axes of the horizon later, they are organized in rows and clusters and form groups, which probably relate to families and kin-groups.

According to ancient practice, which at Aegae survives until the Roman period, earthen mounds (*tumuli*) mark the position of the tombs, while dry stone circular enclosures (*periboloi*) outline their boundaries. The size of these burial mounds varies according to the social status of the deceased. It is thus not accidental that the tomb of Philip II was discovered under the largest burial

Fig. 138 Clay *exaleiptra* (perfume containers) (Cat. nos. 377, 381)

mound in the southern Balkan Peninsula. The use of funerary monuments and of relief or inscribed grave markers, such as those found elsewhere in Greece, becomes common practice from the fifth century BC onwards. In exceptional cases, such as, for example, the tomb cluster of Philip II, next to the burial mound impressive above ground burial monuments are erected with sculptures and reliefs similar to those found in Attica.

Diachronically, the most common burial practice is inhumation. The deceased take with them whatever they wear and whatever characterises them (their clothes, adornments, and weapons); the ritual vessels, characteristic and necessary for the funeral (aromatic-oil and perfume containers (fig. 138)); cups and jugs to extinguish their everlasting thirst in the underworld. These are occasionally accompanied with other banquet vessels. There are also objects related to religious practices and social symbolism – the coins for Charon, figurines (figs. 139–153), models of carts (fig. 88) and others.

Wealth is apparent, especially in the funerary assemblages of the royal clusters and in the tombs of the companions (*hetairoi*). Yet, it is worth remarking that in jewellery, as well as in weapons and metal vessels – expensive objects and thus prestige items – a Doric severity and austerity is observed which distinguishes them from comparable assemblages found in regions outside the limits of the Macedonian kingdom (e.g. at Trebeniste, etc.).

The systematic investigation of the archaic and classical necropolis in the last twenty years offers a basis for comparison and some secure criteria for the identification of royal tomb clusters which are distinguished from the other groups in the following ways: a) in the persistent and diachronic use of a particular space, which can last for up to two and a half centuries; b) in the size and luxury of the funerary monuments, as well as the quality, quantity and diversity of their funerary assemblages – such as gold jewellery, gold-gilded weapons, fine silver and bronze vessels, exotic products, furniture in gold and ivory (fig. 154), and others – which, despite the looting of most tombs, still

Fig. 139 Group of felines attacking
deer (Cat. no. 192)

Fig. 140 (above) Bird-shaped
perfume vessel (Cat. no. 379)

Fig. 141 (right) Clay dove
(Cat. no. 146)

Fig. 142 Clay figurine of a seated goddess (Cat. no. 145)

Fig. 143 Female *protome* found with the burial of the Lady of Aegae (Cat. no. 210)

Fig. 144 Clay figurine of a crouching satyr found in a royal tomb in the cluster of the queens (Cat. no. 216)

Fig. 145 Female clay busts
(Cat. nos. 147–49)

The clay figurines in figs. 146–153 were found in a royal tomb in the queens' cluster – they are part of a large group of terracottas buried with a queen

Fig. 146 Figurine of a woman with traces of paint still visible on its surface (Cat. no. 165)

Fig. 147 Hades and Persephone banqueting (Cat. no. 154)

Fig. 148 Female bust (Cat. no. 163)

Fig. 149 A couple embracing (Cat. no. 155)

Fig. 150 Two boys (Dioskouroi?) (Cat. no. 156)

Fig. 151 Two female figures (Cat. no. 158)

Fig. 152 Seated goddess (Cat. no. 157)

Fig. 153 The god Pan (Cat. no. 159)

Fig. 154 Bearded man with outstretched arms – decoration from a gold and ivory couch (*kline*) found in the tomb of Alexander IV (Cat. no. 486). Shown enlarged

Fig. 155 Exquisite lamp carrier (*lychnouchos*) from the tomb of Philip II

Fig. 156 (above left) Iron
cauldron (Cat. no. 222)

Fig. 156 (above left) Iron
cauldron (Cat. no. 222)

Fig. 157 (above right) Bronze
tripod stand with legs ending
in lion paws – the cauldron
was placed on top of the stand
(Cat. no. 186)

amaze us with their superb craftsmanship, deservedly being described as 'treasures' (fig. 155); c) in the presence of vessels which were used in the washing
of the deceased (fig. 159) – for example, cauldrons, tripod stands, basins, pans,
and others (figs. 156–158) – and of insignia of power – such as the hieratic
sceptre and diadem, libation vessels, etc.; d) in the practice of cremation.

The practices attested at Aegae find parallels in the archaic necropoleis of
Aiane, Archontiko and probably Sindos, echoing the organization of the tribal
kingdoms of the time, which recall the picture of the smaller 'kingdoms' of
the Homeric epics. A few of these kingdoms would be subdued to Alexander
I (498–454 BC) and at the end all of them would be annexed to and unified
under the strong leadership of Philip II (360/359–336 BC), in order to form the
powerful state of Macedon of the fourth century BC.

Fig. 158 Iron tripod and bronze
cauldron from the burial of the
Lady of Aegae (Cat. nos. 198–99)

Fig. 159 Vessels used in the washing of the dead as found in the
main chamber of the tomb of Philip II

Fig. 160 Racing frieze – part of the funeral
games in honour of the deceased (Cat. no. 85)

Fig. 161 Cauldron with an inverted cup as lid – it held the cremated remains of a man, a member of the Temenid royal family (Cat. no. 103)

Three royal tomb clusters have so far been identified at Aegae. The Temenids' cluster, the queens' cluster and the cluster of Philip II. In these clusters the pick-axe of the archaeologist meets Homer. Similar to Patroclos, the dead Temenids are placed on grandiose funeral fires (*pyres*) alongside their rich gifts, while the queens descend to Hades wrapped in purple and gold, similar to the women at Mycenae, almost a millennium earlier. The funeral games (*athla*) are also performed in honour of the deceased, a practice attested until the end of the fourth century BC. These funeral games inspired the painted chariot frieze in the tomb of Alexander IV, dated to around 310 BC, as well as the contemporary relief frieze of a marble monument located somewhere within Aegae (figs. 160, 251).

In the Temenids' cluster twelve tombs came to light: five pits, six monumental cists and a Macedonian tomb. These tombs date from 570 to about 300 BC. Next to and around two of the earliest tombs (570–550 BC and 550–530 BC) the remains of the two earliest funeral pyres at Aegae were discovered (fig. 161): fragments of clay and metal vessels; half-melted helmets; silver-riveted swords, similar to those mentioned in the Homeric epics; swords with ivory handles; purposefully bent swords, ritually 'killed'; spears and lance heads (fig. 162); even fragments from a horse's bridle. All these objects, offered complete to the rage of the flames, were purified by the fire (fig. 70). They provide evidence for the continuity of a burial custom, which inextricably links the Macedonians of the archaic period with the world of the Homeric epics.

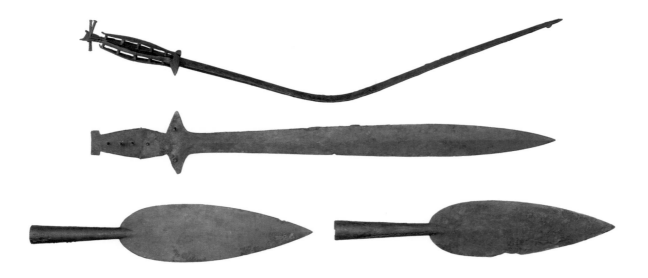

The single Macedonian tomb found in this cluster, dated to the end of the fourth century BC, may have held the bones of Philip III Arrhidaios and his wife, Eurydice, brought back to Aegae by Cassander. Although it is not possible to identify the rest of the deceased, obviously they were all members of the royal family. Some of them lived and acted before the rise to power of Amyntas I (c.540–498 BC), in the age of Aeropos and Alcetas – and all of them led the wars which made the Macedonians lords of the plain of Bottiaia and the plateaux of Eordaia.

In the most privileged and prominent place, far and above the necropolis, next to the north-west gate of the city is the queens' cluster, which received the burials of the most prominent women of the royal family. Nine tombs have come to light there: four large pits (ΛI: 540/30 BC; ΛII: about 500 BC; ΛIII: about 480 BC; ΛIV: 470/60 BC). Among these tombs there is also the intact grave of the Lady of Aegae (figs. 3–4, 41, 88–89, 112–24), the richest burial of this period known to us today; three monumental cists (K1: about 430 BC; K2: about 440 BC; K3: 350–330 BC); the Macedonian tomb of Queen Eurydice (344/3 BC), mother of three kings and grandmother of a world leader; and the Macedonian tomb with an Ionic façade ('tomb of Rhomaios') which stands next to the tomb of Eurydice. The 'Rhomaios tomb' may have belonged to the granddaughter of Eurydice, Thessalonice, who died in 298 BC.

The use of the cluster to bury the family of Philip II, following the tragic fate of the dynasty of the Temenids, is limited only to two generations: starting with the cist tomb I (about 350 BC), which most likely belongs to Nikesipolis, wife of the king and mother of Thessalonice; use continues with the tomb of Philip II himself (336 BC) and concludes with the tomb of Alexander IV about 310 BC (fig. 163), son of Alexander the Great and last of the Temenids, who was assassinated by Cassander while still a boy (fig. 164). The lack of chronological

Fig. 162 Two swords, one ritually 'killed' (purposefully bent and thus made unusable), and a pair of leaf-shaped spear heads from the cremation of a royal man (Cat. nos. 45–46)

Fig. 163 The main chamber of the tomb of Alexander IV as found

Fig. 164 Golden wreath and
silver *hydria* from the tomb of
Alexander IV

depth in this cluster is counter-balanced by the extraordinary wealth of the
funerary assemblages, which offer an unexpected picture of royal grandeur
and splendour.

By honouring its deceased, the family gets an excellent chance to manifest
its position in society, flaunting its wealth and power. Moreover, the ruler's
funeral, a public ritual in which everybody partakes, is an act with great political value that consolidates emotionally the ideological concept of power and
becomes the tangible symbol of status quo; a collective declaration of faith and
acceptance of the system.

The famous burials of the Epic heroes express exactly this notion. It is not
fortuitous that a diachronic demand of democracy is the cut of spending on
funerals and the simplification of the funeral rituals. The citizens of a democratic state – living and dead – are obliged to be and to be seen as equals. Yet, in
the kingdom of Macedon there was never a need to stop the traditional burial
practices. On the contrary, during the time of its peak, the age of Philip II and
Alexander the Great, the old burial custom, nurtured by ambition, power, and

wealth, witnessed a new prestige, acquiring the ideological foundation based on the teachings of Plato and on the convictions of the Pythagoreans and of the Orphics.

The afterlife beliefs of the Macedonian court found their most characteristic expression in the creation of an innovative building, an underground, barrel-vaulted edifice, often with two chambers, with a clearly articulated and regularly monumental façade, onto which a sloping *dromos* (passageway) leads. Following the Platonic call (Plato, *Laws* 947d-e.), a call for the burial of the leaders of the ideal state, the 'idea' of the 'Macedonian tomb' took shape; an indestructible underground chamber, residence of the prominent deceased, the appearance of which recalls a palace and a temple. It is indicative that in the royal necropolis at Aegae a dozen Macedonian tombs have been found, amongst which are not only the oldest but also the most important.

Philip II built for his mother, Queen Eurydice, the woman who handled power like a man, one of the earliest Macedonian tombs, if not the earliest. Inside a magnificent underground chamber, where everything is made for eternity and the gate of Hades exists as an architectural reference in space, the charred bones of the dead queen, wrapped in purple, well protected in their marble chest, would be placed on the splendid marble throne, a trophy in the arms of Persephone, the Mistress of Beyond (figs. 165–166).

With the tomb of Philip II the ideal form of the eternal residence of the ruler is solidified. The companions (*hetairoi*), who came back from the campaign of Alexander the Great and brought with them the gold of the East, imitated the form of this tomb. In the years to follow the barrel-vaulted tombs, to a lesser or greater extent monumental, but always a symbol of status and wealth, became a trend, which perished only at the end of the Hellenistic age, following the fate of the Macedonian kingdom.

The custom of cremation appears at Aegae in the archaic period, alongside the appearance of the Temenids. Initially an exclusive privilege of the king and of his male relatives, from the fifth century BC onwards it extended to the queens and progressively to the companions. By the time of Philip II, cremation had many followers among the lower strata of the population; after the campaign of Alexander, it became the norm for the Macedonians, now spread throughout the *oecoume*.

Like the Homeric heroes, the Macedonian kings are surrendered to the flames accompanied by rich offerings. Polluting and sacred at the same time the remains of the funeral pyre are thrown over the tomb. Tomb and pyre are covered with an earthen mound, recalling the *Iliad* (23.255-257). In the fill of the tomb of Eurydice, the remains of her funeral pyre were discovered. Amongst them were numerous offerings; fragments from at least three panathenaic *amphoras* help us date this event to around 344/343 BC (fig. 168), while hundreds of nails and the bronze-cladding of the intricately decorated door suggest that the Queen was cremated in a wooden *oikos* (house) (fig. 167).

Fig. 165 (opposite) The tomb of
Queen Eurydice

Fig. 166 (above) Detail from the
marble throne in the tomb of
Queen Eurydice

The same practice was also observed above the tomb of Philip II. A huge
pile of half-burnt mud bricks, ashes, charcoal, and hundreds of burnt objects
covered the whole length of the tomb's barrel-vaulted roof. The presence of
this funeral pyre is the most decisive evidence for the identification of the
deceased and excludes any association with Philip III Arrhidaios (see also
9. Musgrave and Prag, this volume). This was the most glorious funerary pyre
ever to have been lit in Greece. The funeral pyre of Philip II also had the form
of a monumental wooden building, perhaps similar to the appearance of the
actual tomb. Inside this wooden building, the dead king was set on fire – lying
on his gold and ivory couch wearing his armour and the golden oak wreath
and placed alongside rich offerings. In the funeral pyre of their master, dogs,
his companions in hunting, were sacrificed along with horses, the presence of
which brings to mind the victories of the Macedonian king at Olympia. And
most importantly: in the flames, one of Philip's youngest wives, most probably
Meda, accompanied her husband to death. According to the tradition in her
country, the Thracian princess followed her master, bed-fellow and companion
forever to Hades. To the eyes of the Greeks, her act made her the new Alcestes,
and this is why Alexander honoured her so much, by giving her, in this journey
with no return, invaluable gifts.

In the ambience of the Heraclid ruler along with the Macedonian tomb, the
idea of the funeral pyre emerges in the shape of a monumental building. This
idea, which started at Aegae, culminated in Babylon with the legendary pyre in
honour of Hephaistion and found imitators in the cenotaph of king Nikokreon
in far-away Salamis on Cyprus.

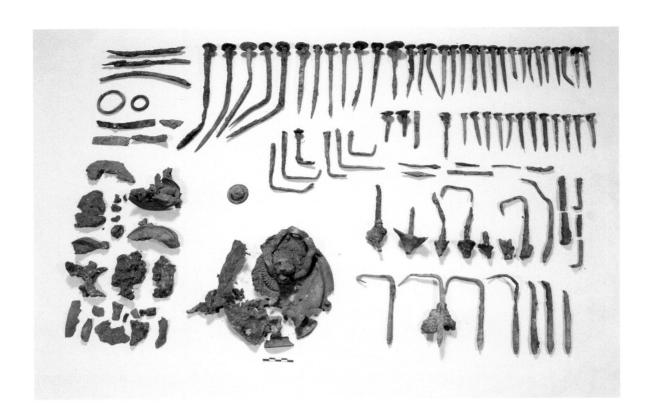

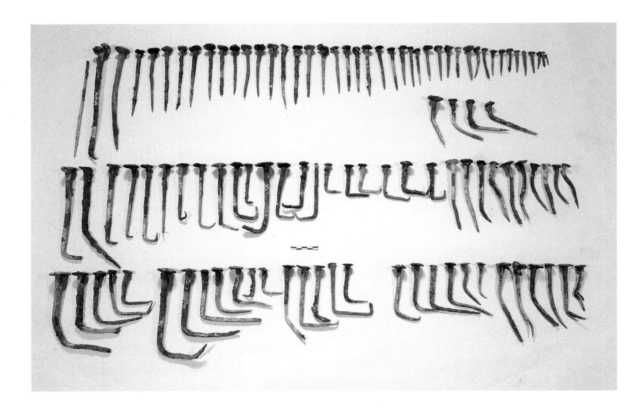

Fig. 167 Hundreds of nails, a doorknob and other metal fragments from the wooden house built to be purposefully burnt in the funeral pyre of Queen Eurydice (Cat. no. 122)

Fig. 168 Fragments from at least three panathenaic *amphoras* (Cat. no. 123) – a few of the fragments bear the name of Archon Lykiskos helping us date the funeral pyre of Eurydice to around 344/343 BC

The grandiose funeral pyres, with the display of power that characterizes them, underline and express in the best possible way the social status of the prominent deceased. It appears that the tendency for emulation of the finest individuals (*aristoi*) and the continuous campaigns helped spread cremation amongst the lower strata of society. Yet, beyond the external conditions, the deeper significance, the meaning and reason (*logos*) – more or less understood even by the participants themselves and hiding behind every funerary ritual – will have to be sought after in the realm of faith, which shapes the relationship of man with the transcendental; and in the realm of myth, which, picturing the unimaginable, tries to sooth the terror of the unavoidable end.

Fire has the power to transubstantiate. The flames abolish the mortal body. The deceased are purified. The gods of the underworld command *holokautomata* (the total incineration of offerings). The animals that are offered to them should be completely burnt. The deceased whose bodies are 'spent' on the fire share the fate of those sacrificial victims – they themselves became offerings for the Lord and Lady of the underworld (fig. 169).

The mythical archetype of cremation is the death of Heracles. At the end of his laborious course on earth the mortal Son of God is preparing, on the peak of Mountain Oete, his thanks-giving sacrifice. The paramount offering

will be himself. The flames of the altar will become his fiery tomb. This act will prove for him an end and a beginning; the end of his earthly existence, and the beginning of a new life. Down in Hades only his shadow will remain. Followed forever by Hebe – the eternal youth – Heracles will enjoy his presence in the banquets of the immortals.

The hero, who in the vase painting of the fourth century BC comes to Eleusis holding in his hand the branch of the supplicant to become the first *mystes* (the initiated one), is the ancestor of the Temenids – and the kings of Macedon will make every effort to recall their relationship with ancestral Heracles (*Heracles Patroos*). The association is apparent; behind it, however, is hidden an ancient faith. A story of Herodotus (5.92) explains the presence of offerings in the funeral pyre: Periander dreamt of his dead wife, Melissa. She complained that she was cold and naked. Then Periander commanded all the women in Corinth to offer her one of their dresses. A large fire was lit and the dresses were burnt, so that Melissa could take them and keep warm in Hades. Cleansed by flames,

Fig. 169 (above) The gold *larnax* of Philip II that held the cremated remains of the king

Fig. 170 (opposite) Demeter lamenting the loss of her daughter Persephone to Hades – detail from a wall painting inside a cist grave under the Great Tumulus at Aegae

the perishable objects can be rendered back to those who have passed to the other side, becoming citizens of the land of dreams.

Kraters, hydrias and chests but mostly pots and cauldrons, became the urns of the Macedonians. In the myths of the Mysteries, which were widespread and popular in Macedonia, these vessels play an important role. Wine is the essence of Dionysus – for the initiated ones, Dionysus is none other than Hades himself. Water dominates in the funeral rituals; the spring of forgetting and remembering delineates the geography of the underworld.

Inside the chest, the mystical *cistus* (fig. 169), lies the quintessence of many mystical myths and rituals; the power of life, the sacred snake, the phallus, the recently cut bud, the beautiful boy that Persephone kept and loved. The sacrificed animals end up in the cauldron; they are reconciliatory victims between mortals and immortals, securing blessing. Inside the boiling cauldron, the dismembered parts of the victim 'come to life' again and the 'hero' rises from the dead – younger and more beautiful than ever before. The wise goddess tries to turn into immortals the sons of the mortals by passing them through fire.

In the Great Eleusinian Mysteries, Demeter (fig. 170) gave to mankind her cherished gift; the wisdom which beats death. With the burnt offering of the breathless body, the deceased, like the sacrificial victims, is offered to the deity. Through their golden bands, the initiated ones greet by name the Lady of Hades, the 'fearsome Persephone' (fig. 171). The 'saved one' returns to the womb of the goddess; 'a kid drowned in milk'. Purified by the sacred fire, the heroes – the deceased – can now start a 'new life' in the land of the Blessed; in the asphodel mead of the Elysian Fields.

Fig. 171 Gold leaf-shaped band inscribed 'Philiste to Persephone, Rejoice!' (Cat. no. 169)

11 Aegae: the Macedonian metropolis

Angeliki Kottaridi

'When Xerxes had reached Therme, he established the army there; and his encampment occupied of the land along by the sea no less than this – beginning from the city of Therme and from Mygdonia it extended as far as the River Loudias and Haliacmon, which form the boundary between the lands of Bottiaeis and Makedonis, mingling their waters together in one and the same stream.'

By describing the size of the Persian army, Herodotus (7.127) offers unique and, for this reason extremely valuable, information regarding the land of Makedonis, the land which the ancient historian knew as the ancestral centre of the kingdom of the Macedonians. The place-name suffixes '-is' and '-idos' denote, in the language of Herodotus, the place that belongs to someone. Thus, Bottiaeis (also known as Bottiaia) is the land of the Bottiaeans, which took its name from its founders and kept it as a geographical term, even when the Bottiaeans were driven away from their land and lived in the Chalkidic peninsula.

Bottiaeis extended to the north of the Rivers Loudias and Haliacmon, the waters of which in the fifth century BC joined in 'one and the same stream'. To the south of the two rivers was Makedonis, the land of the Macedonians: it occupied the southern part of the plain of Emathia and extended to Mount Olympus. A succession of hills and well-watered mountains, with plentiful meadows and fertile plateaux, typify the area's landscape. It is no coincidence that it is here, on the mountain which Herodotus calls *Makedonikon Oros* (Herodotus 7.131) – today known as Pierian mountains – that Lebaia was located; the legendary centre of the Macedonians. Also on the northern slopes of Mount Makedonikon was Aegae, first city of the Macedonians and cradle of the Temenid dynasty.

The oldest settlement in the area surrounding Aegae is attested on the plain, near the River Haliacmon, in an Early Bronze Age (third millennium BC) tumulus. Following the general trend of the time, at the end of the Bronze Age

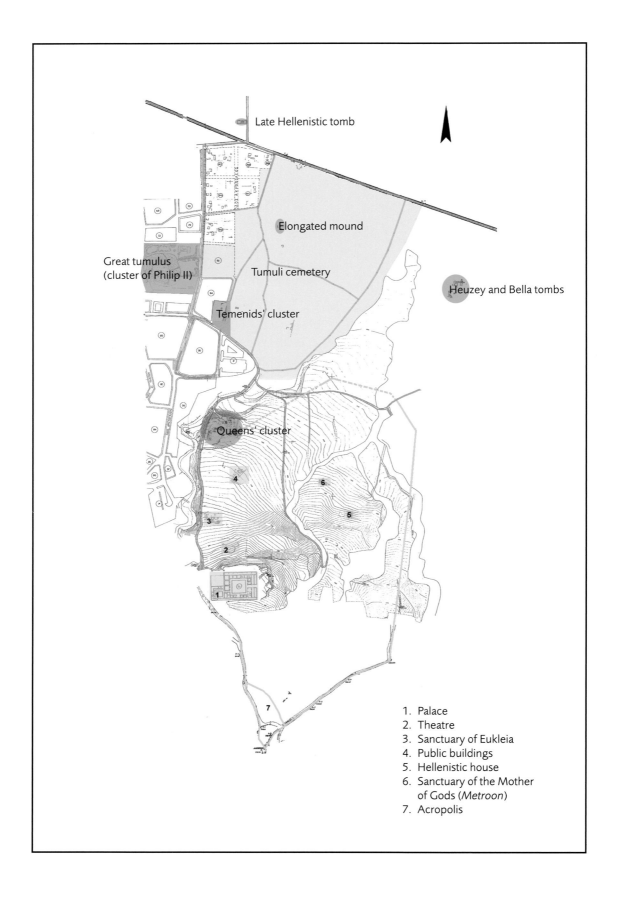

Late Hellenistic tomb

Elongated mound

Great tumulus
(cluster of Philip II)

Tumuli cemetery

Heuzey and Bella tombs

Temenids' cluster

Queens' cluster

1. Palace
2. Theatre
3. Sanctuary of Eukleia
4. Public buildings
5. Hellenistic house
6. Sanctuary of the Mother
   of Gods (*Metroon*)
7. Acropolis

(12th–11th century BC), the settlement moved from the plain to the mountain slopes, to the west of the modern village of Vergina.

The impressive Early Iron Age (1100–700 BC) cemetery, as well as a series of settlements and cemeteries of the same period distributed throughout the plain and especially on the hills in a radius between 2 and 7 km around the main cemetery, testify to the intense use and dense habitation of the surrounding area, which from the beginning of the first millennium BC was already an important and populous centre.

The Pierian mountain range to the south, River Haliacmon to the west and north and River Askordos to the east, define geographically the historic site of Aegae, the first city of Macedon. In this vast area of more than 6,500 ha, surface fieldwork and salvage excavations over the last seventeen years have shown that Aegae,[1] as suggested by the plural form of its name, had an 'open' town plan with small and large settlements scattered around a central core, the *asty*. This is the case with all ancient Greek centres, such as Athens, Thebes, Mycenae, Amyklae, Pherae, whose beginnings are lost in the mist of legend. Centre of a state whose ancient structures recall the society of the Homeric epics, Aegae remained until the end a city '*kata komas*' – an agglomeration of loosely connected settlements that developed naturally, without a strictly delineated plan. This spatial formation suggests a society based on the aristocratic structure of kin-groups in which royal presence and power formed the primary cohesive factor.

Within an area of about 80 ha, the walled *asty* was built at the centre of Aegae, at the meeting point of the old access route which, crossing the mountains, connected the basin of Makedonis and Thessaly, with the road that led from the western coast of the Thermaic Gulf to the hinterland of the kingdom. Here, on the slope that extends between the modern villages of Vergina and Palatitsia, outside the fortified acropolis and the sanctuaries, the palaces and tombs of the kings were located (fig. 172). The settlements begin next to the walls and extend over the entire area. They are scattered across the low hills, as well as the plain, marking with their presence the routes of ancient roads. In the somewhat more remote areas away from the central settlements, one also finds small independent cemeteries.

The word Aegae (ancient Greek *Aigeai*) derives from the same root as the word 'aiga' (which in Greek means goat) and can thus be explained as denoting 'the place with many herds'. As this name testifies, the basis of the city's economy was animal husbandry. The forest offered abundant game and plentiful timber, which in the hands of the king became the basic tool of his foreign policy; the nearby river facilitated the transport of timber and offered abundant fish. The landscape thus provided the area's wealth and secured Aegae's prosperity. While the uncontrollable development of the necropolis in the plain appears to suggest that agriculture may not have played the foremost role, this activity, along with viniculture and the cultivation of fruit-bearing trees, for which this hilly region even today provides ideal conditions, secured Aegae's self-sufficiency (fig. 181).

Fig. 172 Plan of the city and the cemeteries of Aegae. Yellow indicates the extent of the *asty* (city); red and pink indicate the area of tombs and cemeteries

Fig. 173 Lifesize clay heads. The unexpectedly 'realistic' features of the male demons surprise the viewer and herald a development that would take another century and a half to complete (Cat. nos. 175–77)

Fig. 174 (opposite) Lifesize female clay heads – made by the same artist as the male heads, these female heads are more conservative in their overall treatment. All the heads would have originally been placed on wooden poles thus forming statues (*xoana*). After the burial of the queen they were deliberately destroyed and thrown into her tomb (Cat. nos. 173–4, 178–80)

The old Macedonian capital with its traditional economic structure was largely based on the possession and use of land and never became a prominent production and export centre. Yet until the Hellenistic period Aegae, because of the overall prosperity of its citizens and especially the presence of the populous royal court, was a significant market for both products and high-quality services.

In the seventh century BC, the Temenids made their presence felt and, under their guidance, the Macedonians established their position and expanded their power in Bermion and the plain of Bottiaia until the end of the sixth century BC, either by subduing or driving away the local populations. Aegae, the royal seat of power, was inextricably interwoven with the dynasty's fate. Aegae's period of prosperity can be broadly traced in finds from the necropolis, since only a fraction of the core settlement itself has been properly investigated. What is clear is that at Aegae there was no grid plan with *insulae* and vertical road axes. The *asty* developed freely on the slopes of the Pierian mountains, to the north of the acropolis, in successive shallow terraces with building complexes in asymmetrical axes and empty spaces in between.

From 513 to 480 BC, Aegae was part of the empire of the Great King of Persia. Under the suzerainty of the distant master, Amyntas I succeeded in retaining a degree of autonomy for his state by adroit political manoeuvring and even managed to extend its territory. Throughout the first half of the fifth century BC the dominant figure is that of Alexander I (498–454 BC), the king who made the Macedonians lords of the entire land which took from them its name: Macedonia. The kingdom expanded its territory to the east, north, and south. The related, but until then independent, tribal kingdoms of the region became allies and subjects of the Temenid ruler.

It was in the first half of the fifth century BC that Aegae truly became the first city of Macedonia, the heart of the most important northern Hellenic state. Life reached unseen levels of embellishment and luxury. In order to meet the needs of the court, merchants arrived at Aegae with products from all known corners of the ancient world. Precious perfumes came from Phoenicia and Egypt inside ostrich eggs and large *alabastra* (figs. 52, 132). Amber necklaces were brought from the banks of the River Po in Italy (fig. 101). Cosmetics and aromatic oil were transported inside elaborately worked marble vessels (fig. 133). Famous Athenian vase painters sent their creations to Aegae, while local jewellers and metalsmiths worked indefatigably with gold, silver, bronze and iron in order to manufacture intricate weapons for the men, jewellery for the women and furniture and equipment for the households of the elite.

The twenty-six clay heads of wooden statues which were used for the funeral of a queen around 480 BC offer a glimpse of local artistic production on the eve of a new era, when the impact of influences from eastern Ionia was still recognizable in the female forms, despite their unusual linear austerity (figs. 173–74). Yet the unexpectedly 'realistic' features of the male 'demons', the moulds of which were made by the same hand, which manufactured those of the *korai* (female figures), heralded a development that would take another century and

Fig. 175 Painted antefix (Cat. no. 542)

Fig. 176 Antefix from the palace at Aegae
with intricate floral decoration (Cat. no. 546)

Fig. 177 Group of antefixes from the
palace at Aegae (Cat. nos. 544–48)

Fig. 178 Tombstone showing a warrior (Cat. no. 83)

Fig. 179 Painted funerary *stele*

a half to be completed. On the other hand, the conservative form of the bronze *kouros* (male figure) – a handle of a *patera*, a pan-shaped libation vessel from the same tomb – recall an older tradition that draws its inspiration from the source of the Geometric period (fig. 90).

From the buildings of this era only few remains are known as they lie buried under later building phases. Architectural terracottas, such as relief palmette antefixes and painted gutters offer some impression of the lost splendour (figs. 175–177). On the north-western side of the city, just outside the defensive walls of the fourth century BC and next to the tombs of the queens, remains of a large late archaic building of rectilinear plan and elongated spaces surprise us with their sturdiness: with interior and exterior walls one and two metres wide respectively, this building was probably two storeys high, thus dominating the surrounding landscape.

In the middle of the fifth century BC, Perdiccas II acceded to the throne (454–413 BC). Among his other enemies, Perdiccas also had to face the expansionism of Athens. While the king did everything possible to avoid a clash with the superpower of his time, at Aegae – where, among other renowned guests, Hippocrates was welcomed – anything Attic was in fashion. At this time relief and painted grave markers made their first appearance in the necropolis of the capital of the Temenids (figs. 178–179) and the white-ground Attic *lekythoi* brought to the Macedonians the fruits of painting; an art that would become their favourite (figs. 41 and 180).

Most probably during the time of Perdicas II's reign and certainly before the end of the fifth century BC, the city of Aegae acquired a fortification wall built with dressed local stones, but also poros cornerstones from the limestone quarries at Mount Bermion. In the north-western corner of the city, just above the external wall of the large late archaic building mentioned above, part of the defensive wall has been excavated, that includes traces of what may have been a tower, while the north-western city gate was situated next to the tombs of the queens.

At the end of the fifth century BC, Archelaos (413–399 BC), an intelligent and insightful man, decided to 'modernize' his state by opening it up to the artistic and spiritual tendencies of his era. And while life in the crumbling democracy of Athens became increasingly insecure, the court of Aegae proved to be a hospitable harbour for the intelligentsia and artists of the time who found in the face of the Temenid ruler a fervent supporter and benefactor. The new palace of Archelaos was decorated by Zeuxis, the most famous painter of his time. Personalities such as the epic poet Choirilos, the choral poet Timotheos, and the Athenian playwrights Agathon and Euripides graced with their presence the life of the Macedonian city, which by that time must have had a theatre, in which the invited playwrights could have their works performed.

From the 1960s onwards scholars contended that Archelaos moved the capital of the Macedonian kingdom to Pella. However, neither the textual nor

Fig. 180 An Attic white-ground *lekythos* of the Woman Painter (Cat. no. 244)

Fig. 181 Landscape of Aegae

the archaeological evidence appears to support this view. On the contrary, the ever-accurate Thucydides (2.100.1-3), while listing the reforms of Archelaos does not mention the move of the capital. Similarly, the king's companion Euripides, in the tragedy *Archelaos* – which made the homonymous legendary ancestor the founder of Aegae – underlined the connection of Archelaos with the traditional dynastic centre of the Temenids. The king himself also marked out this connection by using the head of a goat, the symbol of Aegae, as his trademark on the coins he issued.

In the turbulent time that followed the assassination of Archelaos, partly to confront the unbearable pressure of the kingdom's many enemies that invaded from the west, north and east, Amyntas III (393–368 BC) frequently took up residence at Pella – a city which, being the largest port on the northern coast of the Thermaic Gulf was developing fast. Amyntas III may have been the first king to build a palace at Pella. This may be reflected in the fact that, until the age of Justinian in the sixth century AD, the place-name 'palace of Amyntas' (*basileia Amyntou*) was associated with the ruins at Pella. However, Aegae, the penultimate refuge of the Temenids, continued to constitute the heart of the kingdom; the widow of Amyntas III, the powerful Queen Eurydice, who managed to secure the throne for her sons and retain power herself, left her mark at Aegae, as numerous epigraphic testimonies confirm.

Despite the development of Pella, a city where the royal family spent a lot of its time, Aegae continued to maintain its full symbolic and ideological significance until the departure of Alexander the Great for his campaign to the East. As the traditional dynastic centre of the Temenids, Aegae also constituted the ancestral ground where all traditional ceremonies and great political events were hosted.

After the death in battle of Perdiccas III in 360 BC, Argaeos – a usurper supported by the Athenians – moved swiftly to Aegae to proclaim himself king of Macedon (Diod. 16.2). However, the people of Aegae rejected Argaeos, and Philip II overcame the usurper's attempt to snatch the throne and established himself as king (360/359–336 BC). Philip also rewarded the city for taking his side by redeveloping and enhancing it.

As suggested by the securely stratified finds – pottery and coins – from the north-western gate, Philip II first attended to rebuilding the defence walls of the *asty* of Aegae in rather elaborate fashion. The new wall (about 3m wide) was reinforced by towers built at regular intervals; the defensive wall was faced with dressed stone up to a certain height. The limestone used in the construction of the wall, the palace and other public buildings was an expensive material. It was brought to Aegae from the quarries on Mount Bermion about 10–13 km to the west of the city. The extensive use of this material for the construction of the wall indicates a considerable outlay, less for practical needs than to grant Aegae a glorious appearance equal to the old capital's fame and significance.

On the eastern part of the wall, where the road from Pydna and Methone reached Aegae, an elaborate gate with circular towers and an internal court-yard was erected – an impressive sight for visitors and passers-by. A smaller gate already existed in the north-western corner above the gate of the older wall. The acropolis, the city's fortified citadel, was situated at the summit of the hill that rises above the city to the south. Here the road over the mountain from the city of Dion and the region of Pieria met a less elaborate gate. In the southernmost extent of the acropolis an internal precinct marked out a large unbuilt space, which probably served military purposes.

Apart from the defence walls, new buildings, such as the sanctuary of Eukleia, the theatre and the palace were built inside the *asty* (fig. 172). New building was also carried out outside – one such, for example, was excavated to the west of the Palaiopanagia stream, just opposite the Sanctuary of Eukleia. The latter was an elaborate structure with dressed stone walls and mosaic floors, spacious rooms arranged in a row and a *stoa* which in a second phase was divided into more spaces. On the western side it opened onto a large court with structures that resembled *exedrae* (niches with pedestals for setting up statues). Undeniably a public building, it may well have been the *gymnasium* of Aegae. It is not a coincidence that in this area the marble complex of the hunter and the boar was found (fig. 63). This marble sculptural complex was perhaps a dedication to Heracles, guardian of the young hunters in commemoration of a successful hunt, which may have underlined the successful passage from boyhood to adulthood of its dedicator. This sculptural complex is dated to the third quarter of the fourth century BC and would fit perfectly in the context of a Macedonian *gymnasium*.

The complete alignment and chronological and structural correspondence of these buildings reveal that they were all conceived as part of a general plan and built within the framework of a large building project, which aimed to modernise and upgrade the overall appearance of the city – and beyond that,

Fig. 182 An intricately decorated mosaic floor from one of the banquet halls of the palace of Philip II at Aegae – notice the raised area around the mosaic floor, where the couches for the banquet would have been placed

behind this planning was a clear ideological move, to connect the centre of political and religious power with the theatre, the centre of art and culture.

Continuing what Archelaos had already started, Philip II, an enlightened ruler according to the Platonic archetype, inaugurated a tradition at Aegae which became a feature of royal cities in the Hellenistic period and which reached a peak in Alexandria with the foundation of the famous library and the museum there, forming the first university of the world. The source of power, the king and his household, became the centre of production of ideology and knowledge. This production can be characterised by its use of space as well as new artistic trends. The household of the Macedonian king became for art and culture what Athens was during the time of Pericles, almost a century earlier. The conservative kingdom under the enlightened guidance of Philip II and his son, Alexander the Great, was transformed into a radical force that changed the ancient world for ever.

At Aegae, above the sanctuaries and temples and next to the newly built theatre, where citizens met collectively and cultural *catharsis* (cleansing) took place – here majestically rose the architectural manifestation of a new era, the *basileion* (palace) of Philip II, a building unique in its time, which was to become an archetype (figs. 182–84). In 336 BC the elected leader of all the Hellenes (Greeks) celebrated his omnipotence here. And at the peak of the feast, Philip II met his destiny. His son, Alexander, was proclaimed king and

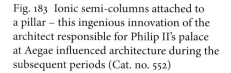

Fig. 183 Ionic semi-columns attached to a pillar – this ingenious innovation of the architect responsible for Philip II's palace at Aegae influenced architecture during the subsequent periods (Cat. no. 552)

Fig. 184 Frontal view of the Ionic semi-column – originally the columns were covered in white stucco (Cat. no. 552)

buried his father in the royal necropolis with honours beyond anything Aegae had ever witnessed before.

It was not by accident that, in the spring of 334 BC, Alexander brought his army to Aegae to initiate his great campaign with feasts and sacrifices to the gods, most likely following the ancestral tradition which dictated that everything should start and end at the ancient Macedonian metropolis – where the body of the world leader was meant to be laid to rest. But this journey was never completed. Alexandria was to keep his body forever and with it the blessing of the new god. To Aegae, the bodies of his assassinated children returned: Heracles, son of Alexander and Barsine, and Alexander IV, son of Alexander and Roxana. Both children were the victims of the greed of Cassander, Alexander's general and a usurper to the throne. These children were also the last of the Temenids.

In the shadow of the royal drama, Aegae prospered, and the resonance of royal luxury left its mark on the everyday life of its citizens. This prosperity did not last long. In 276 BC the Gallic mercenaries of King Pyrrhos conquered the city and pillaged the royal necropolis. Despite the efforts of Antigonos Gonatas, king of Macedon (276–239 BC), the city never again fully regained its strength. Having lost its crucial place within the geopolitical map of the new Hellenistic world, Aegae progressively moved into the sidelines.

After the defeat of the last king of Macedon, Perseus, by the Romans in 168 BC, the old and new capitals of the kingdom were destroyed. The defence walls were razed to the ground; the palace, the theatre and other buildings were burnt and demolished. The destruction was general and affected not only the nearby settlements and villages of Aegae, but also those in the Pierian mountains. Yet life continued. Houses were built over the ruins, often reusing the ancient building materials; some sanctuaries show signs of reuse after restoration. But the palace, the centre and symbol of the abolished monarchy of the Macedonian kings, and the nearby theatre remained in ruins.

In the first century AD a tremendous landslide of the overhanging cliff marked the sudden end of Aegae's *asty*. The inhabitants formed a new settlement in the plain to the north-east of the old necropolis. An early Christian basilica with a baptistery suggests that Aegae was still the regional centre – yet the name was no longer used. The cradle of the Temenids was forgotten – all that remained, as a vague recollection of the palace that once stood there, was the medieval name of the nearby village, 'Palatitsia' (meaning 'little palace'), which survives to the present day.

12 The royal banquet: a capital institution

Angeliki Kottaridi

Fig. 185 Cup with nail-headed handles and high foot (Cat. no. 461)

The banquet (*symposion*) was an indispensable component of every public or private feast or festival and of every convivial assembly.[1] As a rule, the banquet followed the communal meal, and was for the Greeks, from the time of Homer until the end of antiquity, the essence of social life, irrespective of socio-political developments and differences. At once an institution and an obligation, participation in the banquet was, together with war, hunting and politics, a vital element of a man's social identity. Indeed, this is the reason why in Dorian societies the gift that accompanied the rites of passage from adolescence to manhood was a wine cup.

A central subject of life, the banquet also left its mark on death: together with strictly personal paraphernalia, weapons, jewellery and the *unguentaria* (aromatic-oil containers) necessary for funerary rites, the wine cup was included as part of the essential equipment of the 'thirsty' dead on their journey of no return (fig. 185), often with a jug or a pitcher; in exceptional circumstances, a full set of banquet vessels was placed in the tomb.

While those initiated into mystic cults expected eternal life beyond death, the banquet – the most common entertainment in life on earth – became the ultimate promise of the delights of posthumous existence. Free of cares and troubles, the followers of Bacchus and Orpheus, initiates in the secret path to salvation, were not lost in the darkness of Hades but continued to live happily in the eternal banquet of the Blessed, in the jubilant light of the Elysian Fields. And it is not accidental that the central figure of the Bacchic and the Orphic mysteries, the dying and the reborn god whose fate presaged that of his followers, was Dionysus – the god who gave men the gift of wine, the god of intoxication and of ecstasy.

These beliefs, combined with Platonic instruction, were to acquire fervent followers in fourth-century BC Macedonia, where the king and his family as well as his noble companions (*hetairoi*) became initiates of Bacchus and had expectations of the eternal bliss of heroes. The heroised dead were very often accompanied in the tomb by all the necessary tableware, which, in addition to the banquet vessels, some more precious than others, even included the compulsory couch. As a result, the royal necropolis of Aegae constitutes an everlasting source of information on the Macedonian banquet that complements, in a very eloquent way, the scant textual evidence.

Amyntas I (*c.*540–498 BC) informed the Persian legates of Darius that, according to the Macedonian custom, women of the family did not sit down at the banquets of men (a story given to us by Herodotus). However, the presence in the tombs of the queens of objects associated with the procedure of sacrifice and the ensuing meal, and of the banquet overall – iron spits, pitchers, cups, bowls, jugs, *amphoras*, couches, and so forth – indicate that, in special circumstances of festive rites and celebrations, these women must have graced banquets with their presence just like the Homeric Queens Helen and Arete. And if this practice was the case with the queen-priestesses of the archaic period, there is no reason to suppose that it would not hold true for wives, mothers and sisters of kings, such as Eurydice, Olympias and Thessalonice. The Macedonian queens of the Hellenistic *oecoumene*, paramount amongst them Cleopatra the Great, are known not only to have attended banquets, but also frequently to have hosted them, sometimes with fateful historical consequences.

However, apart from 'royal exceptions', the banquet was for the Macedonians, as indeed for all the Greeks, an entirely male affair and in fact, in order to attend them as equals a Macedonian had to have slain a boar without using a hunting net; that is, he had to complete successfully the basic initiatory test in the rite of passage from adolescence to manhood.

Being the most extroverted activity of public and private life, the banquet was the best arena for the conspicuous display of social status, wealth and power. At the same time the banquet as a group activity was frequently repeated and exercised great influence on the formation of the tangible reality that is characterised as material culture. The royal palace, the areas where priests gathered, the best rooms of the houses, the courtyards, the gardens and groves became the banquet space, to which the most valuable and luxurious furniture and vessels of every household were destined.

Homer often describes the preparation for a banquet: the heroes take their bath with water which is heated in a bronze cauldron; they are rubbed with aromatic oils and they put on clean clothes. They then sit down together to delight in the pleasures of food and drink. The feast is accompanied by music: a bard sings of the adventures and feats of men and gods, while the diners discourse.

In the time of the epics, from the tenth to the seventh centuries BC, the banquets of the Macedonians were rather simple. The vessels are clay, often of local handmade manufacture and without any decoration – small *amphoras* and *hydrias* for the transportation of wine and water (fig. 186), the characteristic jugs with the raised spout (cut-away neck jugs) (fig. 187), used for serving, large and sometimes massive cups, bowls with their distinct mushroom-shaped or

Fig. 186 Clay *hydria* for the transportation of wine and water (Cat. no. 381)

Fig. 187 Jug with cut-away neck (Cat. no. 457)

Fig. 188. Bowls with nail-headed handles (Cat. nos. 428, 436, 455)

nail-headed handles and the favourite cup of Dionysus and of the Macedonians, the *kantharos* in all its variants (figs. 188, 191, 193). There are also cups with long handles for ladling the wine and water, which resemble their wooden prototypes and bring to mind similar vessels used diachronically by transhumant pastoralists. The ceramic repertoire also includes clay soup-bowls and basins (fig. 190).

In the transition from the second to the first millennium BC, large *kraters* are also used, in which wine was mixed with water and which recall their Mycenaean prototypes (fig. 189). There are also a few local pots decorated with simple matt-painted geometric patterns. In the course of time, the local matt-painted pottery gives way to the wheel-made, mostly imported, pottery. Typical examples of this new pottery are the *skyphoi* and the *amphoriskoi* decorated with the extremely popular pattern of concentric circles, which introduce to the Macedonians the fashion of the geometric period (fig. 48).

In the aristocratic societies of the archaic period, the banquet, which had developed into an arena of critical, philosophical as well as political ferment that would lead to unprecedented changes for the world, acquired its 'classic' form (fig. 198): when the evening meal is over, the diners wash and perfume themselves, put on a wreath, and recline, usually in pairs, on couches, in order to enjoy wine, which is always diluted with water in the proportions ordered by the master of the banquet (*symposiarch*), so as to control the time and degree of inebriation.

In the seventh century BC the Temenids introduced new trends to Aegae with regard to banqueting accoutrements. Next to the traditional cut-away jugs and the *kantharoi* (deep cups with impressive handles), large and small black-figure column *kraters* (wine-mixing bowls) (fig. 192), *kotylai* and *skyphoi*

Fig. 189 An early *krater* alluding to
Bronze Age prototypes (Cat. no. 463)

Fig. 190 Protogeometric bowl (Cat. no. 431)

Fig. 192 Black-figure column krater with a
representation of an octopus (Cat. no. 503)

Fig. 191 *Kantharos* with raised handles
(Cat. no. 450)

Fig. 193 *Kantharos* (bowl/cup)
(Cat. no. 438)

Fig. 194 Clay Attic cups from the burial of a royal
lady in the queens' cluster (Cat. nos. 196–97)

Fig. 195 Trefoil wine jug (*oinochoe*)
(Cat. no. 493)

Fig. 196 Two red-figure *pelikes*, a type of vessel used as a container for liquids (the one on the left: Cat. no. 528)

(simple bowls with or without handles), small and large *kylikes* (cups with shallow body, horizontal handles and high or low feet) from Corinth (fig. 195), the eastern part of Ionia, the Aegean islands, and the workshops of Athens (fig. 194) and the settlers in the Thermaic Gulf, now appear. The degree of penetration of the products of the commercial centres into the marketplace (*agora*) of Aegae fluctuates following the general historical developments that dictate also the trends of fashion (fig. 196). Yet, beside imported banquet vessels, there are always local imitations, as well as local creations in typical grey colour such as the elegant mixing bowls (*dinoi*) with coil-shaped handles (fig. 204), which apparently imitate metal prototypes. Furthermore, bronze vessels – cauldrons, *hydrias*, jugs, basins, and various dishes – constitute in the archaic period the basic component of these valuable household goods. Metal and clay vessels, products of local workshops, are characterised by their geometric simplicity and the functional clarity of their form as well as by the non-existent or limited decoration – trends which constitute a continuing feature of Macedonian art until the late classical period.

In the democratic cities, excessive extravagance aimed at personal promotion was considered dangerously deviant. This applied principally to banquets given in the homes of private citizens as well as of office holders who had to

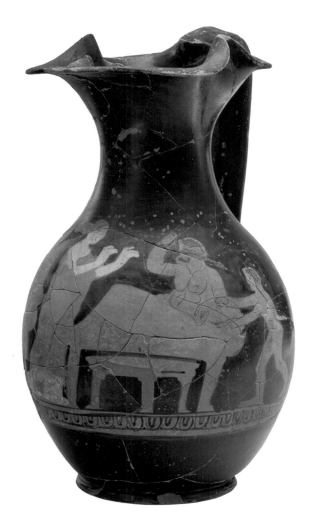

Fig. 197 (left) Two clay *calyxes* (cups) (Cat. nos. 540–41)

Fig. 198 (right) Red-figure trefoil wine jug showing a banquet scene (Cat. no. 539)

be careful not to affront public feeling about equality, either with the luxury of their house or their household goods or with the abundance of drinks and delicacies. However, this practice did not apply to the kingdom of Macedon, where the luxury and the magnificence of the royal presence becomes a vital element of prestige for the state itself. And if in the democratic city the banquet was, along with the *agora*, the venue par excellence for fermenting and generating politics and ideology, the royal drinking party, the banquet of the Macedonian king, was elevated to the most important event not only of the social but also of the political life of the state.

The dynamic expansion and the great prosperity of Macedonia during the reign of Alexander I (498–454 BC) is manifested in the banquet sets: apart from the imported red-figure vases of excellent quality, silver *kylikes*, basins and plates (figs. 199–201) appear along with couches with bronze-covered legs. As suggested by the finds from the queens' cluster dating to the reign of Perdiccas II (454–413 BC), the household effects of the palace of Aegae included gold, ivory and amber couches that bring to mind the passage from Plato, the

Fig. 199 Silver *kantharos* (drinking cup) from the tomb of Alexander IV (Cat. no. 480)

Fig. 200 Silver bowl (*skyphos*) from the tomb of Philip II, with nail-headed handles alluding to earlier forms (Cat. no. 477)

Fig. 201 Silver lion foot from a vessel (Cat. no. 229)

comic poet, who speaks of well-dressed guests reclining on *couches* rich with *ivory* feet and dining on their *purple* cushions (according to Athenaeus, *The Deipnosophists* 2.2.30). In the reign of Archelaos (413–399 BC) the guests of the king, who was the greatest patron of the arts in his time, were hosted in rooms decorated by the most accomplished and most highly paid painter of the day, Zeuxis, and enjoyed the presence of the cream of the Greek intelligentsia, since among the Macedonian sovereign's friends and dining companions were none other than Euripides and the tragic poet Agathon, *amphitryon* (the host of the dinner) of the Platonic *symposion*.

The wealth and largesse of the Macedonian kings may well have provoked the democrats of the south, who looked upon such qualities as a threat that could overturn their own world. However, this does not by any means imply that the royal banquets did not meet the aesthetic demands of the intellectuals of the age, which they sometimes even surpassed. At the royal drinking parties of the young philosopher-king Perdiccas III (368–360/359 BC), brother of Philip II and a pupil of Euphraios, student of Plato, the climate is known to have been especially strict, since in accordance with the royal host's tenets, entry was barred to those who were not conversant with geometry.

Philip II (360/359–336 BC), who was not only the greatest general of his age but also one of the most intelligent and astute Greek statesmen of all time, attached considerable importance to persuasion and to victories that could be won at a diplomatic level. In this context, the court festivals and the banquets of the munificent king, which of course went beyond the bounds of measure and, like many other aristocratic habits of the Macedonians, were criticised by censorious democrats, were not merely the order of the day but proved to be extremely effective political weapons. Through these banquets Philip succeeded in impressing his enemies, who nevertheless lost no opportunity to accuse him of wantonness, drunkenness and barbarity. However, the finds of the royal tombs and the palace of Aegae confute this impression categorically and give us an unexpectedly full and vivid picture of the royal milieu, in which luxury was harmoniously combined with elegance and wealth, with impeccable good taste.

The dining rooms (*andrones*) that occupied most of Philip II's palace at Aegae were luxurious, with elegant and certainly the most spacious banquet halls of their day. Two of these halls occupy an area of about 267sq.m. each. These are the largest halls without internal support known in classical architecture and their roofing constitutes a real technological achievement of ancient engineering. Organised in a tripartite arrangement with ante-rooms, the largest of which open onto the courtyard through impressive columnar façades, they create distinct units within the building and constitute another innovative invention of the architect of Aegae (fig. 267). This new layout of banquet spaces, which evidently served functional needs, soon found imitators and became a trend not only in the palaces and houses of nearby Pella – Macedon's new capital – but also throughout the Hellenistic *oecoume*, creating a point of reference for 'civilised behaviour' both in a private and a public context.

In the 16 banquet halls securely identified in the palace at Aegae, it is estimated that there was space for 224 couches, as suggested by the spatial arrangement and dimension of the halls and the raised platform around the inner walls of the rooms. Thus Philip could hold a banquet for more than 400 guests at once, an unprecedented number by Greek standards, exceeded only by the legendary feasts of Alexander the Great, ruler of the world, and by his successors (*diadochoi*) who were to become kings in the East.

Floors with inlaid marbles (*opus sectile*) and wonderful mosaics, such as that showing the abduction of Europe, heavy bronze-clad wooden doors, walls with brightly coloured stuccoes, adorned with choice paintings, precious furniture and vessels, purple dyed and cloth-of-gold bedsheets and curtains, composed the setting of the royal banquets. The richly ornamented couches, with inlays of glass and gold and ivory reliefs, found in the tomb of Philip II – masterpieces of great artists of their time – allow us to imagine the splendour and sumptuousness of the furnishings of the royal dining halls. Of comparable quality and value was the rest of the royal domestic equipment. Silver was used in abundance for the banquet vessels, which are outstanding not only for their luxury but also for their superb quality: the spare, clean lines of the forms are combined with graceful detail in an ensemble of unrivalled elegance, harmony and charm (figs. 210–219).

Although the Athenians accused the Macedonians of being uncontrolled wine drinkers, all the vessels for the royal banquet, especially the cups, are much smaller than the cups used in Athenian banquets. The tendency for small banquet vessels as well as the use of fancier forms and shapes, which is observed initially in royal equipment and subsequently in all Macedonian households, eventually becoming a fashion of universal appeal, may well denote changes in the procedure of the banquet and the 'ceremony' of wine-drinking. This had apparently become more complex and sophisticated, with a strong tendency towards refinement. This practice is seen for the first time in the court of Philip II and was consolidated in the reign of Alexander the Great, setting the tone for Hellenistic banquets and following the more general rise in living standards.

In place of the voluminous *kraters* (fig. 202), the much smaller buckets (*situlae*), which resemble the large Attic *skyphoi* (fig. 205), are easier to carry and appear with increasing frequency. The cups are much smaller (figs. 197, 203) – the *calyx* is the most typical example, from the bottom of which a relief face usually emerges to the surprise and delight of the drinker, a feature especially cherished in Macedonia; also popular are the miniature *kantharoi*. Elegant cups with nail-headed handles (fig. 200), which reflect traditional Macedonian prototypes, co-exist harmoniously with elegant bronze and silver Attic *kylikes* (fig. 206). The various jugs retain their traditional forms, but along with them one now sees more innovative small *amphora*-bottles (fig. 57), the shape of which resembles an *unguentarium*, underlying therefore the value of their contents. The ladles with their bird-shaped handles and the intricate strainers became decisively the order of the day (figs. 215–216). One such silver-gilded

Fig. 202 Black-figure *krater* (wine mixing bowl) with a representation of a grazing goat (Cat. no. 504)

Fig. 203 Black-glaze cup (Cat. no. 531)

Fig. 204 (left) A mixing bowl (*dinos*) with coil-shaped handles that apparently imitates metal prototypes (Cat. no. 502)

strainer, a veritable masterpiece in miniature signed proudly by the craftsman Machatas, was found in the tomb of Philip II (fig. 216).

The sources refer to the bounty of the host, who instead of estimating beforehand, as was the norm, how much wine would go into a *krater*, so as to keep tabs on the cost of the banquet, gave his guests the opportunity to decide for themselves how much wine and in what proportion of mix they wanted to drink, placing all the necessities on the table of each. This seems to have happened at the royal drinking parties of Philip and Alexander: at the royal banquets choice wine came from the cellar undiluted in elegant silver *oino-choai* (wine jugs), as did fresh cool water. Along with it came honey, myrrh, spices and condiments of aromatic fruits and flowers, essential ingredients for the royal cocktail. This wine was mixed according to the rules of degustation and the desires of the drinker in a bucket (*situla*) (fig. 214) and was served with an elegant ladle into cups (fig. 217), first passing through a strainer.

Fig. 205 Attic red-figure drinking cup (*skyphos*) with himation-clad men (Cat. no. 507)

Fig. 206 Bronze cup (Cat. no. 474)

Thus the enjoyment of wine becomes a true ritual, a highly specialised procedure addressed to the refined palate of a real 'gourmet' who took pleasure in the taste of the drink as well as in the harmony of the music, the beauty of high art, the stimulation of high philosophy (fig. 207). We should not forget that the banquets of Philip II and Alexander the Great were renowned not only for the wealth, luxury and abundance of the vessels, drinks and food but also for the participation of the leading musicians, actors, poets, and intellectuals of the time; and of course the most beautiful and witty courtesans (*hetairai*) were not absent either.

Fig. 207 An exquisite ivory fragment from a gold and ivory funeral couch showing Dionysus escorted by a maenad (female follower) and a flute player

13 Macedonian metallurgy: an expression of royalty

Stella Drougou

According to Herodotus (8.121.2) the Greeks, after their victory against the Persians at Salamis (480 BC), set up a colossal statue of Apollo (about 5.50 m tall) in the sanctuary at Delphi from the spoils and victory offerings of the naval battle.[1] This statue was placed in close proximity to the golden statue of Alexander I (498–454 BC), king of the Macedonians. This information about a golden statue of Alexander I is striking, though 'mythical' kings or powerful tyrants and Eastern satraps often dedicated golden statues or golden offerings to the panhellenic sanctuaries. The shape and appearance of Alexander I's statue is not known, and it is even harder to speculate on its form given that his reign dates to the first decades of the fifth century BC. Yet Herodotus' account appears to correspond very well to the image of this important leader, his actions, life and times. More importantly, it is not refuted by the archaeological finds in Macedonia of the fifth century BC.[2]

Alexander I doubled the size of the country he inherited from his father Amyntas I. He extended the country to the east, securing areas rich in raw materials, especially metals and timber. Despite the oppressing presence of the Persians in Macedonia, as the leading power in the region of the northern Aegean, Alexander I managed to play a crucial role in favour of the Greeks during the Persian wars. He succeeded not only in contributing with his actions to the victory of the Greeks, but at the same time he managed to make the presence of the king noticeable amongst the Greek city-states as a Greek with an ancestry from Argos and a descendant of Heracles.[3]

The information from the textual sources is corroborated by the silver coins, issued by Alexander I, which for the first time bear the name of the king of Macedon (fig. 234). Alexander I issued coins with his name along with symbols well known from the regions of the northern Aegean and Thrace,[4] inaugurating a new form of economy for his kingdom which probably signalled changes on an institutional level. The wealth of the metal mines acquired a different dynamic from that observed in the East, especially in the areas under the rule of the Persian Empire with the hoarding of precious vessels and other objects, already observed in earlier centuries. These actions of the Macedonian king

Fig. 208 Bronze bowls and dishes (*phialai*) (Cat. nos. 151–53, 230, 499, 523)

suggest a gradual removal from Persian dependence and the formation of a new status of political relations with the southern Greek states. At the same time, the new numismatic policy, which the later kings of Macedon would follow and expand over the centuries – with Philip II in the fourth century BC constituting the best example – created a new economic and political landscape not only in the land of Macedon but further beyond.[5]

The archaeological finds from Macedonia that date to this period, especially funerary assemblages from very important centres, corroborate fully the aforementioned observations. In the middle of the 1980s at Vergina,[6] to the northwest of the city of Aegae, the first capital of Macedon, in the area previously known for the Macedonian 'tomb of Rhomaios', a number of large pit graves came to light, yielding rich assemblages. The imported Attic clay vases and the numerous clay heads worked in the round (figs. 173–74) stand out along with the golden strips decorating the funeral garb of the dead women; one can only add to this impressive list the silver shoe soles, the metal vessels, such as the bronze cauldrons, the tripod stands, the silver libation bowls (*phialai*) and the jewellery that accompanied the dead. These are the burials of rich, aristocratic ladies. They stand out because of the quantity, quality and diversity of the funerary assemblages as well as their persistence in the social tradition, as suggested by the shapes of the metal vessels and their jewellery. The finds date to the first decades of the fifth century BC and provide evidence for an outward economy with a vibrant and dynamic exploitation and use of valuable metals, which led to a distinctive metalworking tradition, emblematic of Macedonia.

The example of the late archaic burials at Aegae is not unique for Macedonia, and it does not represent a sudden change. Their similarity with finds from cemeteries at Sindos⁷ near Thessaloniki, of the sixth and fifth centuries BC, especially with regard to the shapes of the clay and metal vessels, has already been highlighted by the excavations and the scholars working on the publication of this corpus of finds, as we progressively build a very impressive picture of the kingdom of Macedon and of its economic and social life during this period.

The rich burials of the extensive cemetery at Archontiko,⁸ to the north-west of Pella – the new capital of the kingdom of Macedon from the late fifth/early fourth century BC – shed light on the earlier periods by going back in time, as early as the middle of the seventh century BC. Plentiful arms and armour, including helmets decorated with golden strips, golden masks with relief ornaments, elaborately decorated shields, metal vessels, *phialai* and numerous Attic, Corinthian and local vases underline in the best possible way the early phase of creative production of the kingdom and, to some extent, fill in the gap of the textual sources. The class of 'warriors' is the most dominant; yet, the quantity, quality and diversity of metals allow, already from this early period, the projection of luxury as a powerful tool of the elite. The bowls with a central boss (*omphalos phialai*) decorated with embossed ornaments of the 'Persian type' that have come to light at Aegae (figs. 208–209), Archontiko and Kozani⁹ reveal the strong ties with the Persian Empire and its western satrapies which

Fig. 209 Silver *phiale* found with the Lady of Aegae (Cat. no. 201)

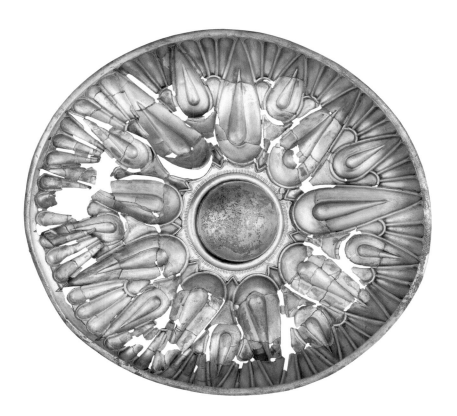

were formed during the reign of Alexander I and which marked the life of the archaic society of Macedonians.

The riches of the Great King of Persia are nearly legendary, especially with regard to the metal resources. With their gold-yielding rivers, the Lydians were probably the first to issue gold coins and impress neighbouring people with their wealth, as suggested by Herodotus. The impact of Persian wealth, and the art it created, radiated further afield, reaching the peoples of the Caucasus and the Black Sea, the Scythians and the Thracians. Relations with the Ionian Greeks in Asia Minor and with the Macedonians require a detailed analysis, since the outcome of the encounter of all these people in their arts is a result of synthesis and economic and political developments in the broader region.[10]

Herodotus (9.80) describes with a critical undertone the riches left behind by the Persians after the battle at Plataea (479 BC): 'and found tents adorned with gold and silver, couches gilded with gold and silver, gold mixing bowls, libation bowls, and other drinking vessels. On the wagons they discovered sacks in which they saw cauldrons of gold and silver. And they stripped the bodies lying there of their bracelets, necklaces and golden daggers, but paid no attention at all to the embroidered clothing.' Yet, in another part of his *Histories*, Herodotus (1.183–188) does not hide his admiration for the wondrous gold and silver works of art – offerings to sanctuaries and part of the Great King's treasures.

Alexander III, one hundred and fifty years later and after the defeat of Darius III, would look at the Persian hoarded treasures; according to Plutarch (*Alexander* 26): 'Alexander after capturing Susa found in the palace forty thousand talents in money already coined, besides an unspeakable quantity of other furniture and treasure'.

The largest part of this treasure consisted of wondrous vessels, furniture and other objects, which recalls the repeated report in the historical sources about luxury gifts from the Great King to his friends and guests, a custom that was followed even in the royal Macedonian court. Golden cups as gifts by Philip II and Alexander III to ambassadors and friends of the court are often mentioned.[11]

The democratic cities of the south were no less impressed by gold and precious metals, but they appreciated them differently. Pheidias, the famous sculptor, was exiled from Athens when he was accused of embezzling the gold that was used to make the gold and ivory statue of the goddess Athena on the Parthenon. In the private life of the citizens, wealth and luxury become more evident at the end of the fifth century BC, at the very end of the Peloponnesian war, as suggested by the extravagant life of Alcibiades of Athens.

In the clash of these two worlds, of Eastern and Greek societies, a decisive, almost emblematic, difference is brought to light: from the late sixth century BC the Persians, as well as the Greeks, adopted coinage for their transactions, which progressively regulated the framework of their economy. The difference lies in the development by the Greek states of an extensive and significant numismatic system directly linked to their poltical system (cf. the characteristics of a democratic *polis* with the Macedonian monarchy). The kings of Macedon are characterised not only by the good craftmanship and processing of their coins but more importantly by the 'political' and 'institutional' use of these coins. The gold-yielding River Gallikos, the metal-rich deposits of Chalkidike and especially the silver mines of Mount Pangaion belong to geographical areas, which the kings of Macedon constantly tried to control, since, along with the forests of the Pieria and Bermion mountains, they offered them the most important resources and the necessary financial means for the development of their kingdom – a task fully achieved in the fourth century BC.[12]

Along with the impressive royal coinage in the fourth century BC, we witness the gradual development of wealth and a luxurious expression of life. The latter is reflected in the material culture, especially the funerary assemblages dating to this period. One observes prolific activity in metalworking and the production of remarkable pieces of art. This production is multi-faceted and innovative.

The rich funerary assemblages of Aegae[13] and a number of other sites in Macedonia, brought to light in the second half of the twentieth century, have caused sensation among specialists and the public alike (fig. 210). More importantly, they made us refocus on the important questions of historical and archaeological research about subjects previously only superficially treated. Our knowledge has increased quantitatively and qualitatively, allowing for better and more informed observations and the setting of new research directions.

Numerous vessels and other objects in silver and bronze, gold wreaths and jewellery, coins hoards, elaborate and rare weapons constitute not only expressions of a powerful elite but also a testimony for the survival of a strong tradition, by placing emphasis on earlier shapes and practices (fig. 200). With regard to their aesthetic value, such as their shape or decoration, the metal production is inextricably interwoven with the older tradition of a society based on clans and tribes, as well as the contemporary economic and political reality of the second half of the fourth century BC. Intricate silver drinking cups decorated with relief heads at the centre or on their handles (figs. 213, 218–220, 223), with some gold used for ornamentation and for colour (see e.g. its use on *calyxes* and *kantharoi*); jugs and small *amphoras*, flamboyant kraters made of bronze, small silver bowls/cups (*skyphoi*) (fig. 217), silver plates (fig. 211), strainers (fig. 216) and *kyathoi*; silver ladles (fig. 215) and silver and bronze buckets (*situlae*) (fig. 214) form a rich assemblage, which can be 'read' and interpreted differently each time, since all these vessels probably had ritual connotations attached to them alongside their use in social events. Shapes from the Athenian Kerameikos are here re-interpreted or copied in metal, while other examples constitute the prototype that would offer inspiration to the Athenian potter attempting to achieve a glimpse of luxury by using not just luxury metals but also the humble clay.[14] The political and social developments in Macedonia during the fourth century BC are best summarised in the developments observed in metalworking, which clearly serves the wealth and luxury of the royal court and of the people surrounding it (fig. 212).

Fig. 210 (opposite) Silver vessels as found in the tomb of Alexander IV

Fig. 211 Silver plate from the tomb of Alexander IV (Cat. no. 484)

Fig. 212 Silver perfume bottle from the tomb of Alexander IV (Cat. no. 483)

Fig. 213 Detail of relief head of a satyr inside a silver cup – from the tomb of Alexander IV

[187]

Fig. 214 Silver bucket (*situla*) from the tomb of Alexander IV (Cat. no. 482)

Fig. 215 Silver ladle ending in a bird's head from the tomb of Alexander IV (Cat. no. 481)

Fig. 216 Silver-gilded strainer from the tomb of Philip II (Cat. no. 478)

Fig. 217 A silver cup from the tomb of Philip II (Cat. no. 479)

The intact royal tombs under the great tumulus at Aegae, the rich tombs at Pydna in Pieria,[15] Derveni[16] to the west of Thessaloniki, and Pella,[17] express a crucial moment for the kingdom of Macedon, as well as for the entire Greek world – from the dynamic reign of Philip II (360/359–336 BC) until the reign of Cassander (305–297 BC) which brought to an end the rule of the Temenids and introduced the Hellenistic age. Philip II managed to expand the kingdom of Macedon to the Black Sea and the valley of Ano Axios. His ambitious and bold policy yielded impressive results, many advantages, power and riches. The historical and social interpretation of the funerary finds is not enough to reveal all the connotations of these rich gifts; nevertheless, they constitute the best clue to this rich society of military men – a society that was able to bring famous artists, philosophers, playwrights and the most skilled craftsmen to the cities of Macedonia and the royal court in order to produce their works.

At the same time, a reverse course is set in motion: for some people this luxury was inaccessible and for this reason they decided to replace the precious metals with clay, covered with a thin foil of gold, silver or tin. For some, this imitation or fake allusion of wealth is enough in order to maintain the 'necessary' illustrious image of the burial. The contrast between wealth and poverty would continue with intensity during the Hellenistic age in the Greek metropolitan cities, where royal wealth was shown off during impressive and extravagant processions, such as the procession of Ptolemy II Philadelphos described by Kallixenos of Rhodes (*FGrH* 627 F 2) with his wonderfully flamboyant vessels, at the time when the ports of the Mediterranean were filled with products of a massive ceramic 'industry'.[18] The kings and the elite continued to give away gold and silver vessels during lavish banquets (*symposia*), a symbolic yet benevolent gesture of their generosity.[19] There are many anecdotes from the time of Philip II and Alexander III. In the funeral pyre of Hephaistion numerous precious vessels accompanied the deceased, while in the famous Macedonian dinners and symposia, Alexander 'gave to each one a golden bowl (*phiale*) in order for them to offer libations to the gods' (Plutarch, *Alexander* 69–70.2).

During the fourth century BC, with the osmosis of the various trends in arts and crafts, the new financial reality and the wide circulation and exploitation of the rich metal deposits, important changes are observed in metalworking. It does not appear to be accidental that the precious vessels attested in funerary assemblages of the fourth century BC, especially in Macedonia, are characterised by the relief heads and other representations on their surfaces. Masks or heads of mythical figures decorate the handles, the interiors of bowls, the rims of precious vessels, offering to their users a new symbolic vocabulary and narrative or '*logon*' (word or speech) exactly as happened in high art. In the silver and bronze vessels from the royal tombs at Aegae, remarkable relief figures and figures in the round were crafted (see e.g. the ram's head at the end of a *patera* handle (figs. 218, 221–222) and the heads of Satyrs and Maenads (figs. 219–223) – the male and female followers of Dionysus respectively, that appear on silver and bronze jugs and kraters). This feature is further corroborated by similar

Fig. 218 A ram's head decorating the end of a *patera* handle

Fig. 220 (opposite) Relief head from a silver *amphora* from the tomb of Philip II

Fig. 219 Silver wine jug (*oinochoe*) from the tomb of Philip II, with a relief head of a *Satyr* under the handle (Cat. no. 475)

Fig. 221 (above) *Patera* (pan-shaped vessel) (Cat. no. 88)

Fig. 222 (below) Detail from the *patera* found in the tomb of Philip II – the handle ends in a ram's head (Cat. no. 88)

Fig. 223 Bronze wine jug (*oinochoe*) decorated with the head of a maenad under its handle – from the tomb of Philip II (Cat. no. 89)

finds from other sites in the broader northern Greek world. Shapes with a different origin, such as the 'Eastern' bowls (*phialai*), the buckets (*situlae*) and the 'angular jugs', acquire a new artistic character by expressing more decisively the value of art, without, at the same time, setting aside the value of the metal itself.[20] The latter is made clear by the frequent attestation of incised weight measurements on the vessels themselves (e.g. on the strainer from the tomb of Philip II on display in this exhibition) (fig. 216).

The picture we have of metalworking based on archaeological finds changes considerably in the Hellenistic age. In contrast to the archaeological evidence, the written sources describe impressive works of art often associated with the royal courts. The concluding chapter is written with the looting of the royal treasury of the kingdom of Macedon by the Romans following the defeat of King Perseus at the battle of Pydna (168 BC). The treasure, the valuable vessels, furniture and other works of art were pillaged with the king of Macedon, Perseus, and his children becoming war booty and the main spectacle of the triumphal parade of Aemilius Paulus in Rome.[21]

14 The royal presence in the agora of Aegae

Chrysoula Saatsoglou-Paliadeli

INTRODUCTION

Despite its large-scale destruction in the mid-second century BC, probably a result of Roman invasion, and subsequent centuries of decline, abandonment, demolition and cultivation, the sanctuary of Eukleia, at Vergina–Aegae, has enriched our knowledge of Macedonia with important and impressive material evidence as a result of the systematic archaeological investigation sponsored by the Aristotle University of Thessaloniki, from 1982 onwards.[1] At present, the location of an Early Iron Age storehouse (*pitheon*),[2] is the only indication of the settlement to which the later phase of the extended tumuli cemetery of Vergina can be related.[3]

The continuous habitation of the site from the early first millennium BC until the first century AD, the loose earth and the dismantling of older buildings to re-use their materials have created problems for dating the architectural remains. It is a happy coincidence, however, that the most important phase of the sanctuary, coinciding with the climax of the Macedonian kingdom, during Philip II's reign, is well documented.

Built on one of the terraces formed to support the structures of the city on its sloping terrain, the sanctuary of Eukleia occupies an area of more than 3,000 square metres, originally probably extending further to the north and to the east. Its proximity to a deep gully, where the western part of the fortification walls should be located, and the discovery within the precincts of the sanctuary of a road that might be extended in the same direction, suggest the possible existence of a gate, whose remains may be hidden under the modern road which leads from today's village to the palace. Remains of another road, leading to the south, suggest a link between the sanctuary and the theatre.[4]

The identification of the sanctuary with part of the agora of the old Macedonian capital was originally suggested in 1987 on the basis of the epigraphic evidence; a dedicatory inscription of Eurydice, daughter of Sirras, queen of Amyntas III, to Eukleia (below no. 2.ia). The latter was a panhellenic deity[5] whose worship in the *agoras* (market places) of the ancient Greek cities[6] and the erection of her temple at the Athenian agora from the spoils of the battle of Marathon (Pausanias 1.14.5) accord with the political connotations of her name, as a protectress of fair repute rather than one of marriage.[7] A second inscribed statuary base, bearing an identical dedicatory inscription, to the same deity by the same queen, suggests the importance of the site as a public place of worship for Eurydice.[8]

The excavation which followed vindicated the original hypothesis: the poorly preserved remains of two temples, an altar, a stoa, two peristyle buildings, three marble bases once supporting monumental dedications[9] and the discovery of the lower part of a colossal marble serpent in the form of Zeus *Meilichios* (the gracious/good-tempered one),[10] emblematic in the agoras of ancient Greek cities,[11] indicate the public and religious character of the site, which is further suggested by its proximity to the theatre and the palace, in a town plan foreshadowing the related features of the Hellenistic *basileia* (palace complexes).[12] The discovery in a deep ditch of fourth-century monumental sculpture[13] and further epigraphic evidence dating to the second century BC[14] attest to the appearance of at least two Macedonian queens in the area. More recently, finds uncovered in the last few years reinforce the importance of the site for the Macedonian dynasties and testify to a royal presence, not only in the palace (where kings and their courts resided), the theatre (where Philip II was assassinated) and the cemetery (where members of the royal family were buried), but also in the agora of the ancient city.

I. EURYDICE, QUEEN OF AMYNTAS III AT VERGINA–AEGAE

Eurydice's presence is attested on three inscribed monuments found in and around the archaeological site of Vergina: two of them (below § 2.i) are dedicatory inscriptions uncovered at the sanctuary of Eukleia; the third, (below § 2.i) although found re-used in an Early Christian basilica at Palatitsia, two kilometres to the north-east of the ancient city, can be associated with a marble female statue discovered in the agora of the ancient city, as explained below.

1. The literary evidence

Originating from the royal family of Lyncestis in Upper Macedonia, Eurydice, daughter of Sirras, was married to Amyntas III in 393/2 BC,[15] and she probably followed him in his flight to the fortified city of Aegae.[16] Eurydice gave birth to a daughter, Euronoe, who married Ptolemy from Aloros,[17] and three future kings of Macedon, Alexander II, Perdiccas III and Philip II (Justin 7.4.5). Although later historians represent her in a rather monstrous way,[18] it is due to her personality that the Macedonian throne was preserved for Amyntas' sons after his death in 370/69 BC. Aischines (II 26–29) records her as queen mother, in connection with the events following her husband's death; according to this source she invited the Athenian general Iphicrates to meet her at court in 368/67 BC, and by appealing to his emotions, she persuaded him to alter the Athenian position towards Pausanias, the pretender to the Macedonian throne, thus saving it for her sons.

Plutarch (*Morals* 14b-c) preserves an epigram accompanying a dedication of Eurydice to the Muses, as an expression of her gratitude for being able to learn how to read and write when her children were already teenagers.

> Εὐρυδίκη Σίρρα, πολιῆτις, τόνδ' ἀνέθηκε
> Μούσαις εὔιστον ψυχῇ ἑλοῦσα Πόθον.
> γράμματα γὰρ μνημεῖα λόγων μήτηρ γεγαυῖα
> παίδων ἡβώντων ἐξεπόνησε μαθεῖν.

I have elsewhere suggested that the term *πολιῆτις* in Plutarch's epigram should be seen as an indication of her permanent residence at Aegae (not as a dedication of the queen 'to or for citizen women' as Carney believes),[19] at least after her husband's death. Such a dedication – the nature of which is not clearly indicated in lines 1–2 of the epigram – might actually represent a statue of *Pothos*, a personification of 'yearning, longing, desire of things usually absent or missing', most fitting to the context of the epigram, with the queen giving thanks to the Muses, protectors of knowledge and learning alluding to her own literacy albeit at an advanced age.[20]

2. The epigraphic evidence

i. Two dedicatory inscriptions to Eukleia

The epigraphic evidence for Eurydice at the agora of Vergina–Aegae consists of two, almost identical dedicatory inscriptions to Eukleia.

a. The first is preserved on a rectangular base consisting of four marble blocks once fastened together by iron Π-shaped clasps in lead:[21] elegantly inscribed on the front widest side of the rectangle, it is framed within an incised band-shaped area, with the strings at the ends also indicated in incision. Destroyed and re-composed in Hellenistic times, the base lacks its mouldings, originally made of separate pieces of marble of which the upper one would have supported a dedication, the kind and form of which we have no further evidence to reconstruct.

b. The second inscription is preserved intact on the front side of a rectangular statuary base,[22] with mouldings on the lower and upper parts and the lead for the safe erection of a statue still preserved on its upper surface. My original suggestion that the marble *peplophoros* (the statue of a woman dressed with the heavy *peplos* garment) discovered in the same ditch might fit into it, due to the similarity in shape and dimensions of its plinth,[23] has recently proven to be wrong, due to a tiny difference in size.

The reason for these two dedications by Queen Eurydice to Eukleia is not easy to trace, due to our poor knowledge about her deeds, apart from those preserved in the literary evidence (above § 1). Born around 410 BC and married to Amyntas III in her late teens, she was certainly alive in 368 BC when she

Fig. 224 Statue of the *peplophoros* as found in the sanctuary of Eukleia at Aegae

met Iphicrates. Nothing about her afterwards survives; that she was still alive during the early years of Philip II's reign should not be excluded,[24] especially if it is accepted that the so-called Macedonian tomb, conventionally named 'the tomb of Eurydice', may be related to her.[25]

In any case the dedications to Eukleia from the agora of Vergina–Aegae according to their lettering cannot be dated to the beginning of the fourth century and therefore related to her marriage with Amyntas III, in 393/2 BC. It seems to me that a later dating,[26] in connection with her successful meeting with the Athenian general Iphicrates in 368 BC, when she managed to secure the Macedonian throne for her sons, fits better the nature of Eukleia, as a political deity and protectress of fair repute.

ii. A base for a statue of Queen Eurydice

The statuary base found re-used as a support for a column at the ruins of an Early Christian basilica in the nearby village of Palatitsia, is almost identical in shape to the second of the dedications to Eukleia (above § 2i.b), although wider and higher than the latter.[27]

One notable difference is the fact that the badly damaged yet securely restored inscription of the Palatitsia base is not dedicatory; its epigraphic formula (*Εὐρυδίκα Σίρρα*) consisting of the name and patronymic of Eurydice only, alludes to a marble statue of the queen which once stood at Vergina–Aegae. Furthermore, the abnormal position of the inscription on the left-hand lateral surface and not on the main face of the slab as one would have expected, suggests that it originally occupied the right-hand end of a larger statuary group.[28]

Due to this evidence and taking into account that a statue of Eurydice was part of the chryselephantine group in the Philippeion at Olympia (Paus. 5.20.9–10), I have elsewhere suggested that a replica of the statuary composition at Olympia might possibly have been erected at Vergina–Aegae.[29] In a forthcoming publication of the ditch and the sculpture it contained, it is suggested that the base at Palatitsia should be related to the statue of the *peplophoros* found in the sanctuary of Eukleia two decades ago.[30]

3. *The marble* peplophoros *from the sanctuary of Eukleia*

The statue (fig. 224) represents a mature female of little more than lifesize, wearing a *chiton* well hidden under the heavy folds of a *peplos*, and the small *himation* which covers the back from head to legs. Only one of the arms survives, originally made of separate pieces of marble and inserted in shallow holes. The head of the statue (fig. 225), found in the same ditch, and also made of a separate piece of marble, fits perfectly on the upper part of the body.[31] Its unusual way of insertion needs further consideration before any firm interpretation can be suggested; yet, its facial features, dated to the third quarter of the fourth century BC, correspond to those of a mature female, thus quite

Fig. 225 Head of the *peplophoros*

Fig. 226 Marble female head from the sanctuary of Eukleia (Cat. no. 170)

Fig. 227 Marble head of a young god,
hero, or heroized mortal found in the
sanctuary of Eukleia (Cat. no. 171)

Fig. 228 Side view of the marble male
head (Cat. no. 171)

possibly representing a portrait of Queen Eurydice.[32] The discovery of this almost complete marble statue along with two other marble heads of the same period found in the same ditch (figs. 226–228) strongly indicate the presence of great – most probably Athenian – sculptors working for Eurydice and her son, Philip II, in the early 30s of the 4th century BC.[33]

II. LAODICE, DAUGHTER OF SELEUKOS, QUEEN OF PERSEUS

Without the epigraphical evidence for the presence of Eurydice at Vergina–Aegae, any attempt to reconstruct a highly fragmentary inscription from the sanctuary of Eukleia would have been impossible.[34] The remaining letters and their monumental size, alongside the dedicatory character of the inscription and its dating to the late third or early second century BC on stylistic grounds, support the suggestion that its text is a dedication of Queen Laodice, daughter of King Seleukos and wife of King Perseus, to an unknown god.[35]

[ΒΑΣΙΛΙΣΣΑ] ΛΑΟ[ΔΙΚΗ]
[ΒΑΣΙΛΕΩΣ] ΣΕΛ[ΕΥΚΟΥ]
[ΤΩ]Ι ΘΕΩ[Ι]

If this is the case then it is evident that the agora of the ancient city of Aegae retained its importance until the end of the Antigonid dynasty on the eve of the Roman invasion.

A colossal marble serpent in the form of Zeus *Meilichios* discovered at the antechamber of Temple II at the sanctuary of Eukleia (where it was intentionally buried along with two coins of King Perseus),[36] should not necessarily be related to Queen Laodice and her dedication 'to the unknown god'. The dating of this monumental sculpture is not easy to ascertain, due to a lack of any certain archaeological data or any other comparable figure in size and style. The coins of Perseus found in the same ditch can only serve as a *terminus ante quem* for the construction of the colossal statue. Its subject matter is found on votive reliefs of the fourth century BC to Zeus in the shape of a serpent and the acclamation τῷ θεῷ in our fragmentary inscription often accompanies these dedications. The colossal size of the sculpture may either indicate a cult statue of Zeus *Meilichios*, possibly sheltered in the main chamber of the temple built in the fourth century BC, or alternatively conceived as a dedication of Laodice to the same deity. Only further material evidence may finally provide an answer to this dilemma.

III. HERACLES, SON OF ALEXANDER III, AT AEGAE?

The gold oak wreath presented in the exhibition (fig. 229) is the most recent, most impressive and most unexpected among the finds at the sanctuary of Eukleia. It was revealed three years ago in the filling of a big rectangular ditch as part of a burial context, consisting of a bronze cylindrical vessel containing a gold ossuary (fig. 230), in the shape of a legless large cylindrical *pyxis* covered with a lid. Inside the latter, apart from the wreath, the cremated bones of a man were found along with remains of gold *lamellae*, as parts of woven cloth.[37]

The anthropological examination of the skeletal remains suggests a teenager no older than 17 years of age, while the exceptional quality of the finds, equal to those of the nearby royal burials of the Great Tumulus, indicate not simply a rich but rather a royal cremation.

The reasons for this assumption are the following:

1. The unexpected burial was discovered within the precincts of a public area – only a few hundred metres away from the nearby necropolis
2. The filling of the ditch was homogenous, without any traces of intervention that might indicate a temporary deposition after a robbery
3. The ceramics of the filling date no later than the late fourth century BC

It was therefore concluded that the find represents a rare case of a royal burial of a cremated young man, which was deliberately hidden in the agora of Aegae in the early Hellenistic period.

The above, in combination with its discovery at the agora of the old capital and royal necropolis of at least the Temenid dynasty, and a short but revealing item of information preserved in Justin (*Epitome of the Philippic History of Pompeius Trogus* 16.2.3) led us to connect this burial with Heracles, son of Alexander III and Barsine (Plutarch, *Alexander* 21.4): born either in 327/6 or 325/4 BC he must have been either 17 or 14 years old when he was murdered by Polyperchon on his way to Macedonia, on the orders of Cassander.[38]

The anthropological and archaeological evidence correspond with the information preserved by Justin, who refers to the tragic death of Alexander's offspring, marking the end of the Temenid dynasty: 'Lest Alexander's son Heracles, who had passed fourteen years, might be called to the throne through the favour with which men regarded his father's name, Cassander ordered that he and his mother Barsine be killed secretly and that their corpses be covered with soil, so that there should be no grave to betray the murder.'[39]

The choice by those who undertook the task to hide Heracles' remains in the agora of the old capital, with no monumental tomb or grave marker to recall the murder, but in the most important part of the city, indicates a special respect for the last of the Temenids and symbolises the end of a dynasty which had established its kingdom three and a half centuries before, on the northern slopes of the Pierian mountains, in the heart of the Μακεδονίς γη of Herodotus (7.127). Further investigation of the vast archaeological site at Vergina–Aegae by the Aristotle University of Thessaloniki may enhance our knowledge about the royal presence in the cradle of the Macedonian kingdom.

Fig. 229 The gold oak and acorn wreath found in
2008 in the area of the agora and the sanctuary of
Eukleia at Aegae (Cat. no. 101)

Fig. 230 The wreath as found
inside the gold ossuary

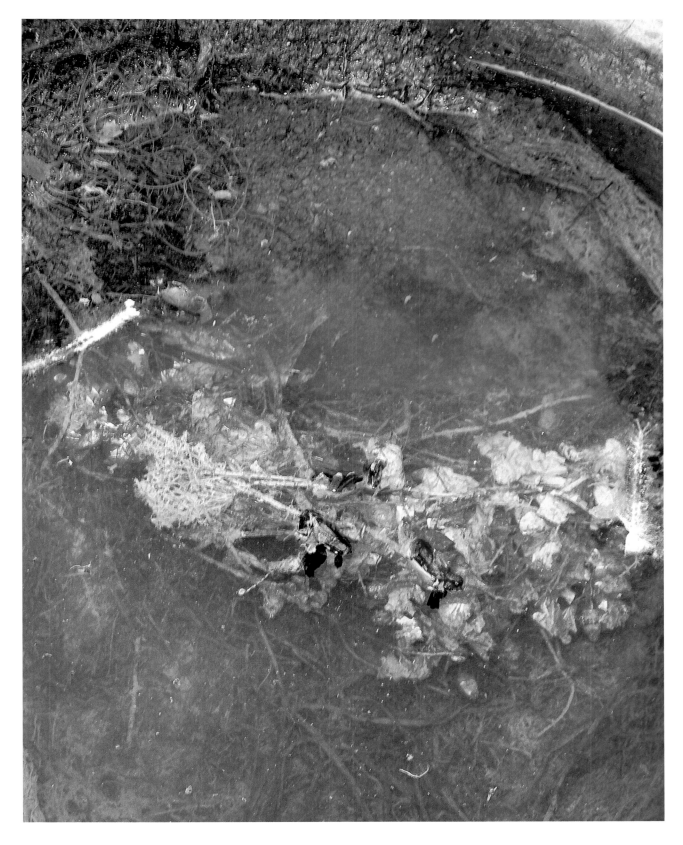

Fig. 231 *Obv.*: Horseman wearing a
petasos and holding two spears

Fig. 232 *Rev*: Helmeted head in
an incuse square. Tetradrachm
of Alexander I (Numismatic
Museum, Athens)

Fig. 233 *Obv.*: Horseman wearing a
petasos and holding two spears. A
dog accompanies the horseman

Fig. 234 *Rev.*: The king's name
in an incuse square. Octadrachm
of Alexander I (Cabinet de
médailles, Paris)

15 Macedonian coinage before Alexander

Sophia Kremydi

The precious metals necessary for coin production by the Greek states were obtained either through direct control over mines or from trade. The inauguration of coinage by the Macedonians under Alexander I (figs. 231–234), not long after the Persian retreat from Thrace in 478 BC, is connected with his temporary control over the silver mines of Mount Dysoron,[1] which as Herodotus (5.17.2) tells us, provided him with a talent of silver per day. In northern Greece, a concentration of appropriate metals was found in eastern Chalkidike and between the Rivers Strymon and Nestos,[2] regions incorporated into the Macedonian kingdom only during the reign of Philip II. How these resources were controlled before Philip is not clear, but evidence shows they were a constant source of rivalry between the Thracians, the Greek colonists, the Athenians and the Macedonians.[3] During the periods when Macedonians did not directly control the mining districts, they certainly imported metal for the production of their coinage, as is the case of Archelaos, who sold timber to the Athenians after the Peloponnesian War (431–404 BC), importing significant quantities of silver in the form of Athenian coinage, which facilitated his own production of silver.[4]

The establishment of a Macedonian coinage by Alexander I was not an innovation in the area. The Thracian *ethne* (tribes) and the *ellenides poleis* (Greek colonies scattered along the coast) had an important monetary production from the last decades of the sixth century BC that naturally influenced Macedonians in their choice of denominational systems and iconographical types. The Macedonians' manipulation of various monetary systems developed in a very sophisticated way. Their fractions were struck according to the Attic system of a drachm subdivided into six obols,[5] but at the same time they created denominations exchangeable with local currencies. The octadrachms of Alexander I followed the 'oriental' standard and were exchangeable with the octadrachms of Abdera, whereas Macedonian tetradrachms were on a local standard, possibly created to facilitate the exchange between silver and electrum.[6] The adaptation of Macedonian coinage to different standards used by

Thracians, Athenians and the northern colonies, reflects, on a monetary level, the complex environment in which this *ethnos* was destined to survive and develop.

The distinction between lighter coins intended for local use and heavier ones used for payments beyond the boundaries of the state was another early Macedonian conception, with obvious benefits for the state. It was first applied to the Macedonian tetrobols issued around the middle of the fifth century BC. The two types of tetrobols – small coins, probably equivalent to a day's pay – can be distinguished by their iconography: light tetrobols bore a horse on the reverse whereas the heavier tetrobols bore a cavalryman. From them we can trace the origins of a monetary policy prevailing in the Hellenistic period: after the death of Alexander 'thraco-macedonian' tetradrachms in the name of Philip were issued for internal circulation or specific regional markets, whereas Alexander's heavier Attic tetradrachms dominated international markets[7] – a practice later adopted by many Hellenistic mints that struck Alexander's coins in parallel to their own local currencies.

Before Alexander, Macedonian coinage did not circulate widely. Fifth-century BC heavy denominations were certainly exported to the Achaemenid Empire, but in relatively small quantities compared with coins from other Greek mints.[8] Fifth-century BC tetrobols have been found in neighbouring regions such as Chalkidike or Paionia,[9] whereas the staters of Archelaos circulated in Eordaia.[10] Silver lifetime issues of Philip II are mainly found within the extended territory of Macedonia and to a small extent in the Peloponnese.[11] Under Alexander they spread in larger quantities to mainland Greece and probably after his death also into the Balkans, where they became popular and were later imitated. The regional circulation of Philip's 'thraco-macedonian' tetradrachms probably influenced Ptolemy, who chose a very similar standard in order to create a closed currency system for his newly founded kingdom in Egypt. The opening of the frontiers by the wars of Alexander's Successors (*Diadochoi*) that created the Hellenistic world enabled the Macedonian coinage to expand considerably outside its borders. Philip, however, had laid the foundations of this expansion by incorporating the mining districts within his kingdom, opening a second mint near the mines of Mount Pangaion, producing coinage on a scale incomparable to that previously minted by the Macedonian state and introducing the Attic standard for gold. Thus, Philip II

Fig. 235 *Obv.*: Head of a hero wearing a *taenia* (headband)

Fig. 236 *Rev.*: Standing horse. Stater of Archelaos (Alpha Bank collection, Athens)

Fig. 237 *Obv.*: Horseman brandishing a spear

Fig. 238 *Rev.*: Lion biting the second spear. Stater of Amyntas III (Ashmolean Museum, Oxford)

took the first crucial steps in transforming Macedonian coinage into an international currency.

The diversity that characterised early Macedonian coinage in terms of metrology and weight standards can also be applied to its iconography: unlike the Greek city-states and their colonies in the north that chose a persistent and unique type, often reproduced in an abbreviated form on smaller denominations, the Macedonians before Alexander followed a different tradition; they used a variety of types modified during periods of dynastic rupture, seemingly snapshots whose meaning is revealed when they are considered as a whole. Fifth-century BC iconography included a warrior-hunter depicted as a mounted horseman, lions, boars, horses, helmets and goats (figs. 231–233, 236–238, 240). With the exception of the goat type, which was a reference to a cult and at the same time to the capital city of Aegae, the rest clearly refer to the Macedonian aristocracy. Hunting and war were the main activities of the Macedonian elite and lions and boars were the pride of the royal hunt. Their connotations reveal their meaning when compared with other elements, such as the wall-painting of the royal hunt of the tomb of Philip at Aegae (figs. 247–248). Their meaning is further clarified by comparison with the staters of Amyntas III (figs. 237–238), father of Philip II, which bear a horseman brandishing a spear on the obverse and a lion grasping a second spear on the reverse. The two images clearly form an iconographic entity, and there is no better argument to prove the existence of the royal lion hunt in the Macedonian court long before Alexander. The head of the local deity *Heracles Patroos* (ancestral Heracles), patron deity of the Temenids, was introduced by Archelaos and used by subsequent rulers (figs. 239–240).

Fig. 239 *Obv.*: Head of *Heracles Patroos* wearing a lion's skin

Fig. 240 *Rev.*: Standing horse. Stater of Perdiccas III (American Numismatic Society, New York)

[207]

Under Philip II, coin types were chosen in order to appeal to a wider Greek public (figs. 241–244). The head of Zeus Olympios was chosen for the obverse of the tetradrachms whereas the mounted warrior-hunter was replaced by the image of an unarmed rider saluting in parade, an obvious reference to the king. Macedonian victories at the panhellenic sanctuary of Olympia were advertised on the tetradrachms as well as on gold staters. The internationally recognisable coin types that survived for centuries show the head of Heracles and the seated figure of Zeus Olympios on the Alexander tetradrachms (figs. 245–246). These types continued to be used on royal, regional and civic issues until the late Hellenistic period.

Fig. 241 *Obv.*: Head of Zeus Olympios wearing a laurel-wreath

Fig. 242 *Rev.*: Victorious jockey holding a palm branch. Tetradrachm of Philip II (Alpha Bank collection, Athens)

Fig. 243 *Obv.*: Head of Apollo wearing a laurel-wreath

Fig. 244 *Rev.*: Charioteer riding a *biga* (two-horse chariot). Posthumous stater of Philip II (Numismatic Museum, Athens)

Fig. 245 *Obv.*: Head of *Heracles Patroos* wearing a lion's skin

Fig. 246 *Rev.*: Zeus Olympios seated on a throne. The goat-head in the field possibly refers to the city of Aegae. Early tetradrachm of Alexander III (Alpha Bank collection, Athens)

16 Painting at the Macedonian court

Harikleia Brekoulaki

Alexander the Great used to visit Apelles's *officina* (atelier) and talk a great deal about painting, provoking the criticism of the legendary painter who would politely advise him to drop the subject (Pliny the Elder *HN*.35.85-86). The authority wielded over the king by Apelles and the honours and affection he received (*HN*.35.86-87) highlight the importance of the painted image – the *eikon* – in the crafting of the king's royal identity and heroic persona. Alexander was already familiar with the impact that 'realistic' images were likely to convey, through the numerous portraits of his father Philip II produced by Apelles and other renowned artists (*HN*.35.93; 35.114). He would also express a personal liking for paintings, for example, by removing from the city of Thebes a work by the painter Aristides to his native house at Pella (*HN*.35. 99). Previous Macedonian kings had also patronized the arts, with prolific artists said to have taken up residence at their court. King Archelaos hired Zeuxis of Heraclea to paint his house, which subsequently became a popular attraction (Aelian *Hist. Misc.* 14.17).

For Alexander's immediate successors painting was still held in very high esteem, serving both as a vehicle for political propaganda and as a precious royal gift. Philoxenos of Eretria was commissioned by King Cassander to paint a battle between Alexander and Darius (*HN*.35.110), while Aratos gained the favour of Ptolemy Philadelphos by sending him drawings and paintings from the Sicyonian school (Plutarch, *Aratus* 12.5; 13.4).[1] King Demetrios Poliorcetes, in order to avoid burning a picture by Protogenes, was said to have abstained from setting fire to Rhodes, when the city could only be taken from the side where the picture was stored (*HN*.35.105).

Although Pliny recalls the activity of noteworthy native Macedonian painters, such as Heraclides of Macedon, who migrated to Athens after the capture of King Perseus in the second century BC (*HN*.35.135; 35.146), the tradition of painting that flourished in late classical and Hellenistic Macedonia (fourth to first centuries BC) is not largely indigenous in origin.[2] Rather, it articulates the cultural and political aspirations of its kings, wishing to assimilate within their court the glory such art had gained through the masterpieces of panhellenic sanctuaries and Athenian public buildings. In the fourth century BC, painting was the art par excellence. Macedonia, as an 'international' cultural crossroad, attracted eminent painters from the well-established schools of southern Greece to produce portraits of its monarchs and images of their gods, decorating their houses and tombs. The funerary use of painting on the façades and interiors of the royal tombs at Aegae enhanced the symbolic function of the monuments, also illustrating the Macedonians' belief in the heroisation of the deceased and the afterlife.

Even though the identity of the artists who produced the masterpieces at the necropolis of Aegae remains doubtful, their exceptional quality is unanimously acknowledged. On the austere façade of Philip's tomb (fig. 247), the monumental composition of the frieze reflects the painter's sophisticated and lifelike use of colour, and at the same time his debt to the sculptural tradition, visible in the skilfully organized hunting groups and in the figures' dynamic, yet static, postures and symmetrical arrangements. Instead of a classical, abstract background, what we see is a realistic landscape where action takes place within a specific time frame, so that the background becomes actively entailed in the picture's narratives. The subtle variations of light pink, yellow, blue and green hues applied in large diluted brushstrokes to the background suggest the pure and cold colours of the dawn, the usual time for hunting (figs. 247–248). An illusion of depth is conveyed through the remarkable depiction of distant objects in paler and bluer colours, contrasting with the warmer earthern hues of the amply displayed bodies and the captured animals in the foreground. The supremacy of the predators over their prey emphasises manly authority

Fig. 247 The façade of the tomb of King Philip II

Fig. 248 Hunting frieze from Philip II's tomb

[210]

Figs. 249–250 Details from the hunting frieze showing the king ready to give the fatal blow to the lion

and heroic strength. Wild beasts are already fatally wounded, while the final death blow to the centrally placed lion in the most impressive hunting scene is further emphasised by the direction of the dead king's gilded spear (figs. 249–250). The crowned youthful successor, Alexander, occupies the middle of the frieze (figs. 30–31), thus anticipating the success of his expedition in the East, while concurrently commemorating the glorious past of his assassinated father. Technically speaking, in this frieze are displayed all those qualities for which Greek painting claimed fame, as listed by Lucian in his work *Zeuxis* or *Antiochus* (VI.5): 'precision of line, accuracy in the blending of colours, taste in the application of the paint, correct use of shadow, good perspective, proportion, and symmetry'. A variety of hues also helps to obtain a delicate chromatic and tonal equilibrium. The artist's application of colour on a dry background in layers, starting with diluted brushstrokes, provides the figures with volume and renders their facial characteristics, with the help of hatching. Mastering the use of shading and manipulating the effects of his light source, coming from the left, the painter of the hunting scene transfers onto the wall his technical knowledge and the current tradition of panel painting. The coloured layers are obtained by mixing various organic and mineral pigments, including lead white and calcite, cinnabar and earthen, iron-based reds, natural copper-based greens and Egyptian blue, organic purple and certainly other pigments, as yet unclassified, coming from the rich mineral resources of ancient Macedonia's mines and subsoil.

Regretting the loss of the painted wooden frieze that was originally fixed on the façade of Tomb III, we may only imagine the appearance of its panel painting, through the scanty remains of the small frieze with floral motif, still visible on the walls of the main chamber. Although, according to Pliny (*HN*.35.118), great fame was confined to artists of panel paintings, they would have certainly managed to paint on the wall, upon request.

Despite their conventional depiction on a dark blue solid background, the 21 chariots surrounding the antechamber's walls of tomb III (fig. 251) reflect the expertise of the painter in memorising and reproducing an impressive range of animal movements and human gestures, even in small-scale compositions.

However, the most powerful expression of free-style painting, abolishing strict contour lines and closed forms, for the benefit of facial expressions and physical gesticulation, is to be seen in the famous abduction scene in the 'tomb of Persephone' (fig. 252). Using a limited range of pigments, the painter distorts perspective in order to fit the figures onto the wall, and displays, despite his hasty execution, the solid background of an expert and talented artist. The modest earthen hues of red and yellow ochres used for the figures and the chariot are counterbalanced by the bright organic pink of the unfolded garment, catching the spectator's eye by its *color floridus*. The youthful Kore's

Fig. 251 Detail from the chariot frieze inside the antechamber walls of the tomb of Alexander IV (tomb III)

Fig. 252 Abduction of Persephone by Hades from the cist grave under the large tumulus at Aegae

nakedness as a sign of submission to the terrible God's will – illustrating the
myth in a most expressive manner – stands out against the majestic figure
of Persephone as the omnipotent Queen of the Underworld, in the tomb of
Eurydice.

Inside the main chamber of this extraordinary monument dated to the mid-
fourth century BC, on the back of a luxurious marble throne, are depicted
in epiphany Hades and Persephone (Kore) on their divine *quadriga* (chariot
drawn by four horses), draped in purple robes and holding golden sceptres
(figs. 253–254). The movement of the horses is cut short, and their bodies are
displayed obliquely, allowing the painter to express his technical abilities in
advanced *chiaroscuro* (contrasts of light and shade) and the lively rendering of
the horses' facial features. Despite the remarkable impasto created by the thick
brushstrokes – visible on the painting's surface – the subtle tonal qualities and
the delicacy in the rendering of outline recall the achievements of the famous
painter Parrhasius (late fifth century BC) in the drawing of the contour line,
which 'ought to round itself off and to terminate as to suggest the presence of
the other parts behind it' (*HN*.35.67).

The reduced chromatic intensities in the figures of the painted scene contrast
with the colourful effect conveyed by the gilded floral frieze of the composition. It is worth noting that the gamut of pigments identified is far from being
a common one: red ochre is entirely substituted by expensive cinnabar, to indicate details, and also mixed with yellow ochre and carbon black to render the
dark brown bodies of the animals. Besides the use of an organic purple, the

rare mineral sandarac and the unusual bone white were also employed, while the choice of lead white as the most appropriate white pigment for painting on a dry stone surface finds here one of its earliest applications.

On the surviving paintings of the monumental tombs at Aegae, royal imagery is clearly expressed through subjects such as hunting, racing, divine abduction and epiphany. The choice of these subjects underscores aspects of self-definition, wealth and hierarchy within an elite society. Apart from their own informative, 'narrative language', royal Macedonian paintings – due to their outstanding quality and remarkable stylistic diversity – serve as the most valuable tangible testimonies of ancient Greek painting at a time when this art had reached its culmination.[3]

17 Pella: the 'greatest of the cities in Macedonia'. The new capital of the kingdom of Macedon

Maria Lilimpaki-Akamati

The capital of the kingdom of Macedon was probably transferred from Aegae to Pella on the coast of the Thermaic Gulf about the end of the fifth century BC – a move primarily to improve communication between the centre of royal power and the rest of Greece, but also because of Pella's advantageous location overlooking a fertile plain and its easy access by both land and sea. Such a choice was not coincidental: the site and surrounding area show signs of occupation from the third millennium BC, testified by the remnants of cemeteries around the new entrance to the archaeological site of Pella, ranging in date from the third and second millennia BC to the sixth and fifth centuries BC (for Pella during the fifth century BC, see Herodotus 7.123 and Thucydides 2.99.3-4). The exact location of any associated settlements is not as yet ascertained, but may well be to the south of the new entrance to the site, still to be explored in detail.[1]

For the older building phase at Pella, when it was first named capital of the Macedonians, the majority of evidence comes from its cemetery, which occupies the south and southeast site of what later became (during the Hellenistic period) the agora of Pella. This cemetery also suggests the presence of a city around the end of the fifth century BC in the southern part of Hellenistic Pella. The north boundaries of the city are marked by the surviving remains of the defence wall with an orientation south-east/north-west, parts of which, were discovered under the *insulae* and the roads of the Hellenistic town. This wall was built on a cemetery of the Early Iron Age (ninth century BC). Further building remains from this early phase of the new Macedonian capital have come to light in the area of the complex of the sanctuary of Darrhon (a local healer god), suggesting that a grid plan existed from the first half of the fourth century BC, a claim further supported by the pottery found in the fills of the earlier layers and the alignment of the external wall of a building from this phase with the external wall of an *insula* of the early third century BC. The notable presence in the earlier layers of imported pottery from Attica underlines the close contacts between the city of Pella and Athens from the end of the fifth century BC, which is further emphasised by the influence of Attic and Athenian art on other media such as sculpture, where it succeeds the influence of the eastern Aegean region. The subsequent development of local pottery and terracotta figures (coroplast's) workshops, metallurgy and floor mosaics, attested in the second half of the fourth century BC, drastically influences the financial buoyancy of life in the city until the end of its period of prosperity in the second century BC.

A large body of excavated material confirms Pella's close contacts with the rest of the Greek world from the end of the fifth century BC. Textual sources offer additional information, mentioning the gathering of many notable, learned people from southern Greece in the royal court of the kingdom of Macedon. The Macedonian kings fostered intellectual activity and art production, creating the conditions for the development of a fertile movement in various sectors of science and art. Archaeological evidence from the fifth–early fourth century BC at Pella also testifies to the worship of gods from the wider Greek pantheon. There is evidence for the use of the Doric dialect and homogeneity in burial practices with those of the rest of the Greek world. Numerous epigraphic evidence also suggests the presence of people from various regions of the Greek world and beyond from the end of the fifth century BC, reaching its peak during the Hellenistic period. In this respect, a multicultural cosmopolitan society was established, transforming Pella into the 'greatest of the cities in Macedonia' during the fourth century BC (Xenophon, *Hellenika* 5.2.13) and the centre of the world empire of Alexander the Great.

Pella, as we know it today, shows the same urban construction that developed in the last quarter of the fourth century BC, occupying an area of about 400ha. The large rebuilding in the years of Cassander (305–297 BC), made possible because of the financial rewards acquired from the campaigns of Alexander the Great, were undertaken with remarkable consistency compared with the pre-existing urban planning of the city. The north wall of the initial phase was destroyed in the last quarter of the fourth century BC so that the city could expand to the north and east. The gradual disuse of the cemetery in the area of the *agora* from the middle of the fourth century BC and its final abandonment in the third quarter of the fourth century BC suggest the coterminous expansion of the city, along with the transference of burial sites to another area, about 800 metres to the east. This new area retained its funerary use until the beginning of the first century BC, when the population began to desert the site following an earthquake, although the southernmost part of the city, closest to the sea, continued to be occupied until the fourth century AD. The new fortification of the city, north of the palace, dated to the last quarter of the fourth century BC, follows the orientation of the older fortification wall, probably in alignment with existing *insulae*.

The Hellenistic urban plan of Pella shows rectangular *insulae* (fig. 255) of about 47m in width and of varying length, evenly divided by vertical streets (north–south) and horizontal (east-west), 6m and 9m wide respectively. This is the most developed plan that we know of for any ancient Greek city,

Fig. 255 Pella – aerial view of
the city

measuring in area about 2.5km (north–south) by 1.5km (east–west). The largest
road, 15m in width, oriented east–west, crosses the city, bisecting the *agora*, the
administrative and commercial heart of Pella. A few vertical streets (north–
south), wider than others at 9–10m, constituted the main arteries of the city,
leading from the port to the *agora*. They were paved and had elevated pave-
ments and *stoas*. Such a clear and functional grid plan, known in Greek cities
since the fifth century BC offered the opportunity for symmetrical expansions
in cities situated on plains, such as Pella, without disruption to their original
construction. Beneath these streets was a dense and well-organised network of
water-supply and drainage. Tunnels cut into the rock brought water from the
mountain springs through clay, stone and stone-lined conduits. The existence
of fountains, wells, cisterns, private and public baths and cleaning shafts reveals
the inhabitants' high standards of living as well as a developed knowledge of
hygiene and attention to the welfare of the population.

The grand palace complex, on the northernmost hill of the city, occupies
an area of some 60,000 square meters (6ha). It comprised large *peristyle* (colonnaded) courts with reception rooms, areas for large gatherings and official functions, including ritual activities. The private quarters include baths,
workshops and storage rooms, with further bathing facilities incorporated in
a large *palaistra*, a peristyle building with an open court. The palace at Pella
was the seat of royal power until the conquest of the kingdom of Macedon by
the Romans in 168/167 BC. The *agora* complex in the centre of the city occupies
an area of some 70,000 square meters (7ha), acting as the heart of the city's
busy commercial activity until the beginning of the first century BC. It was
also the site of the administrative authorities. The features mentioned above,
along with the carefully planned (within the city's grid) sanctuaries, private

Fig. 256 Pella – the 'house of Dionysus'

houses of high-officials with luxury furnishings and houses of average people, highlight the high standards of living at Pella (fig. 256). This point is strengthened further by the tombs of these individuals; the diversity of their design and architectural features as well as their rich funerary assemblages attest to a prosperous economy, rich in intellectual activity and cultural production. This lifestyle is observed throughout the Hellenistic period in the new capital of the kingdom of Macedon.

The use of a grid system for the city's layout, the fortifications and the contacts with southern Greece, especially with Athens, as attested in the archaeological record, support the testimony of Thucydides regarding the innovative activities of King Archelaos (2.100.1-2). On the other hand, the great prosperity of the city could not have been achieved without the grand and multi-faceted vision of Philip II and his son Alexander III. The most original account of Philip II's work and the heritage he left for his son is included in Alexander's speech at Opis in Mesopotamia in 324 BC (Arrian, *Anabasis* 7.9.2 – see also 7. Graekos, this volume). Others factors also contributed, including the unification of the country, the reorganisation of the army and good governance. The amalgamation (*synoecism*) of villages around a single metropolis and the bestowal of a city status on the *ethne* of Upper Macedonia also secured wealth-producing resources. The annexation of Chalkidike and the rich, gold-bearing area around Mount Pangaion formed one of the most influential accomplishments of Philip II in the historic development of the Macedonian kingdom. On the other hand, the cosmopolitan empire established by Alexander the Great and the resulting amalgamation of different civilisations of the ancient world led to a new era, contributing profoundly to the development of the Mediterranean world.

Although very little of the archaeological data can be related to the kings of Pella between the end of the fifth and the last quarter of the fourth century BC, it is nevertheless clear that the urban development of the city's architecture, the composite social structure, the prosperous economy and its intellectual and cultural activity between the last quarter of the fourth century BC until its decline reflect the impact of the policy followed by Philip II and Alexander III (fig. 257), historical figures of the highest importance in shaping Macedon's new capital: 'Pella was a small place until the time of Philip, by whom it was greatly enlarged' (Strabo, *Geography* 7.330.20).

In contrast to Aegae, the old capital of the Macedonian kingdom, a city organised *kata komas* (a collection of villages, not an organised *polis*) that never became a large urban centre, Pella, the new capital, saw the Macedonian kings apply a new model of development in urban planning. In this respect, the Macedonian kings championed the city's determinative contribution and fundamental role in shaping one of the most important cultural expressions of the Hellenistic age (323–30 BC).

Fig. 257 Marble portrait of Alexander the Great found near Pella (Cat. no. 2)

18 From *basileion* to *kaisareion*: the Roman heritage of Philip's palace at Aegae

Susan Walker

For their own imperial experience, especially in the conquest and administration of the lands bordering the eastern Mediterranean, Roman rulers drew upon the legacy of their predecessors in the region: the kings of Macedon and their heirs. This short essay is focused upon a hitherto unexplored role of Philip II's palace at Aegae as a possible source of inspiration for the operation, in Greek lands, of the Roman 'constitutional monarchy' of the first emperors.

PALACE AND GOVERNMENT

Much is known of the fascination of Roman generals and emperors with the image of Alexander the Great, but the influence of Macedonian palatial architecture on Roman imperial public buildings has attracted less attention. Concluding a wide-ranging architectural survey of Hellenistic royal palaces, the Danish scholar Inge Nielsen pointed to Roman public as well as private buildings that had adopted Hellenistic palatial features – theatres, fountains, libraries and the imperial halls whose walls were filled with framed marble images of members of the imperial family set among deities or personifications of personal virtues.[1] Nielsen rightly insisted on understanding the Hellenistic palace as an architectural expression of the ruler's relationship to his or her subjects. She drew an important distinction between the 'national monarchy' of the earlier kings of Macedon, most notably Philip II, and the 'personal monarchies' of Alexander and his successors.[2] The former's palace at Aegae was, if a separate, elevated unit, clearly part of the city plan (figs. 258–259). In contrast, Alexander and his successors tended to occupy larger, self-contained palaces set on islands or in areas of the city that could easily be closed off from the populace in times of insecurity.

Exploring the political relationship between Philip II and his subjects, the historian Miltiades Hatzopoulos has shown how Macedonian cities had already adopted some democratic institutions from Athens and its northern Greek territories.[3] A key quality of a successful constitutional ruler is accessibility:

Fig. 258 Aerial photo of Aegae showing, from top to bottom, the palace, the theatre and the sanctuary of Eukleia

Philip II was praised for his personal interest in his own community (Plutarch, *Demosthenes*, 42.6), while Alexander was judged remote, having learned oriental royal habits (Phylarchos, *Early Greek Historians* 81, Fragment 41; Aelian, *Historical Miscellany* 9.3).

In this respect the later designation of the first Roman emperor Augustus as *princeps rei publicae restitutae* (first citizen of the restored republic) is significant. The title suggests the accessibility of the emperor to his subjects, but in practice the *princeps* received vast numbers of delegations and individual petitions, ruled over huge swathes of territory, and could not be everywhere at once. This is why imperial portrait statues had such great significance in Rome as in distant provinces acting as surrogates for the imperial person – we are told, for example, of petitions for justice and clemency nailed to a statue of Julius Caesar in his forum at Rome.[4] Imperial activities such as the dispensing of justice and the regulation of market prices were managed at a distance from the centre of empire by imperially appointed delegates operating in recognisably Roman buildings.

To Romans conquering Greek lands in the later centuries of the Republic, or maintaining the eastern frontier in the later empire, Alexander the Great offered a military model of vision, purpose and lasting glory. However, in the years following the establishment of the Augustan peace in 27 BC, the more consensual monarchy of Alexander's father, Philip, suggested a viable model of how to rule in peacetime. And it was the form of Philip's palace, not his personal image or his name, that apparently inspired a type of early imperial Roman building whose role might loosely be described as 'connecting the Roman emperor to his Greek subjects' – there is much scholarly debate on the exact nature of these structures.

KAISAREIA: ALEXANDRIA

One Roman building not listed by Nielsen as heir to the Hellenistic palace style is the *kaisareion* (Latin *caesareum*), of which the Alexandrian prototype, begun by Julius Caesar and completed, after his assassination in 44 BC, by the last Ptolemaic ruler of Egypt, Caesar's lover Cleopatra VII, is vividly described by Philo, *de legatione ad Gaium* 22, 150–1 (an address to the Roman Emperor Caligula, AD 37–41):

> *Temples, propylaia (monumental gateways), sanctuaries, porticoes bear witness thereof, so that all cities, be they old or new, which display magnificent works, are surpassed in beauty and grandeur by the kaisareia, and above all by the kaisareion in Alexandria. No sanctuary is comparable to the so-called sebasteion, the temple dedicated to Caesar Epibaterios, opposite the harbours with safe anchorages, built to a great height, of a very great size, very conspicuous and being such that nothing like it exists anywhere else. It is full of paintings and sculptures and decorated all round with silver and gold. It is a very large enclosure adorned with porticoes,*

Fig. 259 Philip II's palace within
the plan of Aegae – buildings
excavated so far are shown in
yellow. All other buildings are
imaginary

*libraries, club rooms, gardens, propylaia, courtyards under the open sky
and provided with everything that could contribute to value and beauty.*

Though the silver, gold and objects of value and beauty have long since
disappeared from the site, all of the Alexandrian enclosure's architectural features – porticoes, libraries, club rooms (if they may be equated to the banqueting suites that were such a striking feature of the palace at Aegae), gardens,
propylaia, courtyards under the open sky, and indeed a sanctuary to Heracles,
the legendary ancestor of the Macedonian royal family – have been recognised
in the excavations of the Palace of Philip II at Aegae (fig. 267).[5] The *kaisareion*
at Alexandria has not been excavated, though its urban location is certain.
Similar projects were begun by Caesar at Antioch, now in south-east Turkey,
and in Athens (see below). This style of building was also adopted in Rome, a
city also transformed by the experience of empire.

KAISAREIA: CYRENE

After Octavian (later Augustus) conquered Egypt in the aftermath of the
battle of Actium, fought against Antony and Cleopatra off the western coast of
Greece in 31 BC, another *kaisareion* was constructed in the city of Cyrene, now
in eastern Libya, by the Roman army commander Marcus Sufenas Proculus
with later work by Gaius Rubellius Blandus.[6] Here a large open enclosure of

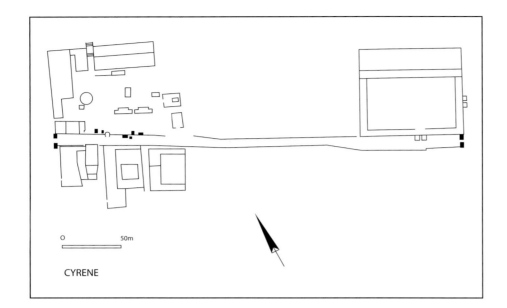

Fig. 260 Plan of the *caesareum* (right) and the old Agora (left) at Cyrene

almost square plan, probably converted from a Hellenistic *gymnasium*, was entered by two grand propylaia (figs. 260–262). In the reign of the emperor Nero (AD 54–68) a basilica was constructed on its north side. Under Nero's Flavian successors the basilica was used to dispense justice. This building was certainly a priority for the Roman imperial authorities to reconstruct at their expense after the disastrous Jewish revolt of AD 115/16. In the following years a temple to the god Dionysus was erected in the open courtyard, and a statue of Hadrian was set up in the basilica's apse, but it is not known where, if anywhere within the precinct, the earlier emperors were venerated. In Cyrene, as in Athens, the old Greek civic agora took on a religious aspect, while some, at least, of its administrative functions appear to have moved to the *kaisareion*. The text of an inscription found in the basilica attests regulation of the activities of businessmen.

Fig. 261 The *caesareum* at Cyrene (view from the south)

Fig. 262 Detail showing the Latin inscription above the monumental entrance

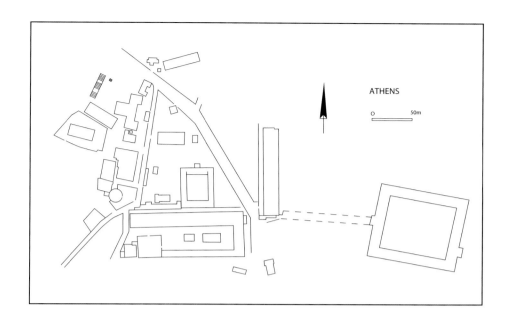

Fig. 263 Plan of the 'Roman' (right) and 'old' Agoras (left) at Athens

Fig. 264 View of the gate of Athena *Archegetis* at the west end of the Roman Agora at Athens. To the right, the edict of Hadrian regulating the sale of oil and fish

A NEW MARKET FOR ATHENS

In Athens, Caesar pledged funds to build a new market, which was not actually constructed until the reign of Augustus, because of the city's vacillating relations with Caesar and other powerful Romans in a protracted period of bitter civil war. Like the *caesareum* at Cyrene, this was an open court, almost square in plan and edged with a colonnade, with two elaborate propylaia dedicated to the city's patron goddess, Athena, the ruling emperor Augustus and his grandson, Lucius Caesar, and the city's patron goddess, Athena *Archegetis* (figs. 263–264). The 'Roman Agora' clearly served as a market, with evidence from the Hadrianic era for imperial regulation of the prices of fish and oil.

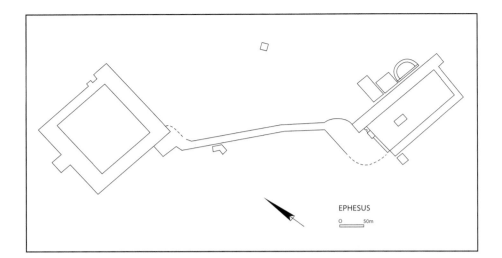

Fig. 265 Plan of the Tetragonal (left) and old Agoras (right) at Ephesus

Fig. 266 View of the gate of Mithridates and Mazaeus from the Agora of Ephesus

Michael Hoff has argued for the presence of a *sebasteion* (a sanctuary for worshipping the emperors) within an open basilica to the east of the market, dedicated to Athena and Augustus' successors in the middle years of the first century AD.[7] In the second century AD, the emperor Hadrian added a second enclosure of similar, if more elaborate design, immediately to the north. This provided the cultural delights of libraries, gardens and club rooms enumerated by Philo in his description of the *kaisareion* at Alexandria and missing from the earlier market. The most immediate inspiration for the design of Hadrian's Library is to be found in Rome, in the Forum of Peace.

A NEW MARKET FOR EPHESUS

In the wealthy city of Ephesus in the Roman province of Asia (western Turkey), a huge colonnaded enclosure was built, its square plan reflected in its modern name of 'tetragonal Agora' (fig. 265–266). Like the buildings in Cyrene and Athens, this too had a commercial function. It was entered via an elaborately decorated gate mimicking a Roman triumphal arch and was originally intended for processional use. The gate was dedicated to Augustus by Mithridates and Mazaeus, two wealthy former slaves of the imperial family. Statues of Augustus, Livia and Tiberius were erected upon it, just as the gate at Athens bore an image of the emperor's heir Lucius Caesar, set up by the Athenian people. In Ephesus as in Cyrene and Athens, the 'old Agora' became a 'heritage centre', the focus of expressions of devotion to the new regime.

SHARED FEATURES WITH PHILIP'S PALACE AT AEGAE

The *kaisareion* at Alexandria, as described by Philo, seems particularly close to the palace of Philip at Aegae in its provision of various features and functions. Some distinctive early imperial constructions in key cities in the Greek east share a number of these features:

- an almost square plan of approximately 100m (the tetragonal Agora at Ephesus is notably larger, but Ephesus was built on the grand scale); rooms opening off an open, colonnaded court
- imposing entrances via one or more monumental gates
- an intrusive appearance within the pre-existing urban plan
- a distance or sense of separateness from the rest of the city: the imperial Roman structures had no immediate street link to earlier Greek Agoras
- some religious function associated with the ruling power
- some provision of functions formerly associated with the Greek civic Agora, such as the dispensation of justice, and/or regulation of prices and trading of commodities and goods
- in Athens, the later addition of the 'twin' library given to the city by Hadrian complements the functional market to offer a closer approximation of the range of features and functions of the Macedonian royal palace.

Essentially, the functional enclosures of the early empire delivered Roman oversight of matters formerly administered locally, while offering local citizens a link with the distant emperor and an opportunity to honour him and his family.

Even in late antiquity these enclosures were valued by the imperial authorities and their local agents: for example, in Athens the 'Roman agora' and Hadrian's Library were included in a defensive system built under Probus in the later third century AD. In contrast, the old Athenian agora was not only excluded but deliberately plundered for construction material.

FROM MACEDON TO ROME VIA EGYPT

The *kaisareia* and early imperial markets have appeared to me, as to many other students of Roman architecture in the Greek East, to be Roman intruders in a Greek urban landscape. Nonetheless, inspiration for their design may be sought at Aegae, in the palace expressing the workings of the 'national monarchy' of Philip II's Macedon.

However, by the time Roman *kaisareia* came to be developed, the palace of Philip at Aegae had been destroyed. There must, then, have been surviving Hellenistic Greek buildings to inspire Caesar and his successors. Hellenistic palaces are described and illustrated by Nielsen. The larger of the two palaces built by Eumenes of Pergamon in the second century BC and identified by Nielsen as a 'public or state palace' combines features of the palace at Aegae with the public functions seen in the early imperial structures.[8] However, a striking example is offered by the monumental colonnaded court excavated at Hermopolis Magna in Egypt. This contained a temple built in 246–221 BC and dedicated by the Greek military garrison to the then ruler Ptolemy III and his sister-wife Berenice, descendants of Alexander's general Ptolemy I.[9] It is also worth noting the Macedonian interest in Hermopolis, where Philip III Arrhidaeos built a monumental portico in Egyptian style within the sanctuary of Thoth.[10] Given that the earliest and most illustrious *kaisareion* we know of was developed by Julius Caesar in Cleopatra's Alexandria, the Ptolemaic rulers of Egypt are likely agents of transmission of the functional ideas expressed in the *basileion* of Philip II to the *kaisareia* of early imperial Rome.

Appendix: The palace of Philip II in Aegae

Angeliki Kottaridi

With an area of 12,500sq.m., the palace at Aegae is not only the biggest, but together with the Parthenon, the most important building of Classical Greece. The systematic investigation and detailed documentation of the building, necessary for its conservation and reconstruction – part of a huge effort begun by the 17th Ephorate of Prehistoric and Classical Antiquities in 2007 and continuing within the framework of works co-funded by the European Union – have shown that this unique monument is part of a large building project of Philip II (360–336 BC).

The large-scale landscaping, terracing and building works commenced around the middle of the fourth century BC and were completed by 336 BC, when Philip decided to celebrate in Aegae his omnipotence as leader of all the Greeks. Alongside the main building, the west peristyle was designed to house services such as sanitary facilities, kitchens, storerooms, stables and staff quarters indispensable for the public use of the main palace (fig. 267). The imposing landmark was visible throughout the plain of Macedonia. It was completely destroyed after the battle of Pydna (168 BC) and the abolition of the Macedonian monarchy by the Romans. Until the twentieth century it provided valuable building material of excellent quality for the entire region.

In the two centuries of its life, the royal establishment of Aegae was only altered by the construction of the south external corridor and the partial reconfiguration of the service peristyle. Thus the palace at Aegae, completed before the palace at Pella – which saw many extensions and changes throughout the Hellenistic period – offers the most authentic evidence for the form and function of Macedonian palaces at their peak. A building entirely revolutionary and innovative for its time, the palace created for Philip in Aegae, perhaps by the ingenious architect Pytheos, who also worked on the Mausoleum at Halicarnassus, would become the archetype for all the *basileia* (palace complexes) of the Hellenistic world and beyond.

The palace façade, like that of a temple, faces east. Two impressive two-storey stoas – the first in the history of Greek architecture – with Doric colonnades at ground level and Ionic semi-column pilasters above (figs. 183–184), harmoniously frame the monumental gabled *propylon* (entrance). Equipped with benches to accommodate a large audience and with fittings for tablets which

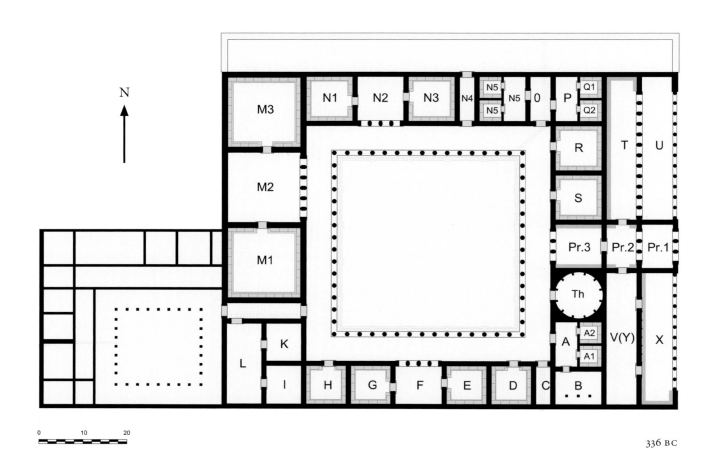

N

0 10 20

336 BC

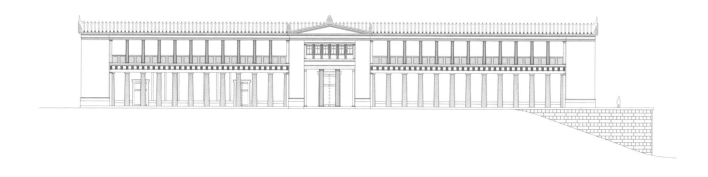

probably publicised laws and decrees, the stoas of the palace were in all likelihood, like the *basileios stoa* in the agora of Athens, the place where the king exercised judicial authority.

From the *propylon* one entered the monumental peristyle – the first in Greek architecture – which with 16 Doric columns on each side represents the geometric and mathematical quintessence of the square. The vast court could accommodate 3,500 people seated. Here select Macedonians gather; the generation that changed the world. The agora, the gathering place for citizens of a democratic city, becomes a court; and the word court acquires a new meaning, synonymous with monarchy.

An important element in the functional organization of the building is the creation of tripartite complexes of two types: the smaller, inward-looking group, inscribed in a square, comprises a rectangular antechamber and two relatively small, square rooms of equal size (e.g. A, A1, A2, P, Q1, Q2, etc.); while the monumental, outward-looking complexes have three large, paratactically arranged spaces, the middle one of which communicates directly with the peristyle through three or five double-sided pillar-columns, forming the antechamber for the other two spaces. These are easily recognised as banqueting rooms (*andrones*). The five-columned antechamber M2 of the large tripartite apartment on the west side, where the largest covered spaces without internal supports of classical architecture are located (room area about 280sq.m.), was, as all the evidence suggests, the throne room. In the well preserved tripartite unit on the south side (E, F, G) the magnificent mosaic floor with flowers and flower-maidens (figs. 182, 269) is situated in room (E), while in room (G) the mosaic with the abduction of Europe has recently been identified.

Next to the propylon, the sacred tholos and the closed complex (A, A1, A2, B), with its small *andrones* and archive, recall the civic idea of a *Prytaneion* (magistrates' hall) but here, the place of the Mother of Gods is taken by *Heracles Patroos*, the father of kings; the mortal son of a god who changed his destiny and through his virtue triumphed over death.

For the palace more than 20,000 cubic meters of poros stone were transported to Aegae from the quarries of Mount Bermion, some 13km distance, with tonnes of valuable timber from the forests of the Pierian mountains. Walls and architectural elements, all worked with astonishing accuracy, were covered with refined marble stucco. Thousands of tiles and decorated antefixes of excellent quality, hundreds of metres of marble inlays and mosaics (about 2,000sq.m. are still preserved, some of which are fine works of art), expensive pigments, bronze and every kind of luxury material were employed to create a whole to satisfy the ruler's ambition. Still, beyond the luxury of its materials, the originality and perfection of the work, the unexpected accomplishments of technology that can be traced at all levels, the most exciting aspect of this unique building remains its ingenious architectural conception.

By combining traditional elements and ground-breaking inventions in such an original way, the brilliant architect of the palace created a building that was clearly shaped and functional but also monumental and impressive. The clarity

Fig. 267 (opposite top) Detailed plan of the palace at Aegae (December 2010)

Fig. 268 (opposite bottom) Elevation showing the monumental entrance to the palace at Aegae with its imposing two-storey façade

of its geometric form was combined with the joy of detail to create a whole of unsurpassed calm and harmony. Everything is subjected to the 'charm of measure.' In its geometry of structure, the quintessence of 'good living' is encapsulated.

The golden Pythagorean triangle 3:4:5 is incorporated in the plan. 4 as a number is either multiplied by itself and its multiples, but is also present as a regular geometric shape (a square). It plays a central role in the architect's calculations. Starting at the centre of the peristyle, the enigmatic sequence of 'Platonic' numbers 1, 2, 3, 4, 9, 8, 27, corresponding to a sequence of inscribed and circumscribed canonical shapes – squares and dodecagons – in concentric circles, seems to define the planning of the building. Then, the ratio 1.6 defines the relation of the height of the storeys and the arrangement of the spaces and also of all other elements, from the heights of different columns to the triglyphs and the metopes and the undercutting of the thresholds.

The number φ, the ratio of beauty or 'divine proportion', is the 'common denominator' that runs through this fascinating building, designed for its enlightened ruler. In it nothing is left to chance. Even the smallest detail obeys the harmony of the world of Pythagoras and conforms to the golden rule that marks the presence of God in the Platonic universe.

An extended article by Angeliki Kottaridi on the palace at Aegae will be published in *History of Macedon,* edited by Robin Lane Fox (forthcoming from E. J. Brill in 2011)

Fig. 269 (below) An intricately decorated floor from banquet hall E

Fig. 270 (opposite) The Lady of Aegae (Cat. nos. 328–339)

List of Exhibits

N.B. An effort has been made to follow the object groupings in the exhibition as closely as possible.

Room 1: The world of the king and his companions at Aegae

Heracles to Alexander

1
Marble statuette of Heracles, having successfully killed the Erymanthian boar, Roman copy of a Greek original, AD 100–200, Ashmolean Museum, AN1928.529 (H: 53cm)

2
Marble portrait of Alexander the Great found near Pella, around 300 BC. Archaeological Museum of Pella, ΓΛ 15 (H: 32cm)

Early beginnings

Two bronze swords from the area of Makedonis, 1450–1375 BC
3
BM 1040 (L: 47cm)
4
BM 1041 (L: 53cm)

Two bronze spearheads from the area of Makedonis, 1350–1200 BC
5
BM 1043 (L: 23cm)
6
BM 1042 (L: 16cm)

Clay Mycenaean *alabastra* (aromatic-oil containers) from a pithos burial in the area of Aegae, 1200–1100 BC
7
BΠ 3716 (H: 8.6cm)
8
BΠ 3717 (H: 8.2cm)
9
BΠ 3718 (H: 7.4cm)
10
BΠ 3719 (H: 8.6cm)

11
BΠ 4722 (H: 8.3cm)

12
Clay Mycenaean-style *alabastron* from the tumuli cemetery at Aegae, 1100–1000 BC, BΠ 3031 (H: 14cm)

13
Bronze sword (Naue II) from the tumuli cemetery, 1100–1000 BC, BM 4074 (L: 72cm, W: 24cm at hilt)

14
Iron sword (Naue II) from the tumuli cemetery, 950–850 BC, BM 3723 (L: 110cm)

Two iron spearheads from the tumuli cemetery, 1000–900 BC
15
BM 3192 (L: 27.3cm)
16
BM 3327 (L: 30.9cm)

17
Iron arrowhead from an Iron Age burial in the tumuli cemetery, BM 5105 (L: 5cm, W: 2cm)

18
Iron dagger from an Iron Age burial in the tumuli cemetery, BM 2867 (L: 12.5cm)

19
Three whetstones with suspension holes, 1000–700 BC, BΛ 1620 (L: 8.9cm, W: 3.5cm), BΛ 1688 (L: 8.8cm, W: 2.7cm), BΛ 1689 (L: 9.6cm, W: 2.3cm)

20
Clay cup, 10th century BC, BΠ 3509 (H: 9cm)

Men at war and at court: the making of the kingdom of Macedon

21
Attic black-figure clay 'Sianna' cup (*kylix*) with men-at-arms and riders, 575–550 BC, BΠ 5724 (H: 14cm)

Offerings at the cremation of a member of the royal family from the Temenids' cluster (nos. 22–29), 540–530 BC:

Two iron spearheads
22
BM 1049 (L: 67.3cm)
23
BM 1050 (L: 55.6cm)

Two iron javelin points
24
BM 1053 (L: 35.2cm)
25
BM 1054 (L: 35.5cm)

26
Iron silver-riveted sword with ivory-lined hilt, 550–530 BC, BM 1048 (L: 58cm)

27
Iron sword (*kopis*) with a forward-curving blade and anatomical handle for better grip, BM 1051 (L: 48.7cm)

28
Iron dagger/knife with curved blade, BM 1052 (L: 22.3cm)

29
Bronze 'Illyrian'-type helmet damaged by the fire of the funeral pyre, BM 1060 (H: 21cm, W: 20cm)

Clay Corinthian *aryballoi* (aromatic-oil containers), 6th century BC
30
ВП 3800 (H: 5.7cm)
31
ВП 3801 (H: 5.2cm)
32
ВП 927 (H: 6.4cm)
33
ВП 929 (H: 6.2cm)

34
Clay Corinthian *aryballos* (aromatic-oil container) with men-at-arms, 6th century BC, ВП 928 (H: 6.7cm)

35
Bronze 'Illyrian'-type helmet, 550–530 BC, BM 3180 (H: 20cm, W: 25cm)

Grave offerings from the royal burial cluster of the Temenids (nos. 36–42):

36
Clay black-figure cup (*kylix*), 6th century BC, ВП 285 (H: 3.7cm, W: 11cm)

37
Clay figurine fragment of a seated goddess, late 6th/early 5th century BC, ВП 942 (H: 6.2cm, W: 4.1cm)

38
Clay head, fragment from a figurine, 6th century BC, ВП 940 (H: 4.2cm, W: 3.4cm)

39
Clay figurine of a seated goddess, 6th century BC, ВП 926 (H: 15cm)

40
Clay 'apple', 6th century BC, ВП 930 (H: 12.2cm, W: 6.2cm)

41
Clay figurine of Heracles, 550–530 BC, ВП 939 (H: 8cm, W: 5.2cm)

42
Clay figurine of twin belly-demons, 550–530 BC, ВП 338 (H: 10.5cm)

43
Iron sword (*kopis* or *machaira*), 550–530 BC, BM 3182 (L: 54.8cm)

44
Iron dagger, 550–530 BC, BM 2506 (L: 13.2cm)

Offerings at the cremation of a member of the royal family from the Temenids' cluster, early 5th century BC (nos. 45–49):

45
A pair of iron leaf-shaped spearheads, BM 1071–1072 (L: 31.8cm and 32.1cm respectively)

Two iron swords
46
BM 1070 (L: 52.3cm)
47
BM 1073 (L: 55.5cm)

48
Iron dagger with curved blade, BM 1257 (L: 11.2cm)

49
Gold finger ring, BM 2104 (Diam.: 2.2cm)

Clay Corinthian *aryballoi* (aromatic-oil containers), 6th century BC
50
ВП 3799 (H: 7.5cm)
51
ВП 3814 (H: 13.7cm)
52
ВП 4236 (H: 13.1cm)
53
ВП 3845 (H: 5.7cm)

54
Clay black-figure column *krater* (wine mixing bowl) showing a four-horse chariot with warriors going to battle, 540–530 BC, ВП 4198 (H: 28.6cm)

55
Iron sword (*kopis* or *machaira*) with organic remains from its sheath, late 5th century BC, BM 2398 (L: 51.5cm)

56
Iron sword, BM 5029 (L: 55cm)

57
Iron *sarissa* (long pike) consisting of the butt, middle rib and head respectively, 4th century BC, BM 3016 (L: 44.6cm), BM 3014 (L: 10.5cm), BM 3015 (L: 50.5cm)

58
Iron stylus, 340–330 BC, BM 2300 (L: 10cm)

59
Clay black-glaze inkwell, late 4th century BC, ВП 2299 (H: 3.7cm, Diam.: 5.8cm)

Grave offerings from the tomb of a member of the royal family in the Temenids' cluster, 430–420 BC (nos. 60–62):

60
Gold roundels decorated with stars, BM 2094–2095 (L: 2.5–2.6cm)

61
Gold strip depicting a combat between two warriors, BM 2107 (H: 3.9cm, W: 5cm)

62
Bronze Medusa head, an ornament from a cuirass, BM 1108 (H: 4cm, W: 3.2cm)

63

Bronze finger ring with a representation of the goddess Athena, 4th century BC, BM 2395 (L: 1.5cm)

64

Bronze finger ring showing a man, 380–350 BC, BM 5085 (L: 2.2cm, Diam.: 1.8cm)

65

Iron finger ring showing Heracles killing the Lernaean Hydra, 4th century BC, BM 1103 (L: 2cm)

Two iron *sarissa* heads, 4th century BC
66
BM 3010 (L: 49cm)
67
BM 4997 (L: 47cm)

Two iron spearheads
68
BM 2361 (L: 32cm)
69
BM 5030 (L: 51.5cm)

70

Iron spearbutt, 4th century BC, AE 3013 (L: 14.2cm)

71

Iron ballista arrowhead, 4th century BC, BM 3013 (L: 14cm)

Two bronze strigils, late 5th century BC
72
BM 1800 (L: 17.2cm)
73
BM 1160 (L: 23.2cm)

74

Iron strigil, 4th century BC, BM 1799 (L: 23cm)

Two clay black-glaze squat *lekythoi* (aromatic-oil containers), 4th century BC

75
BΠ 2405 (H: 10.1cm)
76
BΠ 2193 (H: 8cm)

Clay squat *lekythoi* decorated with a net pattern, 4th century BC
77
BΠ 2194 (H: 7.2cm)
78
BΠ 2886 (H: 13.2cm)
79
BΠ 2401 (H: 5.3cm)
80
BΠ 2971 (H: 8cm)

81

Clay miniature Panathenaic *amphora*, 4th century BC, BΠ 2465 (H: 8.3cm)

82

Clay Attic red-figure cup (*skyphos*) – a man training a horse, 430–420 BC, BΠ 968 (H: 8.1cm, W: 16.5cm)

Tomb markers (stelai)

83

Marble funerary relief *stele* crowned with a pediment and depicting a Macedonian wearing a *petasos* (hat), a short *chiton* (tunic) and the Macedonian *chlamys* (short cloak). With his right hand he is holding two spears and with his left a dove. A scabbard with a sword is placed around his waist. 430–420 BC, BΛ 17 (H: 109cm, W: 45cm, thickness: 7cm).

84

Marble funerary *stele* painted with a red band. Two rows of text appear above and under the band with the names of the dead men, reading: 'Xenokratis, son of Pierion' and 'Drykalos, son of Pierion', 4th century BC, BΛ 29 (H: 107cm, W: 44cm, max thickness: 11.5cm)

Marble frieze from a monument found in the area of Aegae

85

Marble relief frieze showing a chariot-racing scene, a feature of funeral games, late 4th century BC. Beroia Museum (L: 138cm, H: 39cm)

Hunter and boar from the area of the gymnasium of Aegae

86

Marble group of hunter, dog and wild boar, 340–320 BC, BΛ 1703 (H [hunter]: 155cm; L [boar]: 140cm)

From the tomb of Philip II – The king as high-priest, 336 BC

87

Silver-gilt adjustable diadem. The larger part is decorated with incised lozenges. Its two ends fit into a smaller section at the back, decorated in relief with the ends of a knot. A unique object, it represents the dual role of the king as political/ military and religious leader. BM 2632 (Diam.: 25cm)

88

Bronze pan-shaped vessel (*patera*), the handle of which ends in the shape of a ram's head. BM 2579 (H: 7.3cm, max L: 43.3cm, rim Diam.: 24.2cm)

89

Bronze wine jug (*oinochoe*) decorated with a female head (maenad) in relief. BM 2576 (H: 23.6cm)

90

Bronze tripod stand with feet ending in lion's claws. The inscription on the rim ('I am from the games of the Argive Hera') suggests that this object was a prize won in the games at Argos in southern Greece organized in honour of the goddess Hera. Dating from about 430–420 BC, it was a cherished heirloom by the time of its deposition in the grave. BM 2626 (max H: 60cm)

From the tomb of King Philip II, 336 BC

91
Gold Medusa-head, one of two found in the tomb. This gold ornament would originally have been attached to the linen cuirass of the king. According to legend, anyone who dared to look in the eyes of Medusa turned into stone. BM 2630 (H: 3.6cm, W: 3.5cm)

92
Gold twin pin (buckle) with case and chain, BM 2638 (L: 21.5cm)

93
Bronze greaves, BM 2589 (Right: L: 42cm; Left: L: 41.8cm)

94
Iron spearhead, BM 2620 (L: 45.5cm)

95
Iron spearhead decorated with a gold strip, BM 1681 (strip L: 8.1cm, W: 4.8cm), BM 1680 (head: L: 38cm)

96
Five arrowheads made of an alloy of copper, tin and lead, BM 2653 (L: 3cm)

97
Two iron swords, one of which is decorated on the hilt with a heavy, solid cast-gold ornament imitating acanthus leaves. BM 2617 (L: 70cm, W: 11.2cm on the hilt), BM 2618 (L: 60.5cm)

From the tomb of King Alexander IV, about 310 BC

98
Iron spearhead decorated with a gold strip, BM 2613 (L: 31cm)

99
Iron strigil for scraping oil and dirt from the body, BM 2605 (L: 19.7cm, W: 2.9cm)

100
Clay pseudo-Cypriot *amphora*, ΒΠ 6303 (H: 25cm, Diam.: 14.5cm)

Golden wreath from the area of the agora and the sanctuary of Eukleia, 325–300 BC

101
Gold wreath with oak leaves and acorns found with the cremated remains of a young man (Diam.: 18.5cm, 16.5cm)

The Royal Funeral Pyres

Remains of Archaic funeral pyres from the royal burial plot of the Temenids

---

102
Bronze cauldron, 550–530 BC, BM 5100 (H: 37cm, W: 54cm)

103
Local clay cauldron (urn) with an inverted cup as a lid, cremation burial, early 5th century BC, ΒΠ 310 (H: 43cm [with lid], W: 37cm)

Four iron twin pins, mid-6th |century BC
104
BM 5069 (L: 18cm)

105
BM 1058 (L: 5cm), BM 1059 (L: 5cm), BM 1207 (L: 19cm)

106
Iron objects (harness fragments), 550–530 BC, BM 1055–1057, BM 1064–1065, BM 1067–1068 (L: 4–11cm)

107
Iron nails, 550–530 BC, BM 1063 (L: 4cm); BM 5076; BM 1215 (L: 4cm)

108
Iron pin fragments, mid-6th century BC, BM 2171–2172, BM 1209, BM 1212, BM 1061–1062 (L: 2.7–8cm)

109
Iron strip and two bronze objects with spiral endings, 550–530 BC, BM 5078, BM 5079–5080 (L: 9.2 and 8.1cm respectively)

110
Iron object, perhaps a spatula, 550–530 BC, BM 1162 (L: 5cm)

111
Bronze wire, 550–530 BC, BM 1069

112
Bronze fragments and iron strips, mid-6th century BC, BM 5077, BM 5081, BM 1210

113
Bronze fragments, 550–530 BC, BM 5072, BM 5074–5075, BM 2173

114
Clay water jug (*hydria*) fragments and other sherds, mid-6th century BC, ΒΠ 6292–6294

115
Clay *amphora* fragments, mid-6th century BC, ΒΠ 6295

116
Restored rim and part of the handles and bodies of four clay *amphoras*, mid-6th century BC, ΒΠ 6470–6473

117
Clay jug (*olpe*), mid-6th century BC, ΒΠ 3009 (H: 17.5cm)

118
One-handled clay jug, mid-6th century BC, ΒΠ 2441 (H: 12cm)

119
Clay fragments from three *omphalos phialai* (bowls) for pouring offerings to the gods, mid-6th century BC, ΒΠ 6285–6287

120
Iron round object with nails inside, early 5th century BC, BM 5068 (Diam.: 3.5cm)

121
Bronze helmet fragments, early 5th century BC, BM 5073

Remains from the funeral pyre of Queen Eurydice, 344–343 BC

122
Bronze doorknob (*roptron*) in the shape of a lion's head, BM 5082 (W: 18cm); bronze rivets, BM 5092–5095 and bronze nail-heads and iron nails from the wooden funeral house in which Queen Eurydice was cremated, BM 1–761 (L: 2–20cm)

123
Clay Panathenaic *amphora* sherds dating to the archonship of Lykiskos, ΒΠ 982–1258 (H: 2–80.7cm), ΒΠ 2521–2547 (H: 2.6–15.7cm)

124
Bronze fragments, BM 5070–5071, BM 5083

125
Sherds from pseudo-Cypriot *amphoras*, ΒΠ 6391–6451

126
Clay sherds from various vessels, ΒΠ 6306–6390

ROOM 2: QUEENS, PRINCESSES AND HIGH-PRIESTESSES

Insignia of religious authority from female burials of the Early Iron Age, 1000–700 BC

127
Bronze diadem decorated with points and circles, the central one inscribing a cross that may represent the sun ('cosmic circle'), 9th century BC, BM 4489 (Diam.: 19.5cm, W: 7.5cm)

Two bronze staff heads decorated with three rows of double-axes
128
BM 4073 (L: 17cm, W: 9cm)
129
BM 4079 (L: 21cm, W: 9cm)

130
Bronze fusiform pendant crowned with a horse, BM 4081 (H: 9.4cm)

131
Bronze fusiform pendant, BM 4080 (H: 5.8cm)

132
Bronze fusiform pendant with a bird-headed top, BM 5028 (H: 5.8cm)

133
Bronze pendant, BM 4082 (L: 4.4cm, W: 1.8cm)

134
Bronze pendant with globular body, BM 5043 (H: 4.8cm)

135
Bronze pendant crowned with horns, BM 4841 (H: 5.8cm)

136
Bronze pendant, BM 4839 (H: 7.1cm)

137
Bronze anchor-like object, BM 4723 (W: 10.6cm)

138
Bronze cauldron-shaped pendant, BM 4725 (H: 5.3cm)

139
Bronze pendant, BM 5063 (H: 4.1cm)

Bronze 'wheel'-shaped ornaments perhaps representing a 'cosmic circle'
140
BM 4906 (Diam.: 3.2cm)
141
BM 4907 (Diam.: 5.1cm)

142
Bronze globular pendant, BM 3178 (L: about 6cm)

Offerings to the gods

143
Clay figurine of a belly-demon, 540–530 BC, ΒΠ 4258 (H: 7.3cm)

144
Clay figurine of a twin belly-demon, 540–530 BC, ΒΠ 4259 (H: 9.3cm)

145
Clay figurine of a seated goddess, 550–530 BC, ΒΠ 1858 (H: 12.2cm, W: 5.2cm)

146
Clay dove, late 6th century BC, ΒΠ 3330 (H: 8.3cm)

Clay female busts, 5th–4th century BC
147
ΒΠ 2667, ΒΠ 2666 (H: 12cm, W: 8.6cm)
148
ΒΠ 2369 (H: 11.5cm, W: 10.5cm)
149
ΒΠ 1863 (H: 13.3cm, W: 9cm)
150
ΒΠ 1860 (H: 13.2cm, W: 7.9cm)

Two bronze boss-centred dishes or bowls (omphalos phialai) with embossed lance-shaped decoration, late 5th century BC
151
BM 3111 (H: 2.3cm, Diam.: 11.5cm)
152
BM 2883 (Diam.: 13cm)

153
Bronze boss-centred plain dish or bowl (omphalos phiale), BM 3397 (H: 4.5cm, W: 17.9cm)

Clay figurines found in the burial of a queen, about 350–325 BC
154
Hades and Persephone banqueting, ΒΠ 316 (H: 14cm, W: 15cm)
155
Couple embracing, ΒΠ 221 (H: 13.2cm, W: 6.8cm)
156
Two boys (Dioskouroi? – the heavenly twins, Castor and Pollux), ΒΠ 317 (H: 14cm, W: 9.5cm)

157
Seated goddess, ΒΠ 331 (H: 18.5cm, W: 10cm)
158
Two female figures, ΒΠ 324 (H: 18cm, W: 12cm)
159
The god Pan, ΒΠ 333 (H: 10cm, W: 6cm)
160
Comic actor, ΒΠ 332 (H: 10cm, W: 4cm)
161
Female bust, ΒΠ 328 (H: 13cm, W: 10.3cm)
162
Female busts, ΒΠ 329 (H: 14.3cm, W: 10.1cm), ΒΠ 335 (H: 24cm, W: 16.5cm)
163
Female bust, ΒΠ 334 (H: 22.5cm, W: 18cm)
164
Female busts, ΒΠ 336 (H: 17.5cm, W: 16.5cm)
165
Female figurine, ΒΠ 320 (H: 20cm, W: 11.5cm)
166
Female figurine, ΒΠ 321 (H: 18cm, W: 11.5cm)
167
Female figurine, ΒΠ 318 (H: 25.5cm, W: 10cm)
168
Female figurine, ΒΠ 327 (H: 19.5cm, W: 10cm)

169
Gold leaf-shaped inscribed band: ΦΙΛΙΣΤΗ ΦΕΡΣΕΦΟΝΗΙ ΧΑΙΡΕΙΝ ('Philiste to Persephone, Rejoice!'), 4th century BC, BM 4894 (L: 3.6cm, W: 1cm)

Marble heads from the sanctuary of Eukleia
_____

170
Marble head of a young female, 340–330 BC, ΒΛ 1702 (H: 37cm)

171
Marble head of a youth, 340–330 BC, ΒΛ 1701 (H: 34cm)

172
Marble table foot decorated with an incised scene of wild animals, 4th century BC, ΒΛ 1700 (H: 51cm, W [above]: 13cm, W [below]: 10cm, L: 81cm).

Life-size clay heads found in the tomb of a queen (burial ΛΙΙΙ), about 480 BC
_____

Twenty-six life-size clay heads were found in this tomb. Two of them belong to demons with accentuated, almost caricature-like facial characteristics. The rest most probably depict the Great Goddesses (Persephone and Demeter). The heads were originally placed on wooden poles forming statues (*xoana*). They were used in an enigmatic burial ritual and then they were deliberately destroyed and thrown into the pit of the tomb of the queen, wife of Alexander I.
173
Female head, ΒΠ 106 (H: 32cm, W: 21cm)
174
Female head, ΒΠ 120 (H: 31.2cm, W: 20cm)
175
Male head, ΒΠ 128 (H: 31.2cm, W: 19.4cm)
176
Male head, ΒΠ 130 (H: 31.3cm, W: 21cm)
177
Female head, ΒΠ 131 (H: 31cm, W: 18cm)
178
Female head, ΒΠ 119 (H: 31cm, W: 20cm)
179
Female head, ΒΠ 124 (H: 31cm, W: 20cm)

180
Female head, ВΠ 126 (H: 29cm,
W: 18cm)

The Queens' Cluster
Burial ΛI, about 540–530 BC
___

181
Gold roundels with wild animals
and embossed rosettes, and gold
strips with embossed decoration,
BM 2121–2132 (L: 2.2–6.3cm),
BM 2146–2148 (L: 3.9–4.1cm),
BM 2154 (L: 23.4cm, W: 2.5cm)

182
Gold vessel-shaped pendant,
BM 2159 (H: 1.9cm, Diam.: 1.3cm)

183
Silver pin crowned with a relief
rosette, BM 1995 (L: 3.8cm)

184
Four iron pins, BM 5064 (L: 18.4cm),
BM 5065 (L: 8.9cm), BM 5066
(L: 4.5cm), BM 5067 (L: 7.2cm)

185
Iron tripod stand, BM 2859
(H: 25.3cm, Diam.: 29.3cm)

186
Bronze tripod stand with legs ending
in lion's paws, BM 1849 (H: 6cm,
Diam.: 14.5cm)

187
Bronze cauldron, BM 2169
(H: 28.5cm, max Diam.: 33cm)

188
Bronze basin, BM 2170 (H: 11cm,
max Diam.: 31.5cm)

189
Clay figurines of *himation*-clad
kouroi (young men), ВΠ 93 (H:
18cm), ВΠ 94 (H: 19.5cm)

190
Clay figurines of *korai* (young
women), ВΠ 95 (H: 14cm), ВΠ 96
(H: 12cm)

191
Clay figurines of seated goddesses,
ВΠ 97–98 (H: 14cm)

192
Clay group of felines attacking deer,
ВΠ 99 (H: 8.5cm, W: 18cm), ВΠ 100
(H: 8.7cm, W: 15cm)

193
Clay Corinthian jug with cut-away
neck, ВΠ 101 (H: 26cm)

194
Clay black-figure aromatic-oil
container (*plemochoe*), ВΠ 104
(H: 10cm, body Diam.: 16.2cm)

195
Clay Corinthian aromatic-oil
container (*exaleiptron*), ВΠ 105
(H: 6.6cm, body Diam.: 17.4cm)

196
Clay Attic cup (Kassel type
kylix), ВΠ 102 (max H: 9cm,
max W: 24.8cm)

197
Clay Attic black-figure 'band cup'
(*kylix*), ВΠ 103 (max H: 10.5cm,
max W: 25.5cm)

Burial ΛII: The Lady of Aegae,
about 500 BC
___

198
Iron tripod stand, BM 3395
(H: 22.8cm, Diam.: 21.5cm)

199
Bronze cauldron, BM 5098
(H: 21.5cm, Diam.: 30cm)

200
Bronze jug, BM 2295 (H: 20.5cm)

201
Silver boss-centred dish (*omphalos
phiale*) bearing on the underside
an inscription in the dative case
(*ΠΕΠΕΡΙΑΣΙ*) showing that the
dish was used to make offerings
to the gods. BM 2855 (H: 3.7cm,
Diam.: 19.5cm)

202
Iron cosmetics container
with an ornate bronze tripod
base (*exaleiptron*), BM 3977
(Diam.: 19cm, max H: 13cm)

203
Iron model of a four-wheeled wagon,
originally covered with thin gold
foil, BM 2167 (L: 29.5cm, W: 9cm,
H: 9.5cm)

204
Iron spits with thin gold foil,
BM 2858 (Largest fragment: 16cm
long)

205
Clay *amphora*, ВΠ 269 (H: 27cm)

Clay female *protomes* (head and
neck)
206
ВΠ 931 (H: 18cm, W: 11.5cm,
thickness: 8.5cm)
207
ВΠ 932 (H: 17.5cm, W: 12.5cm,
thickness: 8.5cm)
208
ВΠ 933 (H: 17cm, W: 12.5cm,
thickness: 8.5cm)
209
ВΠ 934 (H: 17cm, W: 12cm,
thickness: 8.5cm)
210
ВΠ 341 (H: 15cm, W: 10cm)
211
ВΠ 342 (H: 16.7cm, W: 12cm)

212
BΠ 343 (H: 16.5cm, W: 12.5cm)

Burial ΛIII, about 480 BC

213
Gold strips and discs with embossed decoration (dress ornaments), BM 1991 (L: 6.5cm, W: 3.3cm), BM 1977–1990 (L: 1.9–4cm)

214
Gold seed-shaped pendant, BM 1976 (L: 2.1cm)

215
Bronze handle from a pan-shaped vessel (*patera*) decorated with a *kouros* (young man) raising his arms, BM 2857 (H: 14cm, W: 9cm)

216
Clay figurine of a crouching satyr, BΠ 337 (H: 8cm)

217
Two clay female *protomes*, BΠ 340 (max W: 12.3cm, max H: 16.5cm), BΠ 2647 (max W: 5.7cm, max H: 8.6cm)

Burial ΛIV, about 470–460 BC

218
Gold strips and gold roundels decorated with rosettes, gorgoneia (the face of Medusa), guilloche and the star, BM 2145 (L: 4cm), BM 1953–1954 (L: 1.6cm), BM 1955–1958 (L: 3cm), BM 1962–1964 (L: 0.8–0.9cm), BM 2096 (L: 1.5cm)

219
Gold bead, BM 2118 (Diam.: 1.2cm)

220
Iron tripod stand, BM 2860 (H: 19cm, Diam.: 24cm)

221
Bronze cauldron (*lebes*), BM 5099 (H: 19cm, Diam.: 30cm)

222
Bronze basin (*lekanis*), BM 1851 (H: 9cm, Diam.: 26cm)

223
Clay Attic red-figure *pelike* by the 'Hermonax painter' showing Poseidon chasing Aithra, BΠ 344 (H: 34.3cm, W: 26.5cm)

Burial K1, about 430–420 BC

224
Part of a necklace with gold beads, gold rosettes, gold pendants and gold chain, BM 1960 (Diam.: 5cm), BM 1961 (Diam.: 7cm), BM 1965 (L: 1.9cm), BM 1966 (L: 1.5cm), BM 1968 (L: 9cm), BM 1969 (L: 5.3cm), BM 1970 (L: 5.5cm), BM 1971 (L: 3.7cm)

225
Gold bow-shaped brooch (*fibula*), BM 1959 (max W: 3cm)

226
Bronze pyxis, BM 1850 (H: 6.5cm, Diam.: 9.5cm)

227
Bronze cauldron handle, BM 1859 (L: 6.5cm, W: 3cm)

228
Silver cup (*kylix*) handle, BM 1867 (L: 5.3cm, W: 5.2cm)

229
Silver lion claw, probably the foot of a vessel, BM 1967 (H: 2cm, W: 4cm)

230
Two bronze *omphalos phialai* (boss-centred dishes), BM 1848, BM 5084 (H: 3.5cm, Diam.: 13cm)

231
Bronze undecorated dish (*phiale*), BM 2792 (Diam.: 16.4cm)

232
Bronze spindle-hook, BM 1115 (L: 4cm)

Two marble *lekythoi* (aromatic-oil containers) both with traces of paint. Bands of bright red and deep purple decorate different parts of the body, which at mid-height was encircled with an olive branch.
233
BΛ 45 (H: 24.5cm)
234
BΛ 46 (H: 27cm)

235
Marble perfume container (*plemochoe*). Traces of a leaf ornament, painted in deep purple on the lid, suggest that this object was originally intricately decorated. BΛ 48 (H: 18cm, max W: 19.5cm)

236
Alabaster *alabastron* (perfume flask), BΛ 53 (H: 40.8cm)

Two ostrich eggshell perfumed-oil containers. Ostrich eggs probably arrived in Greece from Egypt or the Levant. Dark blue paint is still preserved on the surface of the ostrich egg depicting bands and a multi-petalled blossoming rosette.
237
BO 1422 (H: 16cm)
238
BO 1423 (H: 15cm)

239
Clay Panathenaic *amphora*, BΠ 286 (H: 56cm, max W: 32cm)

240
Clay black-glaze pointed *amphoriskos* (perfume vessel), BΠ 298 (H: 19cm)

241
Clay red-figure *askos* (perfume vessel) decorated with griffins, ΒΠ 297 (H: 6.9cm)

242
Clay Attic red-figure squat *lekythos*, ΒΠ 299 (H: 20.5cm, W: 12cm)

243
Clay female bust, ΒΠ 339 (H: 16.5cm, W: 12.6cm)

Clay Attic white-ground *lekythoi* (aromatic-oil containers) of the Woman Painter and his followers decorated with colourful scenes showing the visit to the tomb.
244
ΒΠ 288 (H: 40cm)
245
ΒΠ 289 (H: 50cm)
246
ΒΠ 290 (H: 48cm)
247
ΒΠ 291 (H: 48cm)
248
ΒΠ 292 (H: 50cm)
249
ΒΠ 293 (H: 46cm)

Burial K2, about 420–410 BC

250
Two gold conical objects, BM 2070 (H: 4.5cm), BM 2071 (H: 5cm)

251
Gold discs decorated with stars and rosettes, BM 2072–2088 (Diam.: 2.1–2.7cm), BM 2149–2151 (Diam.: 2.6–2.7cm)

Burial K3, about 350–325 BC

252
Gold disc with embossed rosette, BM 2143 (Diam.: 1.1cm)

253
Gold bead, BM 2144 (Diam.: 1cm)

254
Silver gilded discs bearing stars with sixteen rays, BM 2133–2142 (Diam.: 2.3–2.5cm)

The tomb of Eurydice, 344–343 BC

255
Bronze palmettes from the doorknob of the interior door of the tomb of Eurydice, BM 5086 (L: 8.1cm, W: 0.7cm), BM 5087 (W: 3.4cm), BM 5088 (W: 7.5cm), BM 5089 (W: 3.4cm)

256
Gold disc with a star, BM 2178 (Diam.: 2.3cm)

Two marble plates
257
ΒΛ 50 (Diam.: 35cm)
258
ΒΛ 1692 (Diam.: 34.5cm)

259
Alabaster *alabastron* (perfume container), ΒΛ 54 (Diam.: 38cm)

260
Clay pointed *amphora* (two-handled wine transport vessel), ΒΠ 3806 (H: 64cm)

261
Clay Attic red-figure squat *lekythos* (perfume vessel) of the Eleusis Painter with a depiction of Triptolemos and the Eleusinian circle, ΒΠ 3815 (H: 41.5cm, W: 20cm)

262
Clay red-figure squat *lekythos* (perfume vessel), ΒΠ 6474 (H: 23cm)

The Wreath of Queen Meda, 336 BC

263
Gold myrtle wreath. Some 80 leaves and 112 flowers still survive. Found in the antechamber of the tomb of Philip II, BM 2633 (Diam.: 26cm)

264
Six gold discs decorated with a star, from the antechamber of the tomb of Philip II, (L: 2.5–2.6cm)

265
Clay pseudo-Cypriot *amphora*, from the antechamber of the tomb of Philip II, ΒΠ 3362 (H: 20cm)

The Five Ladies

1. The woman buried in tomb NX, tumuli cemetery, 1000–900 BC

266
Pair of bronze pins, BM 4118, BM 4558 (L: 32.6cm)

267
Nine bronze rings,
BM 4519 (Diam.: 2.3cm),
BM 4521 (Diam.: 3cm),
BM 4522 (Diam.: 2.7cm),
BM 4523 (Diam.: 2.3cm),
BM 4524 (Diam.: 2.8cm),
BM 4520 (Diam.: 2.6cm),
BM 4525 (Diam.: 2.7cm),
BM 4526 (Diam.: 2.2cm),
BM 4527 (Diam.: 2.8cm)

268
Two bronze buttons, BM 4216 (Diam.: 3.9cm), BM 4159 (Diam.: 4cm)

269
Bronze coil-shaped ornaments (*fistulae* or *syringes*) in fragments, BM 4161, BM 4160, BM 4235

270
Bronze ornament, BM 4108 (L: 7.3cm)

271

Bronze conical object with breast-shaped protrusion, BM 4116 (L: 1.6cm)

272

A pair of bronze bracelets: one with a single spiral (BM 4467, Diam.: 6.2cm) and the other with 13 spirals (BM 4491, L: 10cm, Diam.: 5.8cm)

273

Necklace consisting of 31 cornelian beads, BΛ 1691 (L: 0.7–1.6cm per bead)

274

Bronze triple double axe, BM 4077 (L: 23cm, W: 11cm)

2. The woman buried in tomb AΔI, tumuli cemetery, 900–850 BC

275

Bronze triple double axe, BM 4076 (L: 22.3cm, W: 9.5cm)

276

A pair of bronze coil-shaped ornaments (*fistulae* or *syringes*) (BM 4133-4134) which join together with two bronze buttons, BM 4135 (Diam.: 3.3cm) and BM 4136 (Diam.: 3.4cm)

277

Thirteen cornelian beads (BΛ1625–BΛ 1626, Diam.: 0.9–1.1cm per bead); a necklace consisting of 29 cornelian beads (BΛ 1624, Diam.: 1.1cm–1.3cm per bead); two cornelian beads (both 1.1cm in diameter); one of which is attached to a small gold hair-spiral (*sphekoter*), BΛ 1623, BΛ 1700; one bone bead, BO 1691 (Diam.: 1.2cm) and one glass bead, BO1692 (Diam.: 2cm)

278

Three gold hair-spirals (*sphekoteres*), BM 4875 (Diam.: 1.9cm), BM 4876 (Diam.: 2.2cm), BM 4877 (Diam.: 2.4cm)

279

Iron hook for the suspension of the spindle stick, BM 4508 (Diam.: 2.3cm)

280

Bronze finger ring, BM 4510 (Diam.: 2.2cm)

281

Bronze spiral ornament, BM 4265 (Diam.: 1.3cm)

282

Fifteen nails (*tutuli*) from the decoration of a belt, BM 4509 (Diam.: about 1cm each)

283

A pair of bronze figure-of-eight brooches (*fibulae*) BM 2418 (L: 18.6cm), BM 2417 (L: 18.8cm)

284

A bronze ornament consisting of three circles joined together, BM 4091 (L: 8.6cm, W: 2.2cm)

285

Bronze spiral ornament, BM 4251 (Diam.: 1.3cm)

286

Three bronze bracelets consisting respectively of one spiral (BM 4483, Diam.: 7.5cm), seven spirals (BM 4708, Diam.: 6cm, L: 6.8cm) and eleven spirals (BM 4492, Diam.: 6.9cm, L: 9.1cm)

287

Several bronze nails (*tutuli*) from the decoration of a belt, BM 4092 (Diam.: 1.9cm, H: 0.6cm)

288

Clay spindle whorl, BΠ 6275 (Diam.: 3cm, H: 2.8cm)

289

Four small bronze nails (*tutuli*), BM 5038 (Diam.: 0.4cm)

3. The woman buried in tomb AZVII, tumuli cemetery, 950–850 BC

290

Four gold hair-spirals (*sphekoteres*), BM 4879 (Diam.: 2.7cm), BM 4880 (Diam.: 2.2cm), BM 4902 (Diam.: 0.8cm), BM 4903 (Diam.: 0.8cm)

291

Bronze torque (collar), BM 4559 (Diam.: 12.8cm)

292

Cornelian necklace consisting of 36 beads, BΛ 1621 (Diam.: 0.7–1.7cm per bead) and a glass bead, BO 1693 (Diam.: 1.6cm)

293

Bronze ring-shaped pendant suspended from the belt, BM 4863 (Diam.: 5.9cm)

294

Bronze inter-dependent rings, one of which is decorated with a figure-of-eight motif, BM 4500 (Diam.: 2.6cm), BM 4499 (Diam.: 2.6cm), BM 4501 (Diam.: 2.7cm), BM 4502 (Diam.: 2.75cm), BM 4097 (Diam.: 1.5cm), BM 4098 (Diam.: 1.6cm), BM 4096 (Diam.: 1.9cm)

295

Bronze finger ring, BM 4503 (Diam.: 2.7cm)

296

Several bronze buttons, BM 4497 (Diam.: 1.8–2cm), including a larger button (Diam.: 3.1cm)

297

Three sets of bronze coil-shaped ornaments (*fistulae* or *syringes*), each accompanied by a bronze button for attachment, BM 4145 (*fistulae*), BM 4144 (button, Diam.: 3.7cm), BM 4143 (*fistulae*), BM 4142 (button, Diam.: 3.2cm), BM 4141, BM 4140 (button, Diam.: 3.3cm)

298

Two bronze figure-of-eight ornaments, BM 4253 (L: 3.4cm), BM 4256 (L: 3.7cm)

299

Three bronze figure-of-eight brooches (*fibulae*), BM 4255 (L: 4.2cm), BM 4252 (L: 3.5cm), BM 5039 (L: 1.5cm)

300

Two bronze bracelets with six and twelve spirals respectively, BM 4457 (L: 5.6cm), BM 4458 (L: 8.3cm)

301

Fifty bronze nails (*tutuli*), BM 4498 (Diam.: 1cm)

302

Three bronze shield-boss ornaments (*omphalia*) for the decoration of the belt, BM 4099 (Diam.: 9.2cm), BM 4100 (Diam.: 9.2cm), BM 4101 (Diam.: 13.3cm)

303

Stone spindle whorl, ΒΛ 1620 (Diam.: 3.1cm)

304

Two disc-shaped bronze ornaments decorated with concentric circles, BM 4504 (Diam.: 2.2cm each)

305

Bronze 'wheel'-shaped ornament ('cosmic circle'), BM 4842 (Diam.: 4.2cm)

306

Two bronze figure-of-eight brooches (*fibulae*), BM 2430 (L: 17.4cm), BM 2421 (L: 18.2cm)

307

Five bronze fragments from figure-of-eight brooches (*fibulae*), BM 5040 (Diam.: 1.4cm), BM 5041 (Diam.: 1.6 and 1.3cm), BM 5042 (Diam.: 0.9 and 1cm)

308

Clay spindle whorl, ΒΠ 6284 (L: 3.5cm)

309

Bronze triple double axe, BM 4075 (L: 20cm, W: 10.2cm)

4. The woman buried in tomb ΓΙ, tumuli cemetery, 900–850 BC

310

A pair of gold hair spirals (*sphekoteres*), BM 3686 (Diam.: 2cm), BM 3687 (Diam.: 2cm)

311

Bronze triple double axe, BM 3679 (L: 26cm, W: 9cm)

312

A pair of bronze figure-of-eight brooches (*fibulae*), BM 3345 (L: 18.8cm, W: 8.8cm), BM 3344 (L: 19.1cm, W: 8.8cm)

313

Several fragments of bronze coil-shaped ornaments (*fistulae* or *syringes*), BM 3692

314

Three bronze buttons, BM 3346, BM 3347, BM 3698 (Diam.: 2cm each)

315

Bronze shield-boss (*omphalia*) belt ornaments,

BM 3350 (Diam.: 10.8cm), BM 3351 (Diam.: 6.5cm), BM 3369 (Diam.: 11cm), BM 3370 (Diam.: 10.6cm), BM 3371 (Diam.: 7.6cm), BM 3372 (Diam.: 7.5cm)

316

Bronze bracelet consisting of 13 spirals, BM 3676 (L: 11.4cm)

317

Bronze 'wheel'-shaped ornament ('cosmic circle'), BM 3691 (Diam.: 4.4cm)

318

Bronze figure-of-eight brooches (*fibulae*), BM 3693 (L: 4cm), BM 3695 (L: 3.7cm), BM 3348 (L: 3cm)

319

Bronze ring, BM 3696 (Diam.: 2.8cm)

320

Round bronze object, BM 3697 (Diam.: 3cm)

Several bronze nails (*tutuli*) from the decoration of a belt
321
BM 3708 (Diam.: 1–2cm)
322
BM 3699 (Diam.: 1cm)

323

Bronze finger ring, BM 3373 (Diam.: 2.5cm)

324

Bronze ring-shaped object, suspended from a belt, BM 3690 (Diam.: 6.7cm)

325

A pair of bronze torques (collars), BM 3694 (Diam.: 13.5cm), BM 3382 (Diam.: 12.5cm)

326

Bronze finger rings ending in a figure-of-eight motif, BM 3349 (L: 3.5cm), BM 3374 (L: 3.9cm), BM 3377 (L: 3.2cm)

327

Iron fragments from a pin, BM 3725

5. The Lady of Aegae, about 500 BC

328

Gold strap diadem. The entire surface is decorated with embossed mythological scenes. In eight rectangular plates (*metopes*) one can see a pair of heraldic sphinxes and a pair of rampant heraldic lions; the return of Hephaistos to Olympus guided by Dionysus; Heracles shooting arrows at two centaurs; the two Gorgons, Stheno and Euryale, chasing Perseus in order to avenge him for the death of their sister Medusa; Theseus killing the Minotaur; Heracles combating the Nemean lion; the blinding of Polyphemos by Odysseus and his companions; and two scenes related to athletic games, perhaps the funeral games for King Pelias of Iolkos. BM 2153 (L: 48.9cm, W: 3.9cm)

329

Three gold coil-shaped ornaments (*fistulae*) joined together with finials, each ending in four gold beads; for the adornment of the head. BM 1974 (first finial: L: 3cm, W: 3cm); BM 1975 (second finial: L: 3.1cm, W: 2.9cm); BM 1993 (fistulae: a. L: 16.9cm, b. L: 26cm, c. L: 36.3cm); BM 2024–2031 (gold beads, Diam.: 0.9–1cm each)

330

Gold strap earrings of exquisite craftsmanship (filigree and granulation) and with fine decoration (two buds flanking the blossoming flower on each earring).

BM 2018–2019 (Diam.: 3.3–3.4cm, W of strap: 0.9cm)

331

Gold necklace consisting of 61 beads set in two rows, BM 2023 (small beads: H: 0.8cm, Diam.: 1.2cm; larger beads: H: 1.2cm, Diam.: 1.8cm)

332

Gold pyramidal pendant lavishly decorated with granulation and a tiny narcissus flower at the apex. BM 2022 (L: 2.5cm, W: 1.3cm)

333

Gold bow-shaped brooches (*fibulae*), BM 1972–1973 (L: 6cm, W: 3.5cm)

334

Gold pins. The pins are reinforced along their entire length by a solid silver core. More than one-third of the pin is occupied by the head: three ribbed beads, increasing progressively in size as they reach the top where they are crowned by a blossoming narcissus flower. BM 2016–2017 (L: 28.5cm, Diam. of head: 3.5cm)

335

Gold double pin used to secure the overgarment (*epiblema*) in place around the waist, BM 2020 (L: 7.2cm, W: 1.3cm)

336

Gold spiral bracelets; worn around each arm like a snake, as suggested by the accurate representations of snake's heads finials in repoussé. BM 1997–1998 (Diam.: 10.5 and 7.9cm respectively)

337

Gold strips decorating the entire front of the overgarment (*epiblema*): a long strip with repoussé guilloche (BM 2157, L: 60.2cm, W: 2.6cm); three sheets with embossed mythical representations (BM 2152,

2155–2156, L: 55.7, 30.4, 27.3cm respectively); a damaged strip with an unidentifiable scene (BM 2158, L: 35.8cm, W: 2.6cm); fifteen small strips with repoussé rosettes (BM 2000, L: 7.8cm, W: 2.6cm; BM 2001, L: 8.5cm, W: 2.7cm; BM 2002, L: 8cm, W: 2.6cm, BM 2003, L: 7.1cm, W: 2.7cm; BM 2005, L: 6.7cm, W: 2.7cm; BM 2006, L: 5.5cm, W: 3.1cm; BM 2007, L: 8.2cm, W: 2.7cm; BM 2008, L: 8.4cm, W: 2.9cm; BM 2009, L: 6.7cm, W: 3.4cm; BM 2010, L: 8.6cm, W: 3.1cm; BM 2011, L: 10.9cm, W: 2.8cm; BM 2012, L: 9.8cm, W: 2.9cm; BM 2013a, L: 13cm, W: 2.9cm; BM 2013b, L: 3.2cm, W: 2.8cm; BM 2014, L: 9.5cm, W: 3.5cm; BM 2044, L: 7.8cm, W: 2.4cm). The densely woven *peplos* was adorned with gold strips with geometric motifs and discs with rosettes in repoussé sewn into it; a broad rectangular double strip just below the waist (BM 1992, L: 12.2cm, W: 7cm), under which small discs with rosettes were sewn into the garment in three rows (BM 2004, BM 2045–2066, L: 2.5–3.6cm); two double and four single triangular strips formed a shimmering border on the hem (BM 2038–2043, L: 2.8–5.6cm); sewn on the overgarment and in the area of the arms were two rectangular strips (one on either side) decorated with triple zigzags and repoussé geometric motifs, probably marking the opening where the hands passed through (BM 2034, BM 2037, L: 6.5cm, W: 6.3 and L: 6.7cm, W: 6.5cm respectively). Similar strips with triple zigzags also existed in the bottom corners of the overgarment (BM 2032–2033, L: 7.1 and 6.5cm respectively) as well as on the lady's shoes (BM 2035–2036, L: 6 and 6.4cm respectively). With this group also were the following strips: BM 2044 (L: 7.8cm, W: 2.4cm); BM 2067–2068 (L: 1cm); BM 2069

(L: 30.5cm); also strip BM 2015
(L: 0.6cm, W: 0.5cm)

338
Gold finger ring, BM 2021
(Diam.: 2.1cm)

339
A pair of gold cones in the form
of snake heads decorated with
filigree and two paired terminals
for securing a long braided silver
chain, which hung from the lady's
shoulders down to the abdomen.
BM 2165–2166 (L: 7cm, W: 1cm)

340
A pair of gilded silver shoe-sole
covers. BM 2163–2164 (L: 24.6cm,
W: 8cm)

Jewellery & Toiletry
The Early Iron Age (1000–700 BC)

341
Bronze spindle whorl-shaped bead,
BM 4084 (Diam.: 3.2cm)

342
Bronze torque (collar), BM 3368
(Diam.: 11.4)

Ten pairs of bronze bow-shaped
brooches (*fibulae*)
343
BM 4110–4111 (L: 11.9cm)
344
BM 4362 and BM 4364 (L: 17.5cm)
345
BM 4365 (L: 9.3cm, W: 7cm),
BM 4363 (L: 18.3cm, W: 12.1 cm),
BM 4426 (L: 7cm, W: 5.6 cm),
BM 4456 (L: 6.8cm, W: 4.7cm)
346
BM 4908–4909 (L: 17.5cm)
347
BM 5716–5717 (L: 18cm)
348
BM 4329–4330 (L: 11cm)

Bronze figure-of-eight brooches
(*fibulae*)
349
BM 4295 and BM 4486 (L: 11.8cm)
350
BM 5061 (L: 6.8cm)
351
BM 4662, BM 4378 (L: 14cm each)
352
BM 2428, BM 2429 (L: 15.2 and
16cm respectively)

353
Pair of bronze figure-of-eight
brooches (*fibulae*) and a coil-shaped
ornament (*fistula*), BM 4409–4410
(L: 6.6cm)

354
Pair of bronze pins, BM 4094–4095
(L: 32–33cm)

355
Bronze pin, BM 4919

356
Pair of bronze bracelets, each with
ten spirals, BM 4709 (L: 7.7cm,
W: 7cm), BM 4494 (L: 7.1cm,
W: 7.1cm)

357
Bronze bracelet consisting of
15 spirals, BM 4490 (L: 11.4cm,
W: 6.8cm)

358
Bronze bracelet consisting of
7 spirals, BM 4711 (L: 4.7cm,
W: 4.9cm)

Three bronze single-spiral
bracelets
359
BM 3378 (Diam.: 9.5cm)
360
BM 3707 (Diam.: 9.3cm)
361
BM 3670 (Diam.: 9.5cm)

362
Two bronze rings, BM 4102–4103
(Diam.: 3.2–3.3cm)

363
Soft stone mould for making
jewellery, 1000–800 BC, ВΛ 1690
(L: 8.2cm, W: 6.5cm)

Four clay feeding bottles
364
ВП 4318 (H: 13cm, rim
Diam.: 4.5cm)
365
ВП 4319 (H: 11cm, rim Diam.: 5cm)
366
ВП 4644 (H: 10.5cm, rim
Diam.: 5.8cm)
367
ВП 4645 (H: 11.4cm, rim
Diam.: 4.4cm)

Archaic and Classical toiletry vessels

Clay Corinthian aromatic-oil
containers (*aryballoi*), 6th
century BC
368
ВП 3847 (H: 5.8cm)
369
ВП 5658 (H: 6.2cm)
370
ВП 5657 (H: 5.5cm)
371
ВП 4237 (H: 7.8cm)
372
ВП 4238 (H: 5.6cm)

373
Clay Corinthian pear-shaped
aromatic-oil container (*aryballos*),
6th century BC, ВП 4234 (H: 5cm)

Two clay Corinthian jars
(*amphoriskoi*), 6th century BC
374
ВП 4231 (H: 10.1cm)
375
ВП 4232 (H: 10.3cm)

376
Clay jar (*amphoriskos*), 6th
century BC, ΒΠ 4230 (H: 8cm)

377
Clay Corinthian perfume container
(*exaleiptron*), 6th century BC,
ΒΠ 3813 (H: 6.5cm, W: 16.5cm)

378
Local clay perfume container
(*exaleiptron*), 6th century BC,
ΒΠ 4205 (H: 4.9cm, W: 12cm)

379
Clay bird-shaped perfume vessel, 6th
century BC, ΒΠ 3866 (H: 8.3cm)

380
Clay perfume bottle in the shape of
a seated figure, late 6th century BC,
ΒΠ 3853 (H: 15.1cm, W: 4cm,
thickness: 7.1cm)

Two clay Corinthian perfume
containers (*exaleiptra*), late 6th /
early 5th century BC
381
ΒΠ 2901 (H: 6.3cm, W: 13.5cm)
382
ΒΠ 4204 (H: 5.3cm, W: 14.5cm)

383
Glass perfume vessel found with
the Lady of Aegae, about 500 BC,
ΒΟ 1420 (H: 5.8cm)

384
Local clay perfume container
(*exaleiptron*), 5th–4th century BC,
ΒΠ 2373 (H: 7cm, W: 16cm)

Clay red-figure squat *lekythoi*
(aromatic-oil containers) with
representations of animals (deer,
lion) and mythical beasts (sphinx),
late 5th–4th century BC
385
ΒΠ 1851 (H: 9cm)
386
ΒΠ 1850 (H: 8cm)
387
ΒΠ 2411 (H: 9.6cm)

Clay red-figure *askoi* (perfume
vessels), late 5th–4th century BC
388
ΒΠ 261 (H: 8.8cm)
389
ΒΠ 2199 (H: 8.9cm)
390
ΒΠ 2423 (H: 8.4cm)
391
ΒΠ 2613 (H: 11.2cm)

392
Clay Attic aromatic-oil container
(*alabastron*), 5th century BC,
ΒΠ 2197 (H: 16cm)

393
Bronze perfume bottle
(*unguentarium*), about 425 BC,
BM 1258 (H: 6cm, W: 7cm)

394
Local clay perfume container
(*exaleiptron*), 4th century BC,
ΒΠ 2191 (H: 7.6cm, W: 16cm)

395
Clay black-glaze perfume bottle
(*lekythos* of the Talcott type), 4th
century BC, ΒΠ 2321 (H: 11.3cm)

396
Clay black-glaze *guttus* (a type of
askos – an aromatic-oil container),
4th century BC, ΒΠ 168 (H: 9cm,
base, Diam.: 6cm)

397
Clay Attic red-figure squat *lekythos*
with Aphrodite and Eros (Kertsch
style), about 350 BC, ΒΠ 2906
(H: 19cm)

Clay red-figure squat *lekythoi*
decorated with palmettes, about
350 BC
398
ΒΠ 1835 (H: 6.7cm)
399
ΒΠ 3299 (H: 7.4cm)
400
ΒΠ 973 (H: 6.3cm)

401
Clay *lekythos* (perfume vessel) in the
shape of the head of Adonis, about
350 BC, ΒΠ 2211 (H: 21cm)

Archaic and Classical Jewellery

402
Figure-of-eight brooch (*fibula*) –
found in a late 6th century BC
grave. This brooch underlines
the conservatism of Macedonian
jewellery, BM 1500 (L: 7cm)

403
Bronze necklace consisting of
beads of various shapes alluding to
earlier Geometric prototypes, 6th
century BC, BM 2899 (L: 15cm)

404
Bronze necklace, BM 4797–4799,
BM 4663 (L: 24.9cm)

405
Pair of gold earrings, 7th century BC,
BM 4888 (Diam. of hoop: 1.6cm)

406
Bronze tweezers, BM 3132 (L: 3.2cm)

Twin silver pins, late 6th–5th
century BC
407
BM 3083 (L: 9cm)
408
BM 3085 (L: 10.7cm)
409
BM 3086 (L: 11cm)
410
BM 3087 (L: 12.2cm)

411
Silver pin, 6th–5th century BC,
BM 3088 (L: 10.9cm)

412
Silver tube-shaped object and chain
found with the Lady of Aegae,
about 500 BC, BM 2160 (L: 22.1cm,
W: 1.3cm), BM 2161 (L: 23cm),

BM 2162 (L of chain: 9.5cm; tube:
L: 12.5cm)

417
Bronze tweezers, BM 5002
(L: 5.2cm, W: 2.3cm)

BM 5090–5091 (L: 14.5 and 14.3cm
respectively)

413
A pair of silver omega-shaped
earrings ending in snake heads, late
6th century BC, BM 3056–3057
(L: 5.4 and 5.3cm respectively)

418
Bronze ear-picks, 5th–4th
century BC, BM 2846 (L: 6.3cm),
BM 3633 (L: 6.7cm)

423
Iron finger ring showing a woman
bathing, 4th century BC, BM 1735
(L: 2cm)

414
Amber necklace consisting of beads
in various relief forms found in the
tomb of a queen (ΛIV), 470–460 BC,
BO 1424

419
Silver chain finial, about 425 BC,
BM 1753 (L: 6cm)

424
Two silver pins, 340–330 BC,
BM 1096, BM 1098 (L: 8cm each)

420
Gold finger ring showing a woman
looking at herself in a mirror,
410 BC, BM 1741 (W: 2.2cm)

*A hydria found with the Lady of
Aegae, about 500 BC*

415
A pair of gold omega-shaped
earrings, 5th–4th century BC,
BM 2092–2093 (W: 2.9 and 2.8cm
respectively)

425
Bronze water jar, BM 2168
(H: 35.5cm, W: 36cm)

421
Four silver bracelets ending in
snake heads, 4th century BC,
BM 1405–1407 (L: 6–7cm), BM 1410
(L: 4cm)

416
Two pairs of bow-shaped brooches
(*fibulae*), 5th century BC, BM 1809
(W: 3cm), BM 1408–1409 (W: 5
and 4cm respectively), BM 1403
(W: 4cm)

422
Two silver pins with pear-
shaped heads, 4th century BC,

ROOM 3: BANQUETING AT AEGAE

*Eating and drinking in the Early
Iron Age*

426
Clay footed bowl (*kantharos*),
11th–10th century BC, ΒΠ 4549
(H: 13.3cm, Diam.: 14.5cm)

427
Clay bowl (*kantharos*), 11th–10th
century BC, ΒΠ 2714 (H: 19cm,
Diam.: 20.5cm)

428
Clay bowl (*kantharos*) with two
nail-headed handles, 11th–10th
century BC, ΒΠ 4585 (H: 13.5cm,
Diam.: 13.4cm)

429
Clay bowl (*kantharos*) with incised
decoration, 11th–10th century BC,
ΒΠ 4635 (H: 21.5cm)

430
Clay protogeometric cup (*skyphos*),
11th–10th century BC, ΒΠ 2654
(H: 10cm, rim Diam.: 16cm)

431
Clay protogeometric two-handled
bowl, 11th–10th century BC,
ΒΠ 2772 (H: 15.3cm, rim
Diam.: 16cm)

Two clay jars (*amphoriskoi*) with
painted geometric decoration,
11th–9th century BC

432
ΒΠ 4317 (H: 12cm)
433
ΒΠ 4705 (H: 14cm)

434
Clay jug with cut-away neck,
from burial N X, 10th century BC,
ΒΠ 2811 (H: 22cm)

435
Clay bowl (*kantharos*), from burial
N X, 10th century BC, ΒΠ 2812
(H: 17cm)

436
Clay bowl with two strap nail-headed
handles, from burial N X, 10th
century BC, ΒΠ 2810 (H: 12cm)

437
Clay jug with cut-away neck, 10th century BC, ВΠ 3090 (H: 26cm)

Clay bowls (*kantharoi*) with painted geometric decoration, 10th century BC
438
ВΠ 3091 (H: 12.2cm, Diam.: 16cm)
439
ВΠ 4309 (H: 16cm, Diam.: 12.7cm)
440
ВΠ 2715 (H: 14cm, Diam.: 22cm with handles)

441
Clay jug with cut-away neck, from burial AZ VII, 1000–950 BC, ВΠ 3077 (H: 25cm)

442
Clay bowl (*kantharos*), from burial AZ VII, 1000–950 BC, ВΠ 2944 (H: 15.5cm)

443
Clay protogeometric bowl (*skyphos*) decorated with pendent-semicircles, from burial AZ VII, 1000–950 BC, ВΠ 3089 (H: 8.7cm)

444
Clay twin neck jug, 10th–9th century BC, ВΠ 4463 (H: 21cm)

445
Clay one-handled jug with cut-away neck, 10th–9th century BC, ВΠ 6283 (H: 40cm)

446
Local clay miniature cup (*kyathos*), ВΠ 2827 (H: 4.5cm)

447
Clay bowl with three nail-headed handles, 10th–9th century BC, ВΠ 3022 (H: 24cm)

448
Clay jug with cut-away neck and painted geometric decoration, ВΠ 3702 (H: 12cm)

449
Clay jug with cut-away neck, ВΠ 2782 (H: 12cm)

450
Clay bowl (*kantharos*) with two raised handles and ribbed decoration on the body, ВΠ 3182 (H: 22cm)

451
Clay jug with cut-away neck, from burial AΔ I, 900–850 BC, ВΠ 4480 (H: 20cm)

Clay jugs with cut-away neck, from burial ΓI, 900–850 BC
452
ВΠ 4324 (H: 25cm)
453
ВΠ 4325 (H: 21cm)

454
Clay handleless bowl (*lopas*), from burial ΓI, 900–850 BC, ВΠ 4295 (H: 9.5cm, max W: 23cm)

455
Clay bowl with two strap nail-headed handles, from burial ΓI, 900–850 BC, ВΠ 4420 (H: 11cm)

456
Clay protogeometric jar (*amphoriskos*), 9th century BC, ВΠ 3020 (H: 17cm, rim Diam.: 10cm)

457
Clay jug with cut-away neck, 9th century BC, ВΠ 2766 (H: 17cm)

458
Clay trefoil jug with painted geometric decoration, 9th century BC, ВΠ 2829 (H: 12cm)

459
Clay one-handled cup, 9th century BC, ВΠ 3178 (H: 8cm, rim Diam.: 12cm)

460
Clay two-handled bowl, 9th century BC, ВΠ 2973 (H: 11.5cm, Diam.: 14.5cm)

461
Clay high-footed *kylix* (cup) with two raised nail-headed handles, 9th century BC, ВΠ 4321 (H: 18cm)

462
Clay bowl (*kantharos*) with painted geometric decoration, 9th century BC, ВΠ 4704 (H: 14cm, Diam.: 17cm)

463
Clay wine-mixing bowl (*krater*), 9th–8th century BC, ВΠ 6282 (H: 31cm, max Diam.: 28cm)

464
Clay water jar (*hydria*) with nipple-shaped protrusions at the front, 8th century BC, ВΠ 2779 (H: 24cm)

Clay bowls (*lopades*), 8th century BC
465
ВΠ 2726 (H: 9.5cm, rim Diam.: 23cm)
466
ВΠ 4617 (H: 8.6cm, rim Diam.: 13.3cm)
467
ВΠ 3015 (H: 9.6cm, rim Diam.: 27cm)
468
ВΠ 6288 (H: 7.5cm, rim Diam.: 19cm)

The banquet of the Companions

469
Bronze calyx-shaped *krater* (wine mixing jar) with intricate decoration on the rim, handles and foot. Heuzey tomb β, about 320–310 BC

470
Bronze jug, Heuzey tomb β, about 320–310 BC

471
Bronze pan-shaped vessel (*patera*) with a ram's head decorating the end of its handle, Heuzey tomb β, about 320–310 BC

472
Bronze cup (*kantharos*), Heuzey tomb β, about 320–310 BC

473
Bronze bucket (*situla*), Heuzey tomb β, about 320–310 BC

474
Bronze cup (*kantharos*), 4th century BC, BM 1136 (W: 20.5cm, H: 11cm)

The banquet of the king from the tomb of Philip II, 336 BC

475
Silver wine jug (*oinochoe*) decorated on the rim and handle. This jug is further embellished with the relief head of a Satyr (Silenus) appearing under the handle. BM 2442 (H: 24.4cm, Diam.: 9.2cm)

476
Silver cup (*kylix*), BM 2540 (H: 3.6cm, W: 13.4cm)

477
Silver bowl (*skyphos*) – its shape and especially the nail-headed handles allude to earlier, Geometric, prototypes. BM 2545 (H: 5.7cm, Diam.: 8.5cm)

478
Silver-gilt strainer decorated with guilloche and floral motifs and equipped with elaborate handles ending in goose heads. BM 2553 (H: 2.2cm, W: 21cm)

479
Silver bowl (*calyx*) decorated inside with a relief head of Pan, BM 2542 (H: 6.1cm, rim Diam.: 9.7cm)

From the tomb of Alexander IV, about 310 BC

480
Silver cup (*kantharos*), BM 2536 (H: 9.5cm, rim Diam.: 8.5cm)

481
Silver ladle, the handle of which ends in a bird's head. BM 2550 (L: 25.6cm)

482
Silver bucket (*situla*), BM 2309 (H: 32.5cm, base Diam.: 9.8cm)

483
Silver perfume bottle, BM 2569 (H: 14.6cm, base Diam.: 4.9cm)

484
Silver dish, BM 2560 (H: 3cm, Diam.: 10.1cm)

The gold and ivory couches: masterpieces in miniature

485
Ivory boar from the decoration of the footstool of a gold and ivory couch, from the tomb of Philip II, 336 BC, BO 1696 (H: 4.2cm, W: 8cm)

486
Ivory figure of a man with outstretched arms from a gold and ivory couch. From the tomb of Alexander IV, about 310 BC. BO 1697 (L: 11.5cm, H: 5.5cm)

Banqueting in the Archaic and Classical periods

487
Clay black-figure cup (*kotyle*) from Chios with a lion, 6th

century BC, ВП 4227 (H: 8.5cm, rim Diam.: 12.1cm)

Clay Corinthian deep cups (*kotylai*), 6th century BC
488
ВП 5748 (H: 7.5cm, rim Diam.: 10.8cm)
489
ВП 4226 (H: 6.7cm, rim Diam.: 9.5cm)

Clay deep cups (*kotylai*), 6th century BC
490
ВП 2907 (H: 15.1cm, rim Diam.: 21cm)
491
ВП 4206 (H: 14cm, rim Diam.: 27cm)

492
Clay jar (*amphoriskos*) with horizontal handles, 6th century BC, ВП 5742 (max L: 16cm)

493
Clay Corinthian trefoil wine jug (*oinochoe*), 6th century BC, ВП 3850 (H: 24cm)

494
Clay trefoil wine jug (*oinochoe*), 6th century BC, ВП 4235 (H: 11cm)

495
Clay trefoil wine jug (*oinochoe*) with a representation of a Satyr's head, 6th century BC, ВП 5659 (H: 15.6cm)

496
Clay Ionian footed dish (*lekanis*), 6th century BC, ВП 5664 (H: 4.4cm, W: 10.4cm)

A pair of local clay two-handled bowls (*kantharoi*), 6th century BC
497
ВП 5759 (H: 14.4cm, Diam.: 14.6cm)

498
ВП 4256 (H: 18cm, body
Diam.: 12.5cm)

499
Bronze bowl (*lekanis*),
6th century BC, BM 1790
(Diam.: 23.5cm, H: 9cm)

500
Bronze trefoil jug, 6th century BC,
BM 2882 (H: 10cm, W: 8cm)

501
Bronze lamp, 6th century BC,
BM 2464 (L: 10.6cm)

502
Local clay bowl (*dinos*), 6th
century BC, ВП 3804 (H: 13cm,
Diam.: 14cm)

503
Clay black-figure column *krater*
(wine mixing bowl) with the
representation of an octopus, 6th
century BC, ВП 4215 (H: 21.5cm,
rim Diam.: 22.4cm)

504
Clay black-figure column *krater*
(wine mixing bowl) with the
representation of a grazing goat, 6th
century BC, ВП 5719 (H: 17.8cm,
rim Diam.: 19cm)

505
Clay Attic lip cup (*kylix*) with a
black-figure Medusa head inside,
550–525 BC, ВП 4558 (H: 7.5cm)

506
Clay Attic red-figure drinking cup
(*skyphos*) decorated with a female
head in profile, early 4th century BC,
ВП 974 (H: 8cm, W: 14.8cm)

507
Clay Attic red-figure drinking cup
(*skyphos*) with *himation*-clad men,
4th century BC, ВП 2209 (H: 10.5cm)

508
Clay Attic black-glaze deep drinking
cup (*skyphos*), 5th–4th century BC,
ВП 303 (H: 12.3cm)

Clay Attic black-glaze bowls (*bolsal*),
5th–4th century BC
509
ВП 397 (H: 6.4cm)
510
ВП 2463 (H: 9.5cm)

511
Clay Attic black-glaze deep cup
(*kotyle*), 5th–4th century BC,
ВП 2272 (H: 7.6cm)

Clay low bowls with a horizontal
handle (one-handler or *kanastron*),
5th–4th century BC
512
ВП 1841 (H: 6cm, Diam.: 17cm)
513
ВП 3235 (H: 3.6cm, Diam.: 11cm)
514
ВП 1800 (H: 4cm, Diam.: 10cm)

Clay black-glaze bowls, 5th–4th
century BC
515
ВП 2201 (Diam.: 9.6cm)
516
ВП 956 (Diam.: 8.7cm)
517
ВП 4798 (Diam.: 15.5cm)
518
ВП 4797 (Diam.: 11.3cm)

519
Clay black-glaze bowl with
impressed rosettes inside, 5th–4th
century BC, ВП 2189 (Diam.: 6.5cm)

520
Clay black-glaze bowl with
impressed palmettes inside,
5th–4th century BC, ВП 2284
(Diam.: 14.3cm)

521
Local clay black-glaze bowl, 5th–4th
century BC, ВП 1855 (Diam.: 15cm)

522
Clay black-glaze lamp, 5th–4th century BC, ВП 181 (H: 3.5cm, L: 9cm)

523
Bronze bowl (*lekanis*), 420–400 BC,
BM 1845 (Diam.: 17.7cm, H: 5cm)

524
Bronze footed bowl with two
handles, 340–330 BC, BM 1795 (rim
Diam.: 13.5cm, H: 6.5cm, W: 14cm)

Clay black-glaze plates (*pinakia*),
4th century BC,
525
ВП 62 (Diam.: 13.4cm)
526
ВП 630 (Diam.: 24.5cm)
527
ВП 6291 (Diam.: 20cm)

528
Clay Attic red-figure jug (*pelike* of
the Kertsch type), 340–330 BC, ВП
248 (H: 32cm)

529
Local clay black-glaze jug (*pelike*),
4th century BC, ВП 6475 (H: 13cm)

530
Clay jug with cut-away neck, 4th
century BC, ВП 1792 (H: 24cm)

531
Clay black-glaze one-handled jug,
4th century BC, ВП 2392 (H: 9cm)

532
Clay black-glaze bowl (*kantharos*)
with 'west slope' decoration, late 4th
century BC, ВП 3264 (H: 19cm, max
W: 30cm)

533
Clay black-glaze bowl (*kantharos*),
4th century BC, ВП 2336 (H: 8cm,
max W: 10cm)

Clay black-glaze salt cellars,
5th–4th centuries BC

534
ΒΠ 2190 (Diam.: 6.7cm)
535
ΒΠ 3220 (Diam.: 6.3cm)
536
ΒΠ 1839 (Diam.: 6.2cm)
537
ΒΠ 3329 (Diam.: 6.5cm)

538
Clay black-glaze juglet (*olpe*), 4th century BC, ΒΠ 2894 (H: 7.9cm)

An oinochoe jug with a symposion scene and two clay cups

539
Clay trefoil red-figure wine jug (*oinochoe*) with a *symposion* (banquet) scene, Kertsch style, about 350–330 BC, ΒΠ 6290 (H: 29cm)

Two clay black-glaze wine cups, second half of the 4th century BC.
540
ΒΠ 2339 (H: 8.5cm, Diam.: 7.9cm)
541
ΒΠ 2340 (H: 8.5cm, Diam.: 8.3cm)

Architectural fragments from the city and the palace at Aegae

Two clay relief palmette antefixes with traces of paint, from the *asty*, 420–400 BC
542
ΒΠ 6304 (H: 27cm, W: 21.5cm)
543
ΒΠ 3046 (H: 27cm, W: 21cm, Depth: 15cm)

Clay relief palmette antefixes, from the palace, around 340 BC
544
ΒΠ 3046 (H: 28.5cm, W: 23cm, L: 24cm)
545
ΒΠ 3047 (H: 26.5cm, W: 23cm, L: 39cm)
546
ΒΠ 4984 (H: 26cm, W: 23.5cm, L: 11cm)
547
ΒΠ 4983 (H: 27cm, W: 23cm, L: 15cm)
548
ΒΠ 4982 (H: 28cm, W: 22cm, L: 17cm)

549
Clay painted gutters (*gutti*) with painted palmettes, from the palace, around 340 BC, ΒΠ 3053 (L: 40cm, W: 23cm, thickness: 5cm), ΒΠ 3054 (L: 34cm, W: 22cm, thickness: 5cm)

550
Clay pan tiles, from the palace, around 340 BC, ΒΠ 3050 (L: 67.5cm, W: 20cm, H: 10cm), ΒΠ 3051 (L: 71cm, W: 56cm, H: 8cm)

551
Clay cover tile, from the palace, around 340 BC, ΒΠ 3048 (L: 68cm, W: 19cm, H: 11cm)

552
Capital of a limestone pilaster with Ionic semi-columns on either end. Traces of white stucco are still preserved on the columns. From the upper storey of the *stoa* at the façade of the palace, around 340 BC. ΒΛ 1488 (H: 46cm, L: 112cm)

The Temenid Kings

N.B. In parenthesis the reign date of each king is given.

Perdiccas I (around 650 BC)
Argaeos I (second half of the seventh century BC)
Philip I (second half of the seventh century BC)
Aeropos I (first half of the sixth century BC)
Alcetas I (first half of the sixth century BC)
Amyntas I (*c.*540–498 BC)
Alexander I (498–454 BC)
Perdiccas II (454–413 BC)
Archelaos I (413–399 BC)
Crateros (399 BC)
Orestes and Aeropos II (399–396 BC)
Archelaos II (396–393 BC)
Amyntas II (393 BC)
Pausanias (393 BC)
Argaeos II (393–392 BC)
Amyntas III (392–370 BC)
Alexander II (370–368 BC)
Perdiccas III (368–360 BC)
Ptolemy of Aloros (regent, 368–365 BC)
Philip II (360/359–336 BC)
Alexander III (336–323 BC)
        Antipater (regent, 334–323 BC)
Philip III Arrhidaios (323–317 BC)
Alexander IV (323/317–310/308 BC)

Select Glossary of Terms

agora [pl. *agoras*] market place(s)

aition the first cause

alabastron [pl. *alabastra*] containers for aromatic oil or a more viscous substance, perhaps to anoint the body of the deceased

amphitryon host/organizer of a banquet

andron [pl. *androns*] dining room(s)

apellai regular assemblies

archon ruler; leader

asty the fortified city; the core of a city

basileia palace complexes

basileus part hereditary and part elective head of state

biga two-horse chariot

calyx [pl. *calyxes*] type of handleless cup

chiaroscuro contrasts of light and shade

chiton garment worn next to the skin; tunic

dinoi mixing bowls

diphthera an animal skin

eikon painted image

emporion [pl. *emporia*] trading place(s); market(s)

ephebeia the period of ritual transition from childhood to manhood

ethnos people or tribe

exaleiptron [pl. *exaleiptra*] perfume container(s)

fibula [pl. *fibulae*] brooch(es)

fistulae or *syringes* coil-shaped ornaments that, like locks of 'hair', framed the face of women

gymnasium the grounds where ancient Greeks competed naked in athletic exercises (*gymnos* in Greek means naked). It later developed into the training ground, both educational and military, for future citizens of the ancient Greek cities and acquired a relatively standardised architectural form centred on the *palaistra*, a peristyle courtyard

heroon a shrine dedicated to a hero

heteroi royal companions

hetairos companion, fellow

hetairai courtesans

Heracles Kynagidas Heracles as leader of the hunters

Heracles Patroos ancestral Heracles

Hieros Gamos Sacred Marriage

himation a piece of dress; an outer garment; cloak

hydria water jug

impasto thick paint

insula [pl. *insulae*] literally meaning 'island' in Latin, it refers to the habitation quarter which is bordered on all four sides by roads

kaisareion see under *sebasteion*; also spelt *caesareum*

kata komas referring to a type of settlement organization based on a loose agglomeration of villages around a central core rather than a pre-planned, organized settlement based on a grid system

kline [pl. *klinai*] couch(es)

kome open, unfortified village

kopis slashing sword with a curved blade used by the Macedonian cavalry

kosmos world; decoration

kantharos [pl. *kantharoi*] type of cup with two raised handles

krater bowl used for mixing wine and water

kore [pl. *korai*] maiden(s); stylised representation(s) of young women of the Archaic period (700–490 BC) in Greece

kotyle [pl. *kotylai*] simple bowl(s) with or without handles (see also *skyphoi*)

kouros [pl. *kouroi*] youth(s); stylised representation(s) of male youths of the Archaic period (700–490 BC) in Greece

kylix [pl. *kylikes*] cup(s) with shallow body, horizontal handles

kyrios guardian

lamella [pl. *lamellae*] small metal piece, plate or strip

larnax [pl. *larnakes*] container(s) in which the cremated remains of the deceased, a member of the Macedonian royal family or the elite, were deposited

lekythos [pl. *lekythoi*] aromatic-oil container(s)

logos word or speech; reason

machaira iron knife

maenad[-s] female follower(s) of Dionysus

mystes the initiated one

ochanon a bar or band fastened crosswise on the underside of the shield, through which the bearer passed his arm

oecumene the known inhabited world; for the ancient Greeks it means 'universe' or 'world'; the whole (known) world

oinochoe [pl. *oinochoai*] wine jug(s)

oikos house; the family line

omphalos phiale a dish with a central boss, the vessel par excellence for making libations to the gods

opus sectile inlaid marbles

Orthos Logos right reason

palaistra a peristyle building with an open court

patrooa hiera ancestral rites

patera pan-shaped vessel used for making liquid offerings to the gods

peplos a full-length plain woollen dress fastened over the shoulder with simple pins or heavy bronze brooches

peristylar colonnaded

phiale [pl. *phialai*] silver libation bowl(s); see also *omphalos phiale*

pitheon an Early Iron Age storehouse

Pothos a personification of yearning, longing, desire of things usually absent or missing

polis [pl. *poleis*] city-state(s)

propylaia monumental gateways

protome[-s] bust(s); head and neck figures of humans or animals, a type of offering to the gods

pyxis [pl. *pyxides*] a type of box/container; cosmetic vessel(s) containing white lead powder for whitening the skin

quadriga four-horse chariot

quillons the cross-guard in a sword or knife, i.e. a bar of metal at right angles to the blade, placed between the blade and the hilt for the protection of the user's hand

ricasso the section just above the guard or handle of a sword or knife

sarissa long pike over five metres in length

satyr[-s] ass-eared and tailed followers of Dionysus

sebasteion a sanctuary for worshipping the emperors

situla [pl. *situlae*] bronze bucket(s)

skoidos a judicial post

skyphos [pl. *skyphoi*] two-handled bowl(s)/cup(s)

stele [pl. *stelai*] tomb marker(s)

stoa [pl. *stoas*] ancient Greek type of building; a colonnaded covered walkway at the back of which one often – but not always – finds additional facilities, such as (work-)shops

symposion banquet

symposiarch master of the banquet

synedrion a standing organ of representative government

tang the part of the blade of a sword or knife extending into and usually through the grip that is fastened to it

tholos a round type of building with conical roof

thyrsus[-es] wand(s) or staff(s) wreathed in ivy and vine-leaves with a pine-cone at the top associated with Dionysus and his followers

tumulus [pl. *tumuli*] burial mound(s)

tutulus [pl. *tutuli*] circular nail-looking bronze ornament(s); part of the decoration of a belt

unguentarium [pl. *unguentaria*] aromatic-oil container(s)

xoanon [pl. *xoana*] wooden statue(s)

Zeus Meilichios the gracious; the good-tempered one

Endnotes

Chapter 2

1. It is an honour to write here on Macedon, which I first visited in 1970 when, as a beginner, I boldly identified Vergina as ancient Aegae, partly because of its palace and unexcavated tumulus, surely (I guessed) covering the royal burials. In October 1977 Manolis Andronikos duly uncovered the first royal tombs there, finding them during my first weeks as an Oxford tutor in Greek history. Since then the site has continued to spring so many surprises. The fundamental study of early Macedonian history is Hammond and Griffith (1972) and (1979); Hatzopoulos's work on Macedonian institutions (1996a) is the essential follow-up. Errington (1990) and Borza (1990) are shorter, sometimes unpersuasive, surveys. Hatzopoulos (2006) offers an important corrective in the light of much recent work. On Philip, Hammond (1994) provides the most optimistic narrative, the one which best challenges specialist readers. George Cawkwell's study (1978) is also valuable, as are the opening chapters by Ellis (1976). The most recent general narrative, based on scholarship in English, is by Worthington (2008) with a bust, however, of the Roman emperor Philip the Arab on the cover. Continental scholarship is drawn on by Squillace (2009). Rhodes (revised ed. 2010) offers the best short survey of Philip and the fourth century BC. I have set out and documented my views on the Macedonian kings, 399–323 BC, in four chapters of my edited *History of Macedon*, forthcoming from E. J. Brill in 2011. Its chapters by M. Mari, M. B. Hatzopoulos, A. Kottaridi, S. Psoma and other Greek scholars are also highly relevant to my summary here.

Chapter 3

1. For further reading see Ginouvès and Hatzopoulos 1993; Hammond 1989; Hatzopoulos 1996a; 2006; Kalléris 1976.
2. Hatzopoulos 1993, 19–20.

Chapter 4

1. On the history of research see Andronikos 1987c; 1993; 1997; Drougou and Saatsoglou-Paliadeli 2000; 2006, 50–95; Drougou 2007; Saatsoglou-Paliadeli 2009; Kottaridi 2011.
2. On the early 20th century British and French work in Macedonia see Wace and Thompson 1909; Wace 1913–14; Rey 1916; 1921. See also Picard et al. 1918–19; Casson 1926 with additional references.
3. In 1954-1955 Andronikos studied in Oxford under Sir John Beazley. He received his doctorate from the University of Thessaloniki in 1952; after ten years in private secondary education, Andronikos was appointed in 1957 Assistant Professor, in 1961 Lecturer and in 1964 Full Time Professor of Archaeology at the University of Thessaloniki. He was awarded an honorary DLitt from the University of Oxford in 1986.
4. Hammond 1970; 1997; Hatzopoulos 1996b; 2003. Lane Fox (1973, 19 and notes in p. 504: in September 1970, Lane Fox noted Theophrastus' cloud-phenomenon at modern Vergina: *On Winds* 27).
5. Andronikos 1984; 1997; see also Drougou 2009. On the identification of the occupants see the most recent summary by Hatzopoulos (2008) and chapter 9. Musgrave and Prag, this volume.
6. A date in the middle of the fourth century BC for the palace based on the style of the column capitals was first put forward by A.W. Lawrence (1957, 306, n. 23.3). See also Kottaridi 2006b. Before restoration work started at the palace in 2007, several other scholars had added important information about its appearance, function and use, including Pandermalis (1976; 1987), Kaltsas (1988, 28-31), Velenis (1997) and Hoepfner and Kosse (2002). For the emphasis at the palace at Aegae on sumptuous dining and sympotic displays see the view first expressed by R.A. Tomlinson (1968).
7. Paraphrasing this sentence from Heuzey and Daumet 1876, 226. Important publications include:

Rhomaios 1951; 1953–4; Andronikos 1964; 1969; 1994; Andronikos et al. 1961; Kottaridi 1999a; 2001a; 2004a; 2004b; 2006a; 2007; 2009; Saatsoglou-Paliadeli 2004; Drougou 2005; see also Rhomiopoulou and Kilian-Dirlmeier 1989; Pandermalis 1972; Tsigarida 1992; Tsigarida and Haddad 1993; Drougou 2009a; 2009b; 2009c; Kyriakou 2008. On the lady of Aegae in particular see Andronikos 1988; Andronikos and Kottaridi 1988; Kottaridi 1989; 1996; 2002 (with additional bibliography); 2005b. On Macedonian tombs the most up-to-date list is included in Huguenot (2008), who, however, lists only eleven tombs at Aegae. Several reports by Kottaridi and the University of Thessaloniki team appear annually in the *AEMTh* and *Egnatia*.

CHAPTER 5

1. On Bronze Age Macedonia see Andreou and Kotsakis 1996; Andreou et al. 1996; Andreou 2003; Cambitoglou and Papadopoulos 1993; Jung 2003; Karamitrou-Mentessidi 2003; Koukouli-Chrysanthaki 1993; Pilali-Papasteriou 1999; Wardle 1980; 1993.

2. The typological classification of Aegean swords by G. Karo, A. Furumark, H. Catling, N. Sandars and I. Kilian-Dirlmeier is unanimously accepted in Aegean research. Despite these typologies the ever-increasing corpus of known swords reveals variants that are often difficult to classify by modern classifications. They are thus best described as local variants.

3. Kilian-Dirlmeier 1993, 35–7, pl. 8–9, 60.

4. Type Cii according to N. Sandars or type Ib according to I. Kilian-Dirlmeier. See Sandars 1963, 121–3 and Kilian-Dirlmeier 1993, 45–7, pl. 62.

5. For a useful account on the use of the various types of Aegean swords in combat, see the article by Molloy 2010.

6. Avila 1983, 64.

7. Jung 2002, pl. 10:113.

8. Andronikos 1969, 168.

9. E.g. Livadeia and Ano Komi Aianis, Ag. Dimitrios at Spathes Palaia Chrani, Nea Agathoupoli, Palaia Leptokarya, Ag. Mamas, Assiros, Kastanas, Demir Kapija, Exohi Dramas, Kastri Thasou, Livaditsa, Perivolaki (Sarace) and Servia Kozanis.

CHAPTER 6

1. Hatzopoulos 1996a; Carlier 2000; Kottaridi 2006b.

2. Archibald 2000.

3. Edson 1970, 17.

4. Picard 2000.

CHAPTER 7

1. Translation by N. G. L. Hammond in Hammond and Griffith 1979, 6–7.

2. Burkert 1985.

3. Hatzopoulos 1994, 89–91.

4. Hammond 1989.

5. Hatzopoulos, (n. 3).

6. Gauthier and Hatzopoulos 1993.

7. Greenwalt 1986, 213–4.

8. Kouremenos, Parassoglou and Tsantsanolgou 2006.

9. Translation by P. A. Burnt.

10. Saatsoglou-Paliadeli 2004a.

11. Snodgrass 1964, 135–9.

12. Drougou et al. 1994, 104.

CHAPTER 9

1. This study is a summary of two articles still in press at the time of writing and due to appear in 2011, where the evidence is set out in greater detail: Musgrave et al. (forthcoming 2011) and Prag et al. (forthcoming 2011). On earlier studies see Prag et al. 1984; Prag and Neave 1997.

2. Bartsiokas 2000.

3. See http://www.medsci.org/v07p0os1.htm. Bartsiokas's results were taken at the time to offer support in favour of the identification of Philip III Arrhidaios and his wife Eurydice as the occupants of Tomb II at Aegae; they were soon used by scholars as evidence, most notably by two supporters of the pro-Arrhidaios theory, Borza and Palagia 2007.

4. According to Robin Lane Fox, the length of time between Philip and Eurydice's deaths and their subsequent reburial by Cassander is usually reckoned to be up to four months. However, Anson (2006) has now made a sustainable case for their honorary funeral being as late as winter/spring 315 BC, up to 17 months later. His longer chronology seems not impossible, although it has not been tested fully by counter-arguments as yet. It is independently suggested by Boiy (2007, 113–6).

CHAPTER 11

1. Based on salvage and test excavations and extensive surface fieldwork conducted by the 17th Ephorate of Prehistoric and Classical Antiquities of Greece under the direction of Dr A. Kottaridi; for preliminary results see *AEMTh*, with references.

CHAPTER 12

1. This text is an abridged and revised version of a longer article by the author (Kottaridi 2004a).

CHAPTER 13

1. Many thanks for their valuable help to my colleagues, the archaeologists Giannis Touratsoglou and Antigone Zournatzi.
2. On Alexander I and the History of Macedonia see Hammond and Griffith 1979, 98 ff.; Errington 1986, 12; Hammond 1989, *passim*; Hatzopoulos 1996a, *passim*.
3. See note 1.
4. See Papaefthymiou 2000, 37 ff.; Drougou 2009b, 171 ff. (bibliography).
5. Hammond and Griffith 1979, *passim*; Hatzopoulos and Loukopoulou 1980, *passim*; Wirth 1985, 35; Worthington 2008, 194 ff.
6. On the excavation in Vergina-Aegae: Andronikos 1984, *passim*; Andronikos 1987a, 1 and 181 ff; Drougou and Saatsoglou-Paliadeli 2000, 39; Kottaridi 1996, 90 ff.; Drougou 2009c, 122 ff; Drougou 2003, 129 ff.; Ch. Saatsoglou-Paliadeli 2000, 387 ff.; Saatsoglou-Paliadeli 2004a, 1 ff.; Drougou 2005, 9 ff., (bibliography); Kottaridi 2001a, 504 ff.
7. On Sindos: Vokotopoulou and Despini 1985, *passim*; Vokotopoulou 1988, 27 ff.; Tsigarida and Ignatiadou 2000, 11 ff.
8. Chrysostomou and Chrysostomou 2008, 477 ff.; Vokotopoulou 1997.
9. See above and Karamitrou-Mentessidi 1993, fig. 3 and pp. 4 ff.
10. Darbandi and Zournatzi 2008, 254 ff; Curtis and Tallis 2005, 132ff. On toreutics see also Sideris 2008, 339 ff.
11. Errington 1986, 99 ff.; Hammond and Walbank 1988, 10 ff; Hansen, Wieczorek and Tellenbach 2010, 111 ff; Kottaridi 2004a, 66 ff; Touratsoglou 1998a, 71 ff.
12. Hammond 1972, 10 ff; Hammond and Griffith 1979, 203 ff; Touratsoglou 2010, 84 ff.
13. See note 5.
14. See note 5 and Barr-Sharrar 1982, 125 ff; 2008, 2 ff and 73 ff; Themelis 2000, 496 ff; Themelis and

Touratsoglou 1997, 158 ff; Vickers and Gill 1994, 165 ff; Vokotopoulou 1997, 240 ff; Touratsoglou 1998b, 235 ff.; Völker-Janssen 1993, 180 ff; Drougou 1998, 305 ff.
15. Besios 2010, *passim*; 1998, *passim*.
16. Themelis and Touratsoglou 1997, *passim*; Barr-Sharrar 2010, *passim*.
17. Lilimpaki-Akamati and Akamatis 2004, *passim*; Lilimpaki-Akamati 1998, 127 ff.
18. Touratsoglou 1998c, 35 ff; Völker-Janssen 1993, 180 ff; on the ceramic industry see Archibald et al. 2005, 52 ff; also the proceedings of the *Scientific Meetings on Hellenistic Pottery* (1986–2006); Rostovtzeff 1972, vol. I, 367 ff.
19. On the symposium see: Avlonitou-Tsimpidou 1999, 114 ff; Kottaridi 2004a, 65 ff.
20. See Andronikos 1984, 145 ff; Murray 1996, 16 ff.
21. See above note 10.

CHAPTER 14

1. Saatsoglou-Paliadeli 1987a; 1989; 1990; 1991; 1992; 1993a; 1994; 1996a; 1999; 2002; 2004b.
2. Saatsoglou-Paliadeli 2002, 486–8.
3. Andronikos 1969.
4. Saatsoglou-Paliadeli 1993a, 56–7.
5. Saatsoglou-Paliadeli 2000, 389 n. 6.
6. Saatsoglou-Paliadeli 2000, 389 n. 7.
7. Saatsoglou-Paliadeli 1987b, 740 ff; Saatsoglou-Paliadeli 2000, 389.
8. Saatsoglou-Paliadeli 1990, 25-26; Saatsoglou-Paliadeli 2000, 395-7.
9. Saatsoglou-Paliadeli 1996a, 58.
10. Saatsoglou-Paliadeli 1991, 12–16.
11. Saatsoglou-Paliadeli 1991, 15.
12. Saatsoglou-Paliadeli 2001.
13. Saatsoglou-Paliadeli 1990, 25-8.
14. Saatsoglou-Paliadeli 2000, 389-392 fig. 2.
15. Carney 2000, 41.
16. Borza 1990, 184.
17. Carney 2000, 39-40.
18. Carney 2000, 42–4.
19. Carney 2000, 46 n. 34.
20. Saatsoglou-Paliadeli 2000, 401–3.
21. Andronikos 1982a; 1982b, 19, fig. 26; Oikonomides 1983; Saatsoglou-Paliadeli 1987b, 733ff.; Saatsoglou-Paliadeli 1996a, 68, fig.1; Saatsoglou-Paliadeli 2000, 393–5, figs. 3–4.
22. Saatsoglou-Paliadeli 1990, 23ff., figs. 2. 3; Saatsoglou-Paliadeli 1993b, 1356-8, figs. 7, 8; Saatsoglou-Paliadeli

2000, 395–7, figs. 5, 6.

23. Saatsoglou-Paliadeli 2000, 396.

24. Carney 2000, 46.

25. Cf. Carney 2000, ibid.

26. Carney 2000, 45, also suggests a dating for the dedication during the period of Eurydice's widowship; she identifies the deity as Artemis Eukleia and suggests that 'Eurydice may have funded the construction of the temple. If the Eucleia cult at Vergina is connected to Artemis and marriage offerings, then we may have an early Argead prototype of royal women as religious patrons'.

27. Saatsoglou-Paliadeli 1993b, 1339–71, figs. 1-6, drawings 1-3 and 8; Saatsoglou-Paliadeli 2000, 397–400, figs. 7–11.

28. Saatsoglou-Paliadeli 1993b, 1371, drawing 8; Saatsoglou-Paliadeli 2000, figs. 10, 11.

29. Saatsoglou-Paliadeli 1993b, 1348–54.

30. Saatsoglou-Paliadeli 1990, 26–7.

31. Saatsoglou-Paliadeli 1990, 27.

32. Saatsoglou-Paliadeli 1990, 27–8.

33. Saatsoglou-Paliadeli 2000, 398, notes 76–81.

34. Saatsoglou-Paliadeli 2000, 389–92, fig. 2.

35. Saatsoglou-Paliadeli 2000, 390, fig. 2.

36. Saatsoglou-Paliadeli 1991, 14 and 21, fig. 9; Saatsoglou-Paliadeli 1996b, 230, n. 50, pl. 45,4; Saatsoglou-Paliadeli, 2000, 391, notes 21–23.

37. Saatsoglou-Paliadeli et al. *in press* a; *in press* b.

38. On the murder of Alexander's legitimate son Alexander IV, cf. Diodorus Siculus, *Library of World History* 19.105.2.

39. Hammond and Walbank 1988, 162–4; Weatley 1998.

Chapter 15

1. For the situation of these mines in the plain of Philippi, see Faraguna 1998, 375–8.

2. Numerous mining areas are mentioned by Herodotus 5.17.2 (Lake Prasias); 6.46.2–3 (Scapte Hyle, opposite Thasos): 7.112 (Mount Pangaion); 9.75.9–11 (Datos-Krenides). Ancient and modern mining areas in Macedonia and Thrace are discussed by Hammond in Hammond and Griffith 1979, 69–73; ancient sources are cited by Psôma 2006, 66–7.

3. Picard 2006.

4. Lykiardopoulou and Psôma 2000, 325–26 (in Greek with an English summary).

5. Psôma 1999.

6. Raymond 1953, 27–37.

7. Le Rider 1993.

8. See the table provided by Liampi 1993, vol. 2, 792–93.

9. Psôma 2009, 110–11 with earlier bibliography. See also Picard (above note 3), 279–80.

10. For the Ptolemais hoard: Westermark 1994, 17–30.

11. Le Rider 1977, 284–319.

Chapter 16

1. Also relayed by Kallixenos of Rhodes in his description of Ptolemy Philadelphos' symposium-tent in Alexandria (Athenaeus, *The Deipnosophists* 196–197).

2. One exception is Pamphilos, one of the masters of the Sicyonian school (*NH* 35.76).

3. On Macedonian painting, especially at Aegae, see Brécoulaki 2001; 2006; 2007; Andronikos 1987b; 1994; Saatsoglou-Paliadeli 2004a.

Chapter 17

1. For the archaeological work in Pella during the last twenty years, see Akamatis 1993; 1999; 2000; 2009; Akamatis 2008; Chrysostomou 1996; 1998; Drougou 1992; 2000a; Lilimpaki-Akamati 1989-91; 1994; 1996a; 1996b; 1998; 2000; 2002; 2007; 2008; Lilimpaki-Akamati and Akamatis 2004; Makaronas and Giouri 1989; Siganidou and Lilimpaki-Akamati 1996; Voutyras 1998.

Chapter 18

1. Nielsen 1994, 216.

2. Nielsen 1994, 15.

3. Hatzopoulos 2001, 189–201.

4. Millar 1977, 516–49

5. Hoepfner and Kosse 2002, 423–8. I am grateful to Dr Angeliki Kottaridi for sharing her interpretation of the new excavations with me.

6. See Walker 1997 for this and further details of what follows.

7. Hoff 1996, 185–200.

8. Nielsen 1994, 107, with fig. 55.

9. Wace, Megaw and Skeat 1959, 4-11, pl. 3; Baranski 1996.

10. Snape and Bailey 1998.

Bibliography

ABBREVIATIONS

AA: Archäologischer Anzeiger
ADelt: Αρχαιολογικό Δελτίο
AEphem: Αρχαιολογική Εφημερίς
AEMTh: Το Αρχαιολογικό Έργο στη Μακεδονία και τη
  Θράκη
AJA: American Journal of Archaeology
AM: Mitteilungen des Deutschen Archäologischen
  Instituts, Athenische Abteilung
BCH: Bulletin de Correspondance Hellénique
BSA: The Annual of the British School at Athens
JHS: Journal of Hellenic Studies
JRA: Journal of Roman Archaeology
REG: Revue des études grecques
RN: Revue numismatique
ZPE: Zeitschrift für Papyrologie und Epigraphik

NOTE

Numerous excavation reports have appeared in *Praktika*
of the Athens Archaeological Society (especially between
1952 and 1961 and in the 1980s); in the proceedings of the
Archaeological Work in Macedonia and Thrace (*AEMTh*,
since 1987); in the *Archaiologikon Deltion* (since 1960); the
Ancient Macedonia conferences (since 1968) and *Egnatia*
(since 1989).

Akamatis, I. M. 1993. *Πήλινες μήτρες αγγείων από
  την Πέλλα. Συμβολή στη μελέτη της ελληνιστικής
  κεραμικής* (Athens).
Akamatis, I. M. 1999. 'Αγορά Πέλλας, 15 χρόνια
  αρχαιολογικής έρευνας', in *Ancient Macedonia* VI
  (Thessaloniki), 23–43.
Akamatis, I. M. 2000. *Ενσφράγιστες λαβές αμφορέων
  από την Αγορά της Πέλλας. Ανασκαφή 1980–1987.
  Οι ομάδες Παρμενίσκου και Ρόδου* (Athens).

Akamatis, I. M. 2009. 'Προϊστορική Πέλλα. Νεκροταφείο
  Εποχής του Χαλκού', in S. Drougou, D. Evgenidou, C.
  Kritzas, N. Kaltsas, V. Penna, I. Tsourti, M. Galani-
  Krikou and E. Ralli (eds.), *ΚΕΡΜΑΤΙΑ ΦΙΛΙΑΣ.
  Τιμητικός τόμος για τον Ιωάννη Τουράτσογλου*
  (Athens), 193–213.
Akamatis, N. I. 2008. 'Ερυθρόμορφη κεραμική από την
  Πέλλα', *AEphem*, 1–78.
Andreou, S. 2003. 'Η μυκηναϊκή κεραμική και οι
  κοινωνίες της κεντρικής Μακεδονίας κατά την Ύστερη
  Εποχή του Χαλκού', in N. Kyparissi-Apostolika
  and M. Papakonstantinou (eds.), *2nd International
  Interdisciplinary Colloquium, 'The Periphery of the
  Mycenaean World'*, Lamia, 26–30 September 1999
  (Athens), 191–210.
Andreou, S. and Kotsakis, K. 1996. 'Η προϊστορική
  τούμπα της Θεσσαλονίκης. Παλιά και νέα ερωτήματα',
  AEMTh 10, 369–87.
Andreou, S., Fotiadis, M. and Kotsakis, K. 1996. 'Review
  of Aegean Prehistory V. The Neolithic and Bronze Age
  of Northern Greece', *AJA* 100, 579–82.
Andronikos, M. 1964. *Vergina: The Prehistoric Necropolis
  and the Hellenistic Palace*, Studies in Mediterranean
  Archaeology 13 (Lund).
Andronikos, M. 1969. *Βεργίνα I. Το νεκροταφείο των
  Τύμβων, Βιβλιοθήκη της εν Αθήναις Αρχαιολογικής
  Εταιρείας* 62 (Athens).
Andronikos, M. 1982a. 'Ανασκαφές στη Βεργίνα', *Praktika*,
  52–6.
Andronikos, M. 1982b. 'Βεργίνα', *Ergon*, 17–20.
Andronikos, M. 1984. *Vergina: The Royal Tombs and the
  Ancient City* (Athens).
Andronikos, M. 1987a. 'Βεργίνα. Ανασκαφή 1987', *AEMTh*
  1, 181–8.
Andronikos, M. 1987b. 'Η ζωγραφική στην αρχαία
  Μακεδονία', *AEphem*, 363–82.
Andronikos, M. 1987c. 'Η Αρχαιολογική Έρευνα στη
  Μακεδονία', *AEMTh* 1, 1–8.

Andronikos, M. 1988. 'Βεργίνα 1988. Ανασκαφή στο νεκροταφείο', *AEMTh* 2, 1–3.

Andronikos, M. 1993. 'Το Χρονικό της Βεργίνας', *AEMTh* 4, 1–4.

Andronikos, M. 1994. *Βεργίνα II. Ο Τάφος της Περσεφόνης, Βιβλιοθήκη της εν Αθήναις Αρχαιολογικής Εταιρείας* 138 (Athens).

Andronikos, M. 1997. *Το χρονικό της Βεργίνας* (Athens).

Andronikos, M., Bakalakis, G., Makaronas, Ch. and Moutsopoulos, N. 1961. *Το ανάκτορο της Βεργίνας* (Athens).

Andronikos, M. and Kottaridi, A. 1988. 'Ανασκαφή Βεργίνας', *Praktika*, 99–107.

Andronikos, M., Saatsoglou-Paliadeli, C., Drougou, S., Faklaris, P., Kottaridou, A., and Tsigarida, B. 1987. 'Ανασκαφή της Βεργίνας', *Praktika*, 126–48.

Anson E. M. 2006. 'Dating the Deaths of Eumenes and Olympias', *Ancient History Bulletin* 20, 1–8.

Archibald, Z. H. 2000. 'Space, Hierarchy and Community in Archaic and Classical Macedonia, Thessaly, and Thrace', in R. Brock and S. Hodkinson (eds.), *Alternatives to Athens: Varieties of Political Organization and Community in Ancient Greece* (Oxford), 212–33.

Archibald, Z., Davies, J. K. and Gabrielsen, V. (eds.) 2005. *Making, Moving and Managing. The New World in Ancient Economies 323–31 BC* (Oxford).

Avila, R. A. J. 1983. *Bronzene Lanzen- und Pfeilspitzen der griechischen Spätbronzezeit*, (*Prähistorische Bronzefunde* 5,1) (Munich).

Avlonitou-Tsimpidou, M. 1999. *Οι μακεδονικοί τάφοι του Αγ. Αθανασίου και του Φοίνικα* (Athens).

Baranski, M. 1996. 'The Archaeological Setting of the Great Basilica Church at Ashmunein', in D. M. Bailey (ed.), *Archaeological Research in Roman Egypt: Proceedings of the 17th Classical Colloquium, Department of Greek and Roman Antiquities, British Museum (JRA Suppl. 19)* (Ann Arbor), 98–106.

Barr-Sharrar, B. 1982. 'Macedonian Metal Vases in Perspective. Some Observations on Context and Tradition', in B. Barr-Sharrar and E. N. Borza (eds.), *Macedonia and Greece in Late Classical and Early Hellenistic Times*, Studies in the History of Art 10 (Washington), 123–38.

Barr-Sharrar, B. 2008. *The Derveni Krater* (Princeton).

Bartsiokas, A. 2000. 'The Eye Injury of King Philip II and the Skeletal Evidence from the Royal Tomb II at Vergina', *Science* 288.5465, 511–14.

Besios, M. 1998. *Πύδνα* (Katerini).

Besios, M. 2010. *Πιερίδων Στέφανος: Πύδνα, Μεθώνη και οι αρχαιότητες της Βόρειας Πιερίας* (Katerini).

Boiy, T. 2007. *Between High and Low: A Chronology of the Early Hellenistic Period* (Frankfurt).

Borza, E. N. 1990. *In the Shadow of Olympus: The Emergence of Macedon* (Princeton).

Borza, E. N. and Palagia, O. 2007. 'The Chronology of the Macedonian Royal Tombs at Vergina', *Jahrbuch des Deutschen Archäologischen Instituts* 122, 81–125.

Brécoulaki, H. 2001. 'Observations sur la course des chars représentée dans l'antichambre de la tombe III à Verghina', in A. Barbet (ed.), *La peinture funéraire antique, Actes du VIIe Colloque de l'Association internationale pour la peinture murale antique, Vienne 6–10 oct. 1998* (Paris), 51–7.

Brécoulaki, H. 2006. *La peinture funéraire de Macédoine. Emplois et fonctions de la couleur, IVᵉ–IIᵉ s. av. J.-C., ΜΕΛΕΤΗΜΑΤΑ* 48 (Athens).

Brécoulaki, H. 2007. 'Suggestion de la troisième dimension et traitement de la perspective dans la peinture ancienne de Macédoine', in. S. Decamps-Lequime (ed.), *Peinture et couleur dans le monde grec antique* (Paris), 81–94.

Burkert, W. 1985. *History of Greek Religion* (Cambridge, MA).

Cawkwell, G. 1978. *Philip of Macedon* (London).

Cambitoglou, A. and Papadopoulos, J. K. 1993. 'The Earliest Mycenaeans in Macedonia', in C. Zerner, P. Zerner and J. Winder (eds.), *Proceedings of the International Conference 'Wace and Blegen. Pottery as Evidence for Trade in the Aegean Bronze Age, 1939–1989'* (Amsterdam), 289–302.

Carlier, P. 2000. 'Homeric and Macedonian Kingship', in R. Brock and S. Hodkinson (eds.), *Alternatives to Athens: Varieties of Political Organization and Community in Ancient Greece* (Oxford), 259–68.

Carney, E. D. 2000. *Women and Monarchy in Macedonia* (Norman, OK).

Casson, S. 1926. *Macedonia, Thrace and Illyria: Their Relations to Greece from the Earliest Times down to the Time of Philip, Son of Amyntas* (London).

Chrysostomou, P. 1996. 'Το ανάκτορο της Πέλλας', *AEMTh* 10, 105–42.

Chrysostomou, P. 1998. *Μακεδονικοί τάφοι Πέλλας, I. Τάφος Β΄, ο ασύλητος* (Thessaloniki).

Chrysostomou, A. and Chrysostomou, P. 2008. 'Τα νεκροταφεία του αρχαίου οικισμού στο Αρχοντικό Πέλλας', AEMTh 20 Years, 477–90.

Cohen, A. 2010. Art in the Era of Alexander the Great: Paradigms of Manhood and Their Cultural Traditions (Cambridge).

Curtis, J. and Tallis, N. (eds.) 2005. Forgotten Empire: The World of Ancient Persia (London).

Darbandi, S. M. R. and Zournatzi, A. (eds.) 2008. Ancient Greece and Ancient Iran Cross-Cultural Encounters, 1st International Conference, Athens, 11–13 November 2006 (Athens).

Drougou, S. 1987–1990. 'Ένας ασημένιος κάλυκας από τη Βεργίνα', Thrakike Epeteris 7, 57–64.

Drougou, S. 1992. Ανασκαφή Πέλλας 1957–1964. Οι πήλινοι λύχνοι (Athens).

Drougou, S. 2000a. 'Krieg und Frieden im Athen des späten 5 Jahrhunderts v. Chr. Die rotfigurige Hydria aus Pella', AM 115, 147–216.

Drougou, S. 2000b. 'Ο εφήμερος πηλός και ο αιώνιος χρυσός. Επίχρυσα και επάργυρα πήλινα αγγεία στον 4ο αι. π.Χ.', in P. Adam-Veleni (ed.), ΜΥΡΤΟΣ. Μελέτες στη μνήμη της Ι. Βοκοτοπούλου (Thessaloniki), 305–14.

Drougou, S. 2003. 'Βεργίνα. Η πόλη των Αιγών. Συμβολή στην ερμηνεία των αρχαιολογικών ευρημάτων', Egnatia 7, 129–161.

Drougou, S. 2005. Βεργίνα. Τα πήλινα αγγεία της μεγάλης Τούμπας, Βιβλιοθήκη της εν Αθήναις Αρχαιολογικής Εταιρείας 237 (Athens).

Drougou, S. 2007. 'Vergina. On the Traces of the Macedonian Kings', in P. Valavanes (ed.), Great Moments in Greek Archaeology (Los Angeles), 256–71.

Drougou, S. 2009a. 'Βεργίνα. Οι τάφοι Heuzey', in 20 Χρόνια. Το Αρχαιολογικό Έργο στη Μακεδονία και στη Θράκη. Επετειακός Τόμος (Thessaloniki), 63–73.

Drougou, S. 2009b. 'Εικόνες και Σύμβολα περί των Αιγών', in S. Drougou, D. Evgenidou, C. Kritzas, N. Kaltsas, V. Penna, I. Tsourti, M. Galani-Krikou and E. Ralli (eds.), ΚΕΡΜΑΤΙΑ ΦΙΛΙΑΣ. Τιμητικός Τόμος για τον Ιωάννη Τουράτσογλου (Athens), 171–9.

Drougou, S. 2009c. 'Βεργίνα – Η εικόνα του τέλους της πόλης των Αιγών: πρώτες σημειώσεις από μια νέα ανασκαφική απόπειρα', Egnatia 13, 121–32.

Drougou, S. and Saatsoglou-Paliadeli, C. 1984. Βεργίνα. Ο Τόπος και η Ιστορία του (Athens).

Drougou, S. and Saatsoglou-Paliadeli, C. 2000. Vergina: Wandering through the Archaeological Site (Athens).

Drougou, S. and Saatsoglou-Paliadeli, C. 2006. Vergina: The Land and its History (Athens).

Drougou, S., Saatsoglou-Paliadeli, C., Faklaris, P., Kottaridou, A. and Tsigarida, E. B. 1994. Βεργίνα. Η Μεγάλη Τούμπα (Thessaloniki).

Drougou, S., Kallini, C. and Trakatelli, L. 2009. 'Βεργίνα 2008–2009. Η πόλη των Αιγών. Ανασκαφή στον αγρό Τσακιρίδη', Egnatia 13, 227–30.

Edson, Ch. 1970. 'Early Macedonia', Ancient Macedonia I (Thessaloniki), 17–44.

Ellis, J. R. 1976. Philip II and Macedonian Imperialism (London).

Errington, R. M. 1986. Geschichte Makedoniens: von den Anfängen bis zum Untergang des Königreiches (Munich).

Errington, R. M. 1990. A History of Macedonia (California).

Faraguna, M. 1998. 'Aspetti amministrativi e finanziari della monarchia macedone tra IV e III secolo A.C.', Athenaeum 86, 349–95.

Gauthier, P. and Hatzopoulos, M. B. 1993. La Loi Gymnasiarchique de Beroia (Athens).

Ginouvès, R. and Hatzopoulos, M. B. (eds.) 1993. Macedonia from Philip II to the Roman Conquest (Princeton).

Greenwalt, W. 1986. 'Macedonia's Kings and the Political Usefulness of the Medical Arts', Ancient Macedonia IV (Thessaloniki), 213–22.

Hammond, N. G. L. 1970. 'The Archaeological Background to the Macedonian Kingdom', Ancient Macedonia I, 53–67.

Hammond, N. G. L. 1989. The Macedonian State: the Origins, Institutions, and History (Oxford).

Hammond, N. G. L. 1994. Philip of Macedon (London).

Hammond, N. G. L. 1997. 'The Location of Aegae', JHS 117, 177–9.

Hammond, N. G. L. and Griffith, G. T. 1972. A History of Macedonia, vol. 1 (Oxford).

Hammond N. G. L. and Griffith, G. T. 1979. A History of Macedonia, vol. 2 (Oxford).

Hammond, N. G. L. and Walbank, F. W. 1988. A History of Macedonia, vol. 3 (Oxford).

Hansen, S., Wieczorek, A. and Tellenbach, M. (eds.) 2010. Alexander der Grosse und die Öffnung der Welt: Asiens Kulturen im Wandel (Mannheim).

Hatzopoulos, M. B. 1993. 'The Natural and Human Resources', in R. Ginouvès and M. B. Hatzopoulos (eds.), *Macedonia from Philip II to the Roman Conquest* (Athens), 19–23.

Hatzopoulos, M. B. 1994. *Cultes et rites de passage en Macédoine*, MELETHMATA 19 (Athens).

Hatzopoulos, M. B. 1996a. *Macedonian Institutions under the Kings*, vols. 1 and 2. ΜΕΛΕΤΗΜΑΤΑ 22 (Athens).

Hatzopoulos, M. B. 1996b. 'Aigéai. La localisation de la première capitale Macédonienne', *REG* 109, 264–269.

Hatzopoulos, M. B. 2001. 'Macedonian Palaces. Where King and City Meet', in I. Nielsen (ed.), *The Royal Palace Institution in the First Millennium BC: Regional Development and Cultural Interchange between East and West* (Aarhus).

Hatzopoulos, M. B. 2003. 'Herodotus (8.137-8). The Manumissions from Leukopetra, and the Topography of the Middle Haliakmon Valley', in P. Derow and R. Parker (eds.), *Herodotus and His World. Essays from a Conference in Memory of George Forrest* (Oxford), 203–18.

Hatzopoulos, M. B. (ed.) 2006. *La Macédoine. Géographie historique, langue, cultes et croyances, institutions* (Paris).

Hatzopoulos, M. B. 2008. 'The Burial of the Dead (at Vergina) or the Unending Controversy on the Identity of the Occupants of Tomb II', *Tekmeria* 9, 91–118.

Hatzopoulos M. B. and Loukopoulou E. (eds.) 1980. *Philip of Macedon* (Athens).

Heuzey, L. A. and Daumet, H. 1876. *Mission archéologique de Macédoine* (Paris).

Hoepfner, W. and Kosse, A. 2002. 'Bauordnung und Weltwunder', in F. Zimmer and J. C. Eule (eds.), *Die griechische Klassik. Idee oder Wirklichkeit* (Mainz), 399–436.

Hoff, M. C. 1996. 'The Politics and Architecture of the Athenian Imperial Cult', in A. Small (ed.), *Subject and Ruler: The Cult of the Ruling Power in Classical Antiquity*, JRA Supplementary Series 17 (Ann Arbor).

Huguenot, C. 2008. *Eretria XIX. La Tombe aux Érotes et la Tombe d'Amarynthos* (Gollion).

Jung, R. 2002. *Kastanas. Ausgrabungen in einem Siedlungshügel der Bronze- und Eisenzeit Makedoniens 1975-1979. Die Drehscheibenkeramik der Schichten 19 bis 11, Prähistorische Archäologie in Südosteuropa* 18 (Kiel).

Jung, R. 2003. 'Η μυκηναϊκή κεραμική της Μακεδονίας και η σημασία της', in N. Kyparissi-Apostolika and M. Papakonstantinou (eds.), *2nd International Interdisciplinary Colloquium, 'The Periphery of the Mycenaean World'*, Lamia, 26–30 September 1999 (Athens), 211–25.

Kalléris, J. N. 1976. *Les anciens Macédoniens*, vol. 2 (Athens).

Kaltsas, N. E. 1988. *Πήλινες Διακοσμημένες Κεραμώσεις από την Μακεδονία* (Athens).

Karamitrou-Mentessidi, G. 1993. *Kozani, City of Elimiotis. Archaeological Guide* (Thessaloniki).

Karamitrou-Mentessidi, G. 2003. 'Μυκηναϊκά Αιανής – Ελιμιώτιδας και Άνω Μακεδονίας', in N. Kyparissi-Apostolika and M. Papakonstantinou (eds.), *2nd International Interdisciplinary Colloquium, 'The Periphery of the Mycenaean World'*, Lamia, 26–30 September 1999 (Athens), 167–90.

Kilian-Dirlmeier, I. 1993. *Die Schwerter in Griechenland (ausserhalb der Peloponnes), Bulgarien und Albanien (Prähistorische Bronzefunde 4,12)* (Stuttgart).

Kottaridi, A. 1989. 'Βεργίνα 1989. Ανασκαφή στο νεκροταφείο και στα βορειοδυτικά της πόλης', *AEMTh* 3, 1–11.

Kottaridi, A. 1990. 'Βεργίνα 1990. Ανασκαφή στο νεκροταφείο και στο ΒΔ τμήμα της αρχαίας πόλης', *AEMTh* 4, 35–44.

Kottaridi, A. 1991. 'Βεργίνα 1991. Τοπογραφικές έρευνες στην ευρύτερη περιοχή και ανασκαφή στο νεκροταφείο των Αιγών', *AEMTh* 5, 23–30.

Kottaridi, A. 1992. 'Σωστικές ανασκαφές της ΙΖ΄ ΕΠΚΑ στη Βεργίνα', *AEMTh* 6, 67–84.

Kottaridi, A. 1993. 'Ανασκαφή Βεργίνας. Η τακτική ανασκαφή στα ΒΔ της αρχαίας πόλης', *AEMTh* 7, 77–88.

Kottaridi, A. 1996. 'Βεργίνα 1997', *AEMTh* 10, 79–92.

Kottaridi, A. 1997. 'Το αρχαιολογικό έργο της ΙΖ΄ ΕΠΚΑ στη Βεργίνα. Το ιστορικό της εκθεσης των θησαυρών των βασιλικών τάφων', *AEMTh* 11, 129–37.

Kottaridi, A. 1998. 'Το αρχαιολογικό έργο στη Βεργίνα το 1998. Νέα ευρήματα από τη νεκρόπολη των Αιγών', *AEMTh* 12, 405–12.

Kottaridi, A. 1999a. 'Βασιλικές πυρές στη Νεκρόπολη των Αιγών', *Ancient Macedonia VI*, 631–42.

Kottaridi, A. 1999b. 'Γυναικεία αρχέτυπα στον αρχαιοελληνικό μύθο', *Archaiologia & Technes* 68, 6–13.

Kottaridi, A. 1999c. 'Macedonian burial customs and the Funeral of Alexander the Great', in Πρακτικά Συμποσίου "Αλέξανδρος ο Μέγας – από την Μακεδονία στην Οικουμένη", Veroia 27–31/5/1998 (Veroia), 37–48.

Kottaridi, A. 2000. 'Από τη νεκρόπολη των Αιγών στον νεολιθικό οικισμό των Πιερίων', AEMTh 14, 527–36.

Kottaridi, A. 2001a. 'Το έθιμο της καύσης και οι Μακεδόνες', in N. Stampolides (ed.), Καύσεις στην Ελλάδα από την Εποχή του Χαλκού ως την Πρώιμη Εποχή του Σιδήρου (Athens), 359–71.

Kottaridi, A. 2001b. 'Οι σωστικές ανασκαφές της ΙΖ΄ ΕΠΚΑ στην νεκρόπολη και την ευρύτερη περιοχή των Αιγών', AEMTh 15, 503–12.

Kottaridi, A. 2002. 'Discovering Aegae, the Old Macedonian Capital', in M. Stamatopoulou and M. Yeroulanou (eds.), Excavating Classical Culture. Recent Archaeological Discoveries in Greece (Oxford), 75–81.

Kottaridi, A. 2003. The Museum of the Royal Graves of Aegae. Searching the Lost Memory (Athens 2003).

Kottaridi, A. 2004a. 'The Symposium', in D. Pandermalis (ed.), Alexander the Great. Treasures from an Epic Era of Hellenism (New York), 65–72.

Kottaridi, A. 2004b. 'The Lady of Aigai', in D. Pandermalis (ed.), Alexander the Great. Treasures from an Epic Era of Hellenism (New York), 139–47.

Kottaridi, A. 2004c. 'Η ανασκαφή στην πόλη και την νεκρόπολη των Αιγών το 2003–2004', AEMTh 18, 527–42.

Kottaridi, A. 2004d. 'Οι νέες ανασκαφικές έρευνες στην ορεινή Μακεδονίδα και η ταύτιση της ηροδότειας Λεβαίης', AEMTh 18, 543–50.

Kottaridi, A. 2004e. 'Αιγαί. Η πρώτη πρωτεύουσα των Μακεδόνων', in Πρακτικά Ημερίδας "Γνωριμία με τη γη του Μεγαλέξανδρου. Η περίπτωση του νομού Ημαθίας", (Thessaloniki), 81–102.

Kottaridi, A. 2006a. 'Couleur et sens. L'emploi de la couleur dans la tombe de la reine Eurydice', in A.-M. Guimier-Sorbets and M. B. Hatzopoulos (eds.), Rois, cités, nécropoles: institutions, rites et monuments en Macédoine. Actes des colloques de Nanterre (déc. 2002) et d'Athènes (2004), ΜΕΛΕΤΗΜΑΤΑ 45 (Athens), 154–68.

Kottaridi, A. 2006b. 'Η έρευνα στις Αιγές, μία πόλη κατά κώμας', AEMTh 20, 773–80.

Kottaridi, A. 2007. 'L'épiphanie des dieux des Enfers dans la nécropole royale d'Aigai', in S. Decamps-Lequime (ed.), Peinture et couleur dans le monde grec antique (Paris), 27–46.

Kottaridi, A. 2009. 'Η νεκρόπολη των Αιγών στα αρχαϊκά χρόνια και οι βασιλικές συστάδες', in P. Adam-Veleni and K. Tsakalou-Tzanavari (eds.), 20 Χρόνια. Το Αρχαιολογικό Έργο στη Μακεδονία και στη Θράκη. Επετειακός Τόμος, (Thessaloniki), 143–53.

Kottaridi, A. 2011. Macedonian Treasures: A Tour through the Museum of the Royal Tombs of Aigai (Athens).

Kottaridi, A. 'The ainigma of the ivory heads from the grave of Philip II', in Proceedings of a workshop held at the Onassis Cultural Center, New York, 12 March 2005 (forthcoming).

Koukouli-Chrysanthaki, Chr. 1993. 'Macedonia in the Bronze Age', in I. Vokotopoulou (ed.), Greek Civilization: Macedonia, Kingdom of Alexander the Great (Athens), 108–10.

Kouremenos, Th., Parassoglou, G. M. and Tsantsanolgou, K. 2006. The Derveni Papyrus (Florence).

Kyriakou, A. 2008. Η Στενόμακρη Τούμπα της Βεργίνας. Ταφικές Πρακτικές στη Μακεδονία του 4ου αιώνα π.Χ. (Thessaloniki).

Lane Fox, R. 1973. Alexander the Great (London).

Lawrence, A. W. 1957. Greek Architecture (London).

Le Rider, G. 1977. Le monnayage d'argent et d'or de Philippe II frappée en Macédoine de 359 à 294 (Paris).

Le Rider, G. 1993. 'Les deux monnaies macédoniennes des années 323–294/290', BCH 117, 491–500.

Liampi, K. 1993. 'Κυκλοφορία των όψιμων αρχαϊκών και πρώιμων κλασικών και «Θρακομακεδονικών» νομισμάτων σε «θησαυρούς»', Ancient Macedonia V, 789–808.

Lilimpaki-Akamati, M. 1989–91. 'Ανατολικό νεκροταφείο Πέλλας. Ανασκαφή 1989', ADelt 44–6 (Meletes), 73–152.

Lilimpaki-Akamati, M. 1994. Λαξευτοί θαλαμωτοί τάφοι Πέλλας (Athens).

Lilimpaki-Akamati, M. 1996a. Το θεσμοφόριο της Πέλλας (Athens).

Lilimpaki-Akamati, M. 1996b. 'Κτιριακά συγκροτήματα στην περιοχή του καναλιού της Πέλλας', AEMTh 10, vol. A, 93–104.

Lilimpaki-Akamati, M. 1998. 'Για τη μεταλλοτεχνία της Πέλλας', in Μνείας Χάριν. Στη μνήμη της Μαίρης Σιγανίδου (Thessaloniki), 127–140.

Lilimpaki-Akamati, M. 2000. *Το ιερό της Μητέρας των Θεών και της Αφροδίτης στην Πέλλα* (Thessaloniki).

Lilimpaki-Akamati, M. 2002. 'Recent Discoveries in Pella', in M. Stamatopoulou and M. Yeroulanou. (eds.), *Excavating Classical Culture: Recent Archaeological Discoveries in Greece* (Oxford), 83–90.

Lilimpaki-Akamati, M. 2007. *Κιβωτιόσχημος τάφος με ζωγραφική διακόσμηση από την Πέλλα, Πέλλης 1* (Thessaloniki).

Lilimpaki-Akamati, M. 2008. *Ο πολυθάλαμος τάφος της Πέλλας, Πέλλης 2* (Thessaloniki).

Lilimpaki-Akamati, M. and Akamatis, I. M. (eds.) 2004. *Pella and its Environs* (Athens).

Lykiardopoulou, M. and Psôma, S. 2000. 'Η αργυρή βασιλική νομισματοκοπία των Τημενιδών της Μακεδονίας από τα τέλη της βασιλείας του Περδίκκα Β΄ έως το θάνατο του Περδίκκα Γ΄ (413–360). Τεχνολογία κατασκευής, ανάλυση μετάλλου, ιστορική προσέγγιση', *Obolos* 4 (2000), 321–38.

Makaronas, Ch. and Giouri, E. 1989. *Οι οικίες αρπαγής της Ελένης και Διονύσου της Πέλλας* (Athens).

Marazou, I. 1998. *Ancient Gold: The Wealth of the Thracians* (New York).

Millar, F. G. B. 1977. *The Emperor in the Roman World* (London).

Miller, M. 2010. 'Luxury Toreutic in the Western Satrapies. Court-Inspired Gift-Exchange Diffusion', in B. Jacobs and R. Rollinger (eds.), *Der Achämenidenhof – The Achaemenid Court* (Wiesbaden), 853–900.

Molloy, B. 2010. 'Swords and Swordsmanship in the Aegean Bronze Age', *AJA* 114, 403–28.

Murray, O. 1996. 'Hellenistic Royal Symposia', in P. Bilde, T. Engberg-Pedersen, L. Hannestad and J. Zahle (eds.), *Aspects of Hellenistic Kingships* (Aarhus), 15–27.

Musgrave, J., Prag, A. J. N. W., Neave, R. A. H., Lane Fox, R. and White, H. (forthcoming 2011). 'The Occupants of Tomb II at Vergina. Why Arrhidaios and Eurydice Must be Excluded', in *International Journal of Medical Sciences. Special Issue on Palaeo Biomedicine. An Evaluation of Ancient Medical Practices and Modern Analytical Techniques* (available online at http://www.medsci.org/v07p0051.htm).

Nielsen, I. 1994. *Hellenistic Palaces. Tradition and Renewal* (Aarhus).

Oikonomides, A. N. 1983. 'A New Inscription from Vergina and Eurydice the Mother of Philip II', *Ancient World* 7, 1983, 62–4.

Pandermalis, D. 1972. 'Ο νέος Μακεδονικός τάφος της Βεργίνας', *Makedonika* 12, 147–82.

Pandermalis, D. 1976. 'Beobachtungen zur Fassadenarchitektur und Aussichtsveranda im hellenistischen Makedonien', in P. Zanker (ed.), *Hellenismus in Mittelitalien*, Kolloquium in Göttingen, 5–7 June 1974 (Göttingen), 387–95.

Pandermalis, D. 1987. 'Η κεράμωση του ανακτόρου της Βεργίνας', in *ΑΜΗΤΟΣ. Τιμητικός τόμος για τον καθηγητή Μανόλη Ανδρόνικο* (Thessaloniki), 579–605.

Papaefthymiou, E. 2000. 'Απόδοση τετρωβόλου με τύπο τράγου στον Αλέξανδρο Α΄ (498–454 π.Χ.)', *Obolos* 4, 37–49.

Picard, Ch., Gardner, E. A., Pryce, F. N., Cooksey, W., Woodward, A. M., Casson, S., Welch, F. B. and Tod, M. N. 1918–19. 'Macedonia', *BSA* 23, 1–103.

Picard, O. 2000. 'Το νόμισμα στο Μακεδονικό χώρο', *Obolos* 4, 15–23.

Picard, O. 2006. 'Mines, monnaies et impérialisme. Conflits autour du Pangée (478–413 av. J.-C.)', in A.-M. Guimier-Sorbets and M. B. Hatzopoulos (eds.), *Rois, cités, nécropoles: institutions, rites et monuments en Macédoine. Actes des colloques de Nanterre (déc. 2002) et d'Athènes (2004)*, *ΜΕΛΕΤΗΜΑΤΑ* 45 (Athens), 269–83.

Pilali-Papasteriou, A. 1999. 'Η μυκηναϊκή παρουσία στη Μακεδονία. Προβλήματα και επανεκτιμήσεις', in Ph. Dakoronia (ed.), *1st International Interdisciplinary Colloquium, 'The Periphery of the Mycenaean World', Lamia, 25–29 September 1994* (Lamia), 103–6.

Prag, A. J. N. W., Musgrave, J. H. and Neave R. A. H., 1984. 'The Skull from Tomb II at Vergina. King Philip II of Macedon', *JHS* 104, 60–78.

Prag, A. J. N. W. and Neave, R. A. H. (1997). *Making Faces Using Forensic and Archaeological Evidence* (London).

Prag, A. J. N. W., Musgrave, J. H. and Neave, R. A. H. (forthcoming 2011). 'A Twenty–First Century Philippic', in G. J. Oliver and Z. Archibald (eds.), *The Power of the Individual in Ancient Greece. Essays in Honour of Professor J. K. Davies* (Stuttgart).

Psôma, S. 1999. 'Monnaies de poids réduit d'Alexandre I et de Perdiccas II de Macédoine', *ZPE* 128, 273–82.

Psôma, S. 2006. 'The Lete Coinage Reconsidered', in P. Van Alfen (ed.), *Agoranomia: Studies in Money and Exchange Presented to John H. Kroll* (New York), 61–85.

Psôma, S. 2009. 'Un petit trésor de Lynkos et Thucydide 4.124', *RN* 165, 107–12.

Raymond, D. 1953. *Macedonian Regal Coinage to 413 BC* (New York).

Rey, L. 1916. 'Les observations sur les premiers habitants de la Macédoine', *BCH* 40 (1916), 257–92.

Rey, L. 1921. 'Observations sur les premiers habitants de la Macédoine. Recueillies par le Service Archéologique de l'Armée d'Orient (Région de Salonique), 1916–1919', *BCH* 41–3 (1917–19).

Rhodes, P. J. 2010. *A History of the Classical Greek World* (revised ed., Oxford).

Rhomaios, K. 1951. *Ο Μακεδονικός τάφος της Βεργίνας* (Athens).

Rhomaios, K. 1953–1954. 'Το ανάκτορον της Παλατίτσας', *AEphem*, 141–50.

Rhomiopoulou, K. and Kilian-Dirlmeier, I. 1989. 'Neue Funde aus der eisenzeitlichen Hügelnekropole von Vergina, Griechisch Makedonien', *Prähistorische Zeitschrift* 64, 86–145.

Roisman, J. and Worthington, I. (eds.) 2010. *A Companion to Ancient Macedonia* (Oxford).

Rostovtzeff, M. 1972. *The Social and Economic History of the Hellenistic World*, vols. I–III (Oxford).

Saatsoglou-Paliadeli, C. 1987a. 'Ανασκαφή στην περιοχή του ιερού της Εύκλειας στη Βεργίνα', *AEMTh* 1, 101–8.

Saatsoglou-Paliadeli, C. 1987b. 'Ευρυδίκα Σίρρα Ευκλείαι', in *ΑΜΗΤΟΣ. Τιμητικός Τόμος για τον καθηγητή Μανόλη Ανδρόνικο* (Thessaloniki), 733–44.

Saatsoglou-Paliadeli, C. 1989. 'Βεργίνα 1989. Ανασκαφή στο ιερό της Εύκλειας', *AEMTh* 3, 25–35.

Saatsoglou-Paliadeli, C. 1990. 'Βεργίνα 1990. Ανασκαφή στο ιερό της Εύκλειας', *AEMTh* 4, 21–34.

Saatsoglou-Paliadeli, C. 1991. 'Βεργίνα 1991. Ανασκαφή στο ιερό της Εύκλειας', *AEMTh* 5, 9–21.

Saatsoglou-Paliadeli, C. 1992. 'Ανασκαφή στο ιερό της Εύκλειας (1982–1992). Σύντομος απολογισμός', *AEMTh* 6, 51–7.

Saatsoglou-Paliadeli, C. 1993a. 'Βεργίνα 1993. Ανασκαφή στο ιερό της Εύκλειας', *AEMTh* 7, 51–9.

Saatsoglou-Paliadeli, C. 1993b. 'Σκέψεις με αφορμή ένα εύρημα από τα Παλατίτσια', *Ancient Macedonia* V (Thessaloniki), 1339–71.

Saatsoglou-Paliadeli, C. 1994. 'Βεργίνα 1994. Ανασκαφή στο ιερό της Εύκλειας', *AEMTh* 8, 109–17.

Saatsoglou-Paliadeli, C. 1996a. 'Το ιερό της Εύκλειας στη Βεργίνα', *AEMTh* 10, 55–68.

Saatsoglou-Paliadeli, C. 1996b. 'Aegae. A Reconsideration', *AM* 111, 225–36.

Saatsoglou-Paliadeli, C. 1999. 'Βεργίνα 1998–1999. Ανασκαφή στο ιερό της Εύκλειας και στη θόλο του ανακτόρου', *AEMTh* 13, 541–51.

Saatsoglou-Paliadeli, C. 2000. 'Queenly Appearances at Vergina–Aegae. Old and New Epigraphic and Literary Evidence', *AA* 2000, 387–403.

Saatsoglou-Paliadeli, C. 2001. 'The Palace of Vergina–Aegae and its Surroundings', in I. Nielsen (ed.), *The Royal Palace Institution in the First Millennium BC: Regional Development and Cultural Interchange between East and West* (Athens), 201–13.

Saatsoglou-Paliadeli, C. 2002. 'Βεργίνα 2000–2002. Ανασκαφή στο ιερό της Εύκλειας', *AEMTh* 16, 479–490.

Saatsoglou-Paliadeli, C. 2004a. *Βεργίνα. Ο τάφος του Φιλίππου. Η Τοιχογραφία με το κυνήγι, Βιβλιοθήκη της εν Αθήναις Αρχαιολογικής Εταιρείας* 231 (Athens).

Saatsoglou-Paliadeli, C. 2004b. 'Εξερεύνηση του αρχαιολογικού χώρου της Βεργίνας με τη μέθοδο της γεωηλεκτρικής χαρτογράφησης, 1984–2004' (in collaboration with G. N. Tsokas, G. Vargemezis, P. Tsourlos, S. Drougou and K. Tokmakides), *AEMTh* 18, 551–60.

Saatsoglou-Paliadeli, C. 2009. 'Βεργίνα 1977/87–2006', *20 Χρόνια. Το Αρχαιολογικό Έργο στη Μακεδονία και στη Θράκη. Επετειακός Τόμος*, 295–306.

Saatsoglou-Paliadeli, C., Kyriakou, A., Mitsopoulou, E. and Tourtas, A. (in press a). 'Old Engagements and New Finds at Aegae', *AEMTh* 22.

Saatsoglou-Paliadeli, C., Papageorgiou, P., Maniatis, G., Triantaphyllou, S., Kyriakou, A. and Tourtas, A. (in press b). 'Microexcavation of an Unexpected Find from the Agora of Aegae: the Interdisciplinary Approach', *AEMTh* 22.

Sandars, N. 1963. 'Later Aegean Bronze Swords', *AJA* 67, 117–53.

Sideris, A. 2008. 'Achaemenid Toreutics in the Greek Periphery', in S. M. R. Darbandi and A. Zournatzi (eds.) 2008. *Ancient Greece and Ancient Iran Cross-Cultural Encounters, 1st International Conference, Athens, 11–13 November 2006* (Athens), 339–53.

Siganidou, M. and Lilimpaki-Akamati, M. 1996. *Πέλλα. Πρωτεύουσα των Μακεδόνων* (Athens).

Simpson, S. J. 2005. 'The Royal Table', in J. Curtis and N. Tallis (eds.), *Forgotten Empire* (London), 104–11.

Snape, S. and Bailey, D. 1998. *The Great Portico at Hermopolis Magna. Present State and Past Prospects* (British Museum Occasional Paper no. 63) (London).

Snodgrass, A. 1964. *Early Greek Armour and Weapons from the Bronze Age to 600 BC* (Edinburgh).

Squillace, G. 2009. *Filippo il Macedone* (Rome).

Themelis, P. 2000. 'Μεταλλοτεχνία Μακεδονική', in P. Adam-Veleni (ed.), *ΜΥΡΤΟΣ. Μελέτες στη μνήμη της Ι. Βοκοτοπούλου* (Thessaloniki), 495–517.

Themelis, P. and Touratsoglou, I. 1997. *Οι τάφοι του Δερβενίου* (Athens).

Tomlinson, R. A. 1968. 'Ancient Macedonian Symposia', *Ancient Macedonia* I (Thessaloniki), 308–15.

Touratsoglou, I. 1998a. 'Back to the Future. Alexander the Great's Silver and Gold in the Balkans: The Hoard Evidence', in A. Burnett, U. Wartenberg, R. Witschonke (eds.), *Coins of Macedonia and Rome: Essays in Honour of Charles Hersh* (London), 71–101.

Touratsoglou, I. 1998b. 'Στην αναζήτηση του ελληνιστικού χρυσού. "Μεγάλοι αντί μικρών και πλούσιοι εκ πενήτων" (App. V 27, 6)', in *Μνείας Χάριν. Στη μνήμη της Μαίρης Σιγανίδου* (Thessaloniki), 235–64.

Touratsoglou, I. 1998c. 'Dated Gold. The Evidence from Hellenistic Macedonia', in D. Williams (ed.), *Art of the Greek Goldsmith* (London), 30–8.

Touratsoglou, I. 2010. A Contribution to the Economic History of the Kingdom of Ancient Macedonia (6th–3rd Centuries BC) (Athens).

Tsigarida, E. B. 1992. 'Ελληνιστικό σπίτι στη Βεργίνα', *AEMTh* 6, 84–91.

Tsigarida, E. B. and Haddad, N. 1993. 'Ανασκαφική έρευνα στη Βεργίνα 1993. Ελληνιστικό κτίριο με εξώστη', *AEMTh* 7, 69–76.

Tsigarida, E. B. and Ignatiadou, P. 2000. *Ο Χρυσός των Μακεδόνων. Αρχαιολογικό Μουσείο Θεσσαλονίκης* (Thessaloniki).

Velenis, G. 1997. 'Τεχνικές στο ανάκτορο της Βεργίνας', in *Μνήμη Μανόλη Ανδρόνικου, Makedonika Suppl.* 6 (Thessaloniki), 25–37.

Vickers, M. and Gill, D. 1994. *Artful Crafts* (Oxford).

Vokotopoulou, I. 1988. *Αρχαία Μακεδονία: Κατάλογος της Έκθεσης* (Athens).

Vokotopoulou, I. 1997. *Ελληνική Τέχνη. Αργυρά και χάλκινα έργα τέχνης στην αρχαιότητα* (Athens).

Vokotopoulou, I. and Despini, A. 1985. *Σίνδος: Κατάλογος της Έκθεσης* (Thessaloniki).

Völker-Janssen, W. 1993. *Kunst und Gesellschaft an den Höfen Alexanders d. Gr. und seiner Nachfolger* (Munich).

Voutyras, E. 1998. *Διονυσοφῶντος γάμοι. Marital Life and Magic in Fourth Century Pella* (Amsterdam).

Wace, A. J. B. 1913/4. 'The Mounds of Macedonia', *BSA* 20, 123–32.

Wace, A. J. B. and Thompson, M. 1909. 'Prehistoric Mounds in Macedonia', *Liverpool Annals of Archaeology and Anthropology* 2, 159–64.

Wace, A. J. B., Megaw A. H. S. and Skeat, T. C. 1959. *Hermopolis Magna Ashmunein* (Alexandria).

Walker, S. 1997. 'Athens under Augustus', in M. C. Hoff and S. I. Rotroff (eds.), *The Romanization of Athens* (Oxford), 67–80.

Wardle, K. 1980. 'Excavations at Assiros 1975–79. A Settlement Site in Central Macedonia and its Significance for the Prehistory of South-East Europe', *BSA* 75, 229–67.

Wardle, K. 1993. 'Mycenaean Trade and Influence in Northern Greece', in C. Zerner, P. Zerner and J. Winder (eds.), *Proceedings of the International Conference 'Wace and Blegen. Pottery as Evidence for Trade in the Aegean Bronze Age, 1939–1989'* (Amsterdam), 117–41.

Weatley, P. V. 1998. 'The Date of Polyperchon's Invasion of Macedonia and Murder of Heracles', *Antichthon* 32, 12–23.

Westermark, W. 1994. 'The Staters of Archelaus. A Die Study', in M. Price, A. Burnett and R. Bland (eds.), *Essays in Honour of Robert Carson and Kenneth Jenkins* (London), 17–30.

Williams, D. and Ogden, J. 1994. *Greek Gold: Jewellery of the Classical World* (London).

Wirth, G. 1985. *Philipp II. Geschichte Makedoniens* (Stuttgart).

Worthington, I. 2008. *Philip II of Macedon* (New Haven).

Zournatzi, A. 2009. 'The Processing of Gold and Silver Tax in the Achaemenid Empire. Herodotus 3.96.2 and the Archaeological Realities', *Studia Iranica* 29, 241–71.

Zournatzi, A. (forthcoming). 'The Vouni Treasure and Monetary Practices in Cyprus in the Persian period', in A. Liampi and D. Plantzos (eds.), *Proceedings of the International Conference Coinage/Jewellery. Uses-Interactions-Symbolism, from Antiquity to the Present, Ios 26–28 June 2009*, KERMA, Athens (available online): http://www.achemenet.com/document/ZOURNATZI_Vouni_Treasure_31-7-2010.pdf

Illustration Acknowledgements

The copyright of the photographs of the exhibits belongs to the Hellenic Ministry of Culture and Tourism – Archaeological Receipts Fund. All images illustrated in this catalogue are courtesy of the Photographic Archive of the 17th Ephorate of Prehistoric and Classical Antiquities, except from the following images:

Figs. 3–4 (pp. 4–5): Drawing by G. Miltsakakis
Figs. 5, 233–234: Courtesy of the Cabinet des Médailles, Paris
Figs. 8, 239–240: Courtesy of the American Numismatic Society, New York
Figs. 9, 11, 25, 235–236, 241–242, 245–246: Courtesy of the Alpha Bank Collection
Figs. 10, 231–232, 243–244: Courtesy of the Numismatic Museum, Athens
Fig. 15 (p. 13): Ashmolean Museum, University of Oxford (Coin Room, HCR7028)
Fig. 24 (p. 22): Ashmolean Museum, University of Oxford (Antiquities, AN1928.529)
Fig. 26 (p. 24): Ashmolean Museum, University of Oxford (Coin Room, HCR6279)
Fig. 30 (p. 36): photography and photomosaic (2010) by J. F. Stephens and
    A. E. Stephens
Fig. 137 (p. 129): University of Manchester
Fig. 248 (p. 210): Drawing by G. Miltsakakis; photography and photomosaic (2010)
    by J. F. Stephens and A. E. Stephens
Figs. 255–256 (pp. 221–222): Courtesy of Professor I. Akamatis and Dr M. Lilimpaki
    Akamati
Fig. 257 (p. 223): Courtesy of the Pella Archaeological Museum
Figs. 260 (p. 228), 263 (p. 229) and 265 (p. 230) were drawn by S. Bird and are
    reproduced by courtesy of Oxbow Publications (reworked by S. Hebron)
Figs. 261 (p. 228), 262 (p. 228), 266 (p. 230) were taken by the author and fig. 264
    (p. 229) by Y. Galanakis